A BASIC THEORY OF
NEUROPSYCHOANALYSIS

W. M. Bernstein

KARNAC

First published in 2011 by
Karnac Books Ltd
118 Finchley Road
London NW3 5HT

British Library Cataloguing in Publication Data

A C.I.P. for this book is available from the British Library

ISBN-13: 978-1-85575-809-4

Typeset by Vikatan Publishing Solutions (P) Ltd., Chennai, India

www.karnacbooks.com

"The whole of science is nothing more than the refinement of everyday thinking."

—Albert Einstein, *Physics and Reality* (1936)

CONTENTS

PREFACE

This book introduces a theoretical framework for studying the mind and brain. Specifically, an attempt is made to frame ideas from psychoanalysis and cognitive-social psychology so that they can be taken readily into the realm of neurobiology. Psychoanalytic theory still represents a very comprehensive description of the human mind. It includes cognitive, emotional, and behavioural variables, plus the idea of unconscious mental operations. The *pleasure principle* and *repetition compulsion* were Freud's most general concepts of mental functioning. These concepts are renovated to get them on the same page with ideas from social cognition and neurobiology. I think the basic theorizing has important implications for diagnosis and treatment of mental illnesses.

The Complete Works of Sigmund Freud contains twenty four volumes. He speculated on basic scientific questions in biology, psychology, and sociology. And, he wrote about applications of his theory to child development, psychotherapy, group behaviour, religion, and art. But the core of the theory is relatively concise. Perhaps all the fundamental and most valid assumptions of Freudian psychoanalytic theory could fit into one or two volumes. It is how the separate assumptions are linked together in a powerful explanatory system that makes psychoanalytic theory so compelling.

Scientific assumptions are testable by scientific methods. For example, there is the hypothesis from "Negation" (Freud, 1925) that claiming one's innocence *too much* is a compensatory behaviour. In other words, the person who feels guilty about having engaged in acts of anti-social behaviour, or who merely has "bad" thoughts, makes a special effort to claim that they have never done or ever had wishes to do such things. This, of course, is the same assumption that Shakespeare made in *Hamlet* (1600): "The lady doth protest too much methinks".

While psychoanalysis dominated Medical Psychology between approximately 1920 and 1975, Behaviourism was mostly dominant during that period in academic psychology departments. When I entered college in 1969, the psychology faculty somehow communicated the idea that psychoanalytic ideas were not testable. But this is not so (e.g., Eysenck & Wilson, 1973; Weston, 1999).

The doctrinaire rejection of psychoanalysis motivated, in part, my doctoral thesis. It involved a laboratory experiment demonstrating that Freud's idea about *negation* was valid under certain conditions (Bernstein, 1981; 1984). Those who feel especially guilty about having anti-social wishes do indeed make more strenuous denials of such wishes than others. But I also found that some young men are not particularly interested in "sex with mother". Oedipal dynamics are central to psychoanalytic theory, but some analysts tended to be ridged in applying the concepts in practice. Anyone disclaiming incestuous wishes was thought to be involved in a defensive operation. This dogmatism rivalled that of the Behaviourists who believed that psychoanalysis was all bunk.

In any case, it is likely that people who made (or even still make) a claim that psychoanalytic assumptions are not verifiable had no knowledge of how such things might be tested by scientific methods. The field of Human Experimental Social Psychology arose shortly after the beginning of psychoanalysis. The experimental social psychologists developed methods that were suited to testing psychoanalytic hypotheses. This is not a coincidence. Kurt Lewin and his students were all knowledgeable of psychoanalysis and were driven to learn how to test and refine psychodynamic assumptions.

A key for developing scientific theory in general is to connect theoretical realms with their adjacent fields. Otherwise, the islands of knowledge become sealed-off or *hermeneutical*. Psychology can develop most surely by linking to cognitive-social theory on one side and biological theory on the other. The linking is not *scientific reduction* defined formally (e.g., Kemeny & Oppenheim, 1956). But, we may ask of a hypothesis about mind–brain: "Is it at least consistent with knowledge of both biology and social psychology?" If not, then the number of plausible paths for future research is reduced. This is a reduction or consolidation in the service of moving ahead with more integrated theories.

Such a theory-making method takes its cue from the brain itself. A reduction occurs in the brain early in life before development can continue. The neonate's brain contains about a trillion cells. Soon after birth, the number of neurons starts to fall. The adult human brain contains only 10% of the neurons in the newborn. Brain–mind development is not merely a function of the number of nerve cells in the brain. But reducing clutter is certainly a temporal precedent of development.

Psychoanalysis, behaviourism, and experimental social psychology have developed on parallel paths that rarely connect (Bernstein, 1995; Whittle, 1999). The "soft science" psychoanalytic school and the "hard" behaviourist and experimental schools are still allergic to each other. Perhaps the greatest barriers to developing theory in psychology are the assumptions that biological and psychological explanations are mutually exclusive; and, that cognitive and motivational explanations are also mutually exclusive. These are false dichotomies for the most part. The theories and methods of experimental, psychoanalytic, and modern neurobiology schools are each powerful. How can more connections be made between them?

The method of this book is to consider some robust, central concepts in psychology, psychoanalysis, and neurobiology. Then, theoretical paths are followed that are at least consistent with tenets in all three fields. Some new assumptions are added to link the basic ideas. Many of the integrating ideas seem logically obvious when the various fields are considered together rather than in isolation.

My argument is built on a fundamental assumption: *Understanding the relationships between repetitive processes and approach pleasure/avoid pain operations (the pleasure principle), is a key to understanding mind–brain.*

Repetitive processes are stimulated when the person fails to develop needed, useful concepts. In mental illness, repetition is often fruitless. But the tendency to repeat gives the person a chance to "get it right". This is what makes mind–brain a "continuous improvement apparatus". Repetition is a normal mind–brain process that can become deregulated by neuropathology, psychopathology, or both.

The mind is a biological and social thing. Psychoanalysis has many terms to describe how biological tendencies to behave are shaped by societal forces such as parents, teachers, and the culture at large. In his great style, Freud labelled these transformations "the vicissitudes of the instincts". Today we say less colourfully that "the mind is the functioning of the brain". Any theory presuming to improve on psychoanalysis must integrate what has been learned about psychology and neurobiology since Freud.

A *reduction* of psychology to biology is impossible because there are no theoretical terms in biology that correspond to the phenomena of "subjective experience". Subjective experiences of thought and feeling, their relations to each other, and to overt behaviours, are our subjects. Understanding relations between biological and psychological events calls for eliminations, additions, and readjustments of theoretical terms in psychology and neurology.

This is not to say that parsimony is not always welcome in a theory. *The Parsimony Principle* is that simple explanations should be preferred to more complicated ones. But when a theory ignores the real complexity of phenomena, it is better described as "incomplete" than parsimonious. Behaviourism provided a valuable pole in the dialectic with psychoanalysis and other theories concerning arcane mental processes. No one besides a few strange characters in psychology departments at mid-century ever believed that thinking and feeling don't occur. Rather, it made some good sense to study what was relatively observable, that is, the stimuli in the environment and how the animal responded to stimuli with overt movement of its body. This last is what behaviourists called "behaviour".

While anyone can see the rat and the cheese, it took behavioural science to develop methods of studying animal behaviour that worked to extend the understanding of psychology beyond common sense and folk wisdom. Modern human experimental psychology, a paradigm strongly shaped by behaviourism, includes cognitive-social psychology and modern neurobiology. Today, it makes sense to consider as "behaviour" any activity of cells or entire organisms that can be observed with or without prosthetic sensory devices, e.g., functional magnetic resonance imaging, (fMRI). Overt, easily observable behaviour is surely affected by less obvious subjective experience, that is, the person's private thoughts and feelings, and the neurological processes that support them.

Neuroscience recognizes all sorts of phenomena and research methods as important for understanding the mind and brain. These include: recording electrical activity in single cells and the entire brain; real-time imaging of physiologic processes in the brain; and identifying the molecular cascades occurring between synapses and neuronal nuclei. Work in the clinic is being supported by extensive efforts to develop psychopharmacological agents (see Stahl, 2008).

This book is an attempt to correlate objectively measurable and hypothetical brain activities to discrete and global subjective experiences of mind, such as "resolving conflict" and "feeling anxious". In this effort to integrate parts of psychoanalytic thinking with neuropsychiatry I am following pioneers such as Solms (e.g., Solms & Turnbull, 2002); Levin (2003); and Carhart-Harris, et al. (2008). Here, I attempt to examine and refine the most general, foundational assumptions of psychoanalysis: *pleasure principle* and *repetition compulsion*.

Correlating an individual's subjective experience with events in the brain would be impossible if we did not listen to patients and research subjects with *the third ear* (Reik, 1948). That is, if we did not query our subjective reactions to information coming from other people. The new biology of mind indicates that aspects of the person's subjective experience are transmitted reliably to the brains and minds of observers. For example, the preverbal infant and the mother use subtle forms of communication that help the parent regulate the experience of the newborn. The parent's competence at sensing and conceptualizing the baby's needs is the most important factor in human development.

Neuroscience research has supported the basic validity of many social, psychological, and psychoanalytic ideas. Biological and social-cognition theoretical systems are prepared as never before for consolidation efforts.

ACKNOWLEDGEMENTS

The talks I have had over the years with Robert Wicklund and David McCraney helped me formulate my ideas for this book. Others who helped were Warner Burke, Mark Davis, Ross Klavan, Dan Kovacevic, Lee Levin, Murray Sokoloff, Mary Stone, Annette Tecce, Elaine Waters, Edward Whitesides, and Mike Wickham. Two dedicated individuals literally sat on the desk as I wrote—the loyal cats *Johnny* and the late *William*.

ABOUT THE AUTHOR

W. M. Bernstein received a BS in Biology from Tufts University and a PhD in Experimental Social Psychology from the University of Texas at Austin. He was a Research Associate in Psychology and Psychiatry at Dartmouth College and Medical School; and, a NIMH Post-Doctoral Fellow in Basic and Applied Social Psychology at Columbia University. Dr. Bernstein is a graduate of The Center for Psychoanalytic Studies, Massachusetts General Hospital-Harvard Medical School; and, a Diplomate of the American Board of Medical Psychology. He was one of the first psychologists in the United States licensed to prescribe psychotropic medicines.

INTRODUCTION

A model of mind is developed from concepts in psychoanalysis, brain biology, and experimental social psychology in Chapters One through Three. The ideas are applied in Chapter Four in the context of emergency responses. In Chapter Five I use the basic framework to explain the results of a laboratory experiment involving approach and avoidance conflict. In Chapters Six through Nine, the model is used in the context of the treatment of Mr. K, a sixty five year-old man. The case of Mr. C, a fourty five year-old man, is described in Chapter Ten. Relevant psychopharmacology and neurobiology are included throughout the book. Chapter Eleven takes a look at the processes involved in thought suppression and its affect on executive function, especially memory. Chapter Twelve describes a diagnostic scheme based on the theory.

Chapter One looks back at psychoanalysis and other psychological theories. I take as representative of mainstream psychoanalytic theorizing the final book of the late Charles Brenner, *Psychoanalysis or Mind and Meaning* (2006). My argument begins with what are some deficiencies in Brenner's theorizing; especially that he does not recognize the need to include a principle of mental functioning in addition to a *pleasure principle*. His book is a succinct description of what might be called "neo-classical" psychoanalytic theory.

Chapter Two considers important contemporary theories of the mind. These include the Affect Regulation School (e.g., Fonagy et al., 2004; Schore, 2003) and the Cognitive Therapy School (e.g., Beck et al., 2004). The affect regulation writers are on the right track. But despite the effectiveness of some cognitive treatment methods, the theories of the Cognitive Therapy School are problematic. This is because they do not consider energy or motivational variables, or unconscious processes. There is logically no doubt that thinking, like all other biological processes, uses energy. If logic isn't convincing enough, empirical studies punctuate the point. In research where subjects were asked to perform effortful mental control tasks such as the Stroop Test, it was found that, "relatively small acts of self-control are sufficient to deplete the available supply of glucose" (Gailliot et al., 2007, p. 335).

Affect regulation theories and psychoanalysis both include cognitive and motivational variables in their theorizing. That is, they are concerned with mental processes and structures that guide and shape the use of biological energy for feeling, thinking, and behaving. It should be obvious that theories of the mind and brain must account for both cognitive and energy or motivational processes. In any case, some of the features of the Cognitive Therapy School are reviewed and critiqued.

Chapter Three spells out the general framework of the model. Figure 2 depicts the assumed causal relationships between data coming from the sense organs and viscera; and concepts, expectations, feelings of pain and pleasure, and overt behaviour. An important part of the model comes from the experimental and theoretical work of Allan Snyder and his group at the Centre for the Mind in Sydney, Australia (e.g., Snyder & Mitchell, 1999; Snyder et al., 2006). Snyder's group studies processes of concept-activation in autistic and normal subjects. Clearly, central mechanisms in conceptual processing involve concept activation, that is, how concepts become conscious or "switched on" and then "switched off".

The chapter then examines the role of awareness and self-awareness in executive functioning. Four conditions in which mind–brain functions either with few or no concepts, or with some disorder of concept usage, are discussed: autism, neonatal life, animals, and post-traumatic disorders. Such naturally occurring "conceptless minds" are invaluable when attempting to understand cognition in normal and pathological conditions.

A key executive function of mind is to generate expectations, essentially probability estimates, regarding the potential of situations to cause pain and pleasure. Concepts or "theories of reality" are the proximal generators of expectations. Normally, the person's concepts of "what causes what" are "valid enough" to generate reasonable expectations or predictions of events in the biological, psychological, and social worlds. Situations may be expected to yield pleasure, pain, or both. But how does the person decide what to do when expectations conflict?

Expectations are the net result of thinking, and the summary material used for executive decisions regarding conflicts between a situation's pain and pleasure potential. Conflict is maximal when the options are of a zero-sum variety, that is, when only two, mutually exclusive options are considered for solving a conflict. I assume that minds regulated by many "black and white" conceptual categories are less developed than those able to imagine more than two solutions to a problem.

The belief that a conflict can have only two possible solutions rather than many is an important cause of anxiety seen in both normal and pathological conditions. Mind–brain decision-making processes operate in parallel, constantly, consciously, unconsciously, and at varying levels of intensity, in order to resolve conflict. The brain is a calculator of pleasure and pain. All thinking has hedonic causes and effects.

Decisions are resolved by what psychoanalysts call *compromise formations*. The compromise is between the person's need to solve the problem and their need to regulate the mind itself. Some solutions may be unthinkable (e.g., "Stop smoking? Not me!"). Compromises in the face of conflict are strongly affected by both the individual's personality and their knowledge of the world. I assume that if an important conflict cannot be resolved by some satisfactory compromise, the mind–brain will process the conflict again. That is, *there is a tendency to repeat the psychobiological processes of conflict resolution. These processes will keep repeating at some level of mind–brain if no better concepts for resolving the conflict are developed.*

Depending on the competence of decisions, the person will be more or less successful in the biological, psychological, and social worlds. Executive functions such as directing attention, especially towards the self, work more and less well to regulate the person's subjective experiences of sensation, thought, and feeling. Mental competence depends, in part, on the durability under stress of conscious, executive functions.

The prototypical stress is caused by conflicting pleasure and pain expectations. Animals want to approach pleasure and avoid pain. Of course, if a situation or person promises only all pain or all pleasure there is no problem. But the idea that any thing or any person is "all good" or "all bad" is preposterous. In truth, things are more complex. There is always some stress between the mind–brain systems striving to approach an object, and the systems wanting to avoid the same object. The "object" can be a person in the social world or a thought in one's own mind. Bio-psychological health depends upon the degree of regulation of approach and avoidance tendencies by means of learned Executive or Ego Functions. Brain–mind is the manager of stress regulation but all organ systems are involved more or less.

Decisions are made in milliseconds and over years. But in life-threatening emergency situations, time is at a premium. I assume in **Chapter Four** that *the fear of not having enough time to make and enact a competent decision is the deepest fear.*

Chapter Five reviews briefly the work of Kurt Lewin and Neal Miller on Approach and Avoidance Motives. Lewin and Miller were influenced by Freud's theories and, in turn, built the foundation of today's School of Experimental Social Psychology. This book has been influenced by the early scholars in the experimental school including: Leon Festinger, Stanley Schachter, Edward Jones, Harold Kelly, John Lanzetta, and Jack Brehm. Lewin, Miller, and their students devised concepts and experimental methods to study conflict in the laboratory. They described clearly for the first time the asymmetry in the temporal and spatial dynamics of Approach and Avoidance Motives.

Ambivalence and conflict about approaching pleasure and avoiding pain are at the centre of most clinical disorders. In normal psychological functioning the person is always attempting to resolve conflicting expectations about moving towards or away from ideas, situations, or other people. The late Melvin Snyder wrote about how people generate and exploit conceptual ambiguity in response to conflict (e.g., Snyder & Wicklund, 1981). I use the results of a study in

Snyder's Attributional Ambiguity tradition (Bernstein, Stephenson, Snyder & Wicklund, 1983) to demonstrate the use of the model in Figure 2.

Chapter Six explores how attentional control and the regulation of thoughts and feelings are hampered in anxiety disorders. The case of Mr. K, who has anxiety, is used to illustrate my approach. The patient's problematic object relations history and his early experience of talk and pharmacological therapies are described.

Ideas from both Freudian Drive Theories and Self-Psychoanalytic Object Relations Theories are needed to explain the person (e.g., Bernstein, 1984; 2001). Despite some moderately extreme traumas and conflictual relationships with family members, Mr. K developed "good enough" conceptual competences to lead a relatively successful life. But his control system, that is, part of his personality, was not good enough to regulate anxiety reliably. This chapter builds on the ideas of Melanie Klein and David Winnicott to describe the development of the first self-concepts that comprise the personality. The chapter also includes some additions to the basic model described in Chapter Three. The revised model appears in Figure 6.

Chapter Seven looks at how self-concepts, developed early on, must continue to develop in order to make the person competent to regulate sexual and aggressive behaviours in adulthood. Freud's Oedipus Theory is examined. The need to resolve Oedipal conflict is described as a more general problem involving integration of new concepts and regulatory processes into the developing self-system.

Chapter Eight describes the "vicissitudes" of the aggressive instincts in the case of Mr. K. Ideas from the previous chapters are used to explain Mr. K's difficulties at both the psychological and neurochemical levels of analysis.

Chapter Nine reviews psychological and neurobiological aspects of Eye Movement Desensitization and Reprocessing (EMDR) treatments. Processes proposed to explain the therapeutic action of EMDR, including the activation of rapid eye movement sleep-like processes (REM), and alterations in the function of working memory are reviewed. The use of EMDR with Mr. K is described.

Chapter Ten describes the Case of Mr. C, a fourty five year-old theoretical scientist. Psychodynamic diagnoses, cognitive methods, drugs, and EMDR produced an alteration in executive functioning as measured by neuropsychological testing. Relationships between memory processes, psychiatric symptoms, and mind–brain change are illustrated in this chapter. The argument is made that mind–brain change depends, in part, on relatively disorganized, high entropy brain conditions such as REM sleep and states induced by hallucinogens.

Chapter Eleven offers an explanation for the results of a recent study of thought suppression employing Semantic Priming methods (Najmi & Wegner, 2008). The relations between thought suppression processes, stress, memory problems, and anxiety disorders are discussed.

Chapter Twelve uses ideas from the basic theory to develop a model of causal relationships between etiological factors and six reliable categories of functional psychopathology.

The Epilogue adds some final thoughts about evolution, executive functioning, somatoform disease, and health care.

CHAPTER ONE

Historical foundations

Freud, a neurologist, began his work at the end of the 19th century. He predicted accurately that technologies to study the biology of brain processes would not be developed for a hundred years (Kandel, 2006). In the meantime, he devised a psychological model of mental structures and processes. Psychoanalysis understands the mind's tasks as aiding biological survival and reproduction. Freud described how instinctual, biological drives for security and sex become transformed in the course of living in a social environment. For example, the human infant's hunger drive is enacted by shameless eating. Later, sucking, grabbing, and gurgling are supplanted by more civilized eating behaviours such as using utensils and "table manners".

Freud's most general theoretical constructs were presented in "Beyond the pleasure principle" (1920). He made a distinction between two basic mental arrangements: *the pleasure principle* and *the repetition compulsion*. Simply enough, the pleasure principle states that we are motivated to behave in ways that produce pleasurable feelings and thoughts. I assume in the psychoanalytic tradition that feelings of pleasure and pain are always involved, at various levels of consciousness, as both causes and effects of thoughts and behaviours.

More generally, feelings, thoughts, and overt behaviour are part of an overall system in which each has bidirectional causal effects on the other. In behaviourist terms, for example, pleasurable feelings associated with food and sex are reinforcing. The association of a stimulus with a good feeling works to build a habit to approach such a stimulus object. And, of course, painful feelings associated with physical or social situations work to create habits of avoiding such things.

Approach and avoidance habits include habits of thought, as well as habits of overt behaviour. For example, specific thoughts implying approach such as "I want to eat some sweets" become associated with overt, appetitive behaviours such as looking for sweets. And, actual approach behaviours can work to promote thoughts and bodily sensation. On the way to dinner, to have sex, to hear one's favourite concerto, or to buy cigarettes, the person imagines the consummation and the thoughts themselves are pleasurable.

But are the motives to approach pleasurable and avoid unpleasurable situations enough to explain the operation of mind? Freud used the case of "war neurosis" to illustrate that a pleasure principle alone is insufficient to explain the mind. Today we would label "war neurosis" a *Post Traumatic Stress Disorder* (PTSD).

Beyond the pleasure principle for Freud was *the repetition compulsion*. The existence of something like a repetition compulsion is consistent with a common symptom of PTSD listed in the latest edition of *The Diagnostic and Statistical Manual of The American Psychiatric Association* or DSM-IV (1994): Patients replay the traumatic events over and over both while awake and in dreaming sleep. Freud felt that the underlying causes of repetition seen in PTSD were different than those in less severe repetition pathologies, such as obsessive counting or compulsive hand-washing. A psychoanalytic explanation for obsessions and compulsions is that they are a form of self-punishment for some guilt-producing thought; and that punishment in the manner of having to perform some ritual is in some sense gratifying. The symptom rectifies an unbalanced situation by punishing the imagined wrongdoing. It is a form of masochism and, hence, explainable by a *pleasure principle*.

But most of Freud's war patients were not responsible for causing their trauma. He felt that the repetition of dreams in these patients is not sufficiently explained by a pleasure principle. Even if there was some pleasure in terrifying dreams or some guilt for surviving when comrades did not, it seemed to Freud that there was an additional factor operating. This he dubbed *the repetition compulsion*.

Freud (1920) did not make much progress in illuminating the nature of this compulsion. Rather, he speculated that there was "an instinct, an urge inherent in organic life to restore an earlier state of things". This he embellished with the idea that "the aim of all life is death". So, the repetition compulsion got its other name— the *Death Instinct*. This Death Instinct was posited as the antithesis of a more creative, Life Instinct. These he called *Thanatos* and *Eros*, respectively. Together, the two forces represent Freud's most general formulation of the dynamics of the mind.

Most psychoanalysts have been critical of the idea of a Death Instinct. For example, Charles Brenner in his final book claimed that: "All the currently available evidence speaks in favour of the conclusion that the mind always works to gain as much pleasure as it can, and, at the same time, to avoid unpleasure insofar as it is possible to do so" (Brenner, 2006, p. 18).

One can't disagree with Brenner that the mind strives to approach pleasure and avoid pain. But psychopathology and neuropathology can inhibit the person's ability to attain pleasure and avoid pain. Psychological conditions that are not adequately explained by a pleasure principle alone were what Freud was trying to explain with the repetition compulsion. Merely rejecting a Death Instinct is not enough. One must do something to explain phenomena that are not adequately characterized by a pleasure principle alone.

A simple, starting assumption of this book is that parts of the brain and mind are not operating merely on a pleasure principle. Processes in cortical association areas involved with cognition and feeling represent the brain and mind functions most regulated by a pleasure principle. Feeling and thinking are more or less equivalent to sensing and interpreting sensations of pleasure and pain. In contrast to these cortical regions, more primitive areas of the brain such as the amygdyla have more specific functional responsibilities. The amygdyla functions to regulate reflex-like, fear and flight responses. In the absence of gross psychoneuropathology, its functions can come to be regulated by the higher regions of the mind and brain. That is, by those brain–mind areas operating under a pleasure principle. In PTSD clearly, and I assume in all other psychopathologies to various degrees, the functioning of cortex and various brain nuclei become disjoined. In other words, the mutual regulatory processes of the brain–mind system are out of order.

Anxiety

A major reason that PTSD is so hard to treat is that sensory stimuli associated with the original trauma reach the amygdyla and hippocampus a millisecond or two before they reach the cortical areas of the brain (Kalivas, Churchill & Klitenick, 1993; Swerdlow & Koob, 1987; Zahm & Brog, 1992). Sights, sounds, and smells associated with the original trauma produce activity in the amygdyla and a sensation of anxiety and dread. For example, the backfiring of a car sends the war veteran into an anxiety state. This fast amygdyla activity, unmediated by logical thought, is also seen in phobias. The arachnophobe does not distinguish between poisonous spiders and others. Rather, all spiders activate a fear response. Similarly, the person with *social anxiety* is not a particularly accurate judge of which groups or places pose real dangers and which do not.

The cortex of the brain is centrally important for conceptual thought. Most often, no amount of reasoning with the trauma patient works to stem their anxiety. They cannot be convinced that there is no real threat in a current environment. Their ability to use thought to regulate anxiety is literally short-circuited by the fast action of the amygdyla, which sets off fear and avoidance reactions before thought can intervene (LeDoux, 1996).

The difference between PTSD and other anxiety disorders might best be considered a quantitative one. All mental disorders are forms of dysregulation between brain–mind functions. Most generally, thoughts can function to regulate sensations coming from the external world and the internal environment of the body. The conscious and unconscious interpretation of sensations, the estimates of their pleasurable and painful or injurious potential, is cognition. What have been variously called *executive functions* or *ego functions* organize and regulate the relations between thought, feeling, expectations, and overt behaviour. The "Executive" also works to relate thoughts to other thoughts, feelings to other feelings, and behaviours to other behaviours. Ideally, an individual's mind–brain system can make the best decisions in line with a pleasure principle.

In trauma, unexpected sensations overwhelm the person. Protective reflexes of avoidance are activated quickly without thought. In refractory cases, traumatic, *one-trial learning* and *stimulus generalization* have taken place. Neuronal circuits supporting the avoidance behaviours fire in response to weak stimuli which only resemble the original, injurious situation in a general way. Once this set of conditions is met, we often diagnose PTSD. PTSD might best be considered a *learning disorder*. At bottom, the patient cannot learn or use what is learned to contain anxiety. All anxiety disorders share this quality of rational thought not working to control sensations. The trauma victim's difficulties are quantitatively greater. And, because the habits formed in response to the injurious stimuli are activated quickly, cortical brain functions are not enlisted fully in anxiety control.

The war veteran "knows" that there are no enemies around the corner, but there is no "realization" of the knowledge. It does not work to reduce anxiety. The pleasure principle can't operate. In its place we see the unregulated operation of other brain regions. When brain sub-systems are operating without input from higher, conceptual processing areas, behaviour tends to repeat.

Many disease symptoms are a result of the body's attempts to heal. The repetition instinct can best be understood as the idea that until brain–mind processes develop to effect higher levels of control, they will repeat. *Trial and error* is a basic sort of animal learning (Thorndike, 1913). Behaviours that lead to increases of pleasure or decreases of pain will become habits. An animal will try this and that until the right behaviour is executed, that is, the one that increases pleasure or decreases pain, or both. It is hard for the anxiety patient to learn. He or she can't do the experiment or can't learn from it. Until the person develops concepts that work to control mental life, the old thoughts, feelings, and behaviours will repeat.

The good news is that our brains will constantly tee-up the lousy old response to a situation until a better response is developed. We are wired for constant improvement. But serious injuries coming from the social or biological environment of the brain can make development difficult or impossible. A concept something like *repetition compulsion* has great theoretical utility. It is needed along with a pleasure principle to explain the mind. Remember Freud's claim was that "the urge to repeat" was "beyond", not "instead", of a pleasure principle. We would locate the tendency to repeat below the cortical processes in the brain, and describe it as a help to development of the mind unless its connections to higher brain regions are disturbed.

Learning

The aim of this book is to describe psychoneurological structures and processes that function to promote and inhibit learning. If there is an overarching monotheism here, it is that *the desire to learn about reality has the most potential of all desires to generate intense feeling and, of course, thought.* Learning about reality involves the development of concepts to interpret data coming from the senses. Conceptual activity takes place in association areas of the brain such as the *parahippocampal cortex* which operates to interpret visual sensations. The proximal causes of pleasurable feelings are events occurring at a cellular level. Opiates such as morphine elicit pleasure when they attach to *mu-opioid receptors* on the surface of nerve cells. The brain makes its own *mu-opioid* agonists called *endomorphins.* Conceptual activity is more pleasurable than merely sensing information. This is because: "The brain's association areas have the greatest density of mu-opioid receptors. In other words, it is the *interpretation* of visual patterns that leads to the feeling of pleasure" (Biederman & Vessel, 2006, p. 253).

McClelland (1978) thought *power* to be the most pleasurable thing. His claim might be altered to say that *the power to get interpretable feedback about the self and the world can promote learning.* People with power can make decisions that are carried out by others (e.g., French & Raven, 1959). This frees the person from almost everything besides making decisions. Making decisions involves primarily the interpretation of data. This is highly pleasurable, especially if one can learn about the quality of their decisions. High offices in public and private sectors are ideal roles to play to learn about one's decision-making competence. This is why people aspire to play such roles.

Of course, the power to get feedback about the self can promote narcissistic grandiosity. In such cases, repetition of mistakes rather than true learning occurs. A famous image of the perversion of learning is Hitler prancing around Berlin, looking at his reflection in the windows of fancy shops while devising diabolical social and biological experiments. But if we remove the generally negative attitude about power, it may be seen as simply instrumental to learning.

The know-how and means to influence conditions in the world of the laboratory are competencies of the experimental scientist. In this book, I adopt Fritz Heider's (1958) characterization of the human as a so-called *naïve scientist*. Heider's use of this as the central assumption for understanding the mind is consistent with the idea that the motive to learn is of the greatest importance.

Freud chose sex as the strongest motive in large part because it was imagined to be the most pleasurable thing. But his theory made it explicit that sex and aggressive drives were transformed mostly to energize and regulate all socially creative behaviours: Art, science, athletics, government, law, and everyone's, everyday social performance—everything. In the psychoanalytic view, behaviour in line with the pleasure principle becomes more sophisticated with development by taking account of the *reality principle*. In the long run, continuing to learn more and more about reality works to promote the goals of the pleasure principle.

The nervous system regulates bodily functions including its own unique function—thinking. Ideally, the executive, decision-making agency of mind works to maximize pleasure and avoid pain. This calls for accurate registration and interpretation of sensations coming from the inside and outside worlds. And, of course, regardless of where the stimulus for a sensation originated—inside or outside the body—it winds up inside the body in the nervous system.

Raw sensory data coming from regions distant from the cerebral cortex must be interpreted. Meaning must be assigned to the sensations. How one feels must be taken into account. This accounting is done consciously and unconsciously. The implications of the sensations for promoting and inhibiting attainment of goals must be judged. This calls for some theories of "how things work". In other words, "How do people make sense of the world?"; "What causes my behaviours and other people's behaviours?"; "What causes my pleasure and my pain?" Cognitive-social psychology, in particular Attribution Theory and research, has been the branch of psychology most concerned with these sorts of questions.

Early attribution writers described their field of study as *phenomenal causality*. "How do people perceive the causes of behaviour?" The field is also-called *person perception* because most research concerned how subjects made attributions for the behaviour of other people or the self. More recently it is called *social cognition* or *neuro-social cognition*. The change is significant for our purposes. Early attribution writers likely used the label "perception" because the religious version of behaviourism was dominant in most academic departments of the day. Behaviourists "allowed" the study of perception but not cognition.

It was never the case that Heider and the others were studying perception. Making inferences about causality is a higher order mind–brain process that is related to, but different from, sensory perception processes. Developing and using concepts is cognition. Our concern is how the mind processes sensory perceptions via cognition, more and less competently. What are the factors promoting accurate causal inferences? What factors, in mental illness especially, lead to invalid causal assumptions? Because cognition including making attributions is based on sensory data, it makes sense to briefly examine the psychology of sensation.

Sensation

The first experimental psychology was the work of the psychophysicists in the 19th century. Their study of the person's subjective experience was tied to events that were relatively easy to observe and control. Gustav Fechner (1860) exposed subjects to various types of stimuli (e.g., light, sound, and touch), and asked them to report on their subjective experience of the intensity of their sensations.

Fechner's Law (also known as the Weber–Fechner Law) was developed from these experiments and is accepted as generally valid today. The law states that: In order that the perceived intensity of a sensation may increase in arithmetical progression, the stimulus must increase in geometrical progression. In other words, if the strength of a light increases from 2 units to 4 units, the perception of the relative intensity of the two stimuli will be some subjective sense that the light has increased 50%, not the 100% of its actual increase in physical intensity.

For us, the importance of the work of the psychophysicists is the demonstration that the nervous system registers events in the world in a systematic, if not an exactly correct or "true" fashion. In a very real way, sensation needs to be corrected by cognition to know the truth of what is going on in the external world and inside of the body and brain.

The "modification system" of the person is distinct from the more automatic system of the brain–mind that registers sensation or perception. It is the "cognitive system". The differences between the perceptual and cognitive systems were first studied by Wilhelm Wundt, a contemporary of Fechner and Weber. Wundt (1874) used a more insightful term for what we now call cognition—*apperception*, that is, perception of perception. Cognition is a reprocessing of raw sensations or somewhat more organized perceptions. Cognition involves the control of attention and assumptions or beliefs that may or may not be conscious.

While the brain automatically processes sensation via certain perceptual rules such as the Weber–Fechner Law, the cognitive system adds an extra perspective on sensation. This extra level of processing allows the person to modify and control behaviour in a more sophisticated fashion than would be possible via mere instinctual, hardwired responses to the world. For example, consider a person wishing to increase the level of light perceived by visitors to their living room by 100%. A decorator with valid scientific cognitions would replace the 20 watt light bulb with an 80 watt bulb, not a 40 watt bulb. Such behaviour based on a valid concept, the Weber–Fechner Law, leads to greater control than behaviour guided by less formal, sensory intuition.

Attribution Theory

Attribution Theory is the branch of cognitive-social psychology concerned with how people infer what causes events in the external, physical, and social worlds, as well as in the internal, mind, and body worlds (see Shaver, 1975 for a classic description). Attribution Theory deals with the systematic, often implicit, rules that are used to relate perception to cognition. It is like psychophysics in relating events in the world to subjective mental phenomena. But it differs in that it is mostly concerned with the correspondence between perception and cognition and feeling, not merely between external stimulus intensity and perceptions of intensity. And, of course, Attribution Theory involves reactions to complex "social stimuli" (e.g., other people, the self), rather than simpler physical stimuli (e.g., light and sound).

Attribution Theory describes the person as a *naïve scientist*. People do not typically use formal logic like formal scientists, but rather commonsensical rules that are "science-like". But the motivation of the naïve and formal scientists is assumed to be roughly the same. That is, to infer causes and thereby to gain control of events. One of the major tasks of the person is to understand the causes of their feelings. Or, in other words, to answer the question: "What brings me pleasurable and painful feelings?"

Towards this end, the person uses causal concepts. For example: "Being a good person causes good things to happen. I am a good person; therefore I expect good things to happen to me. Certain classes of people are no good, so bad things should happen to them". Of course, in these examples "goodness" or some kind of morality is seen as a causal force. In the child or unsophisticated adult, "moral arguments" tend to dominate over logical or scientific arguments when attempting to understand the causes of events.

Attribution Theory and research try to explain how people explain things. Within the Attribution School itself, some researchers prefer "cognitive explanations" to explain "explaining behaviour" (e.g., Miller & Ross, 1975). For example, things that are obvious or salient tend to be seen as causes. So, actors tend to attribute their own behaviour to what others do, but observers tend to see something inside the actor as causing their behaviour. This is the so-called *Fundamental Attribution Error* or *Actor–Observer Difference* (Jones & Nisbett, 1971). Other researchers tend to see the person's motives to feel good and not feel bad as the causes of their explaining behaviour (e.g., Snyder, Stephan & Rosenfeld, 1978).

We will explore these cognitive and motivational issues in more depth later. For now it will suffice to make clear my position which seems to be a non-controversial alternative to the cognitive *vs.* motivational debate: *Both cognitive and motivational forces work together to determine how people explain events in the world and in the self.*

Affect and sensation

As noted above, there was a lack of precision in the early attribution theorists' claim that they were studying "perceptions of causality" rather than thinking. Of course perceptual and cognitive processes are closely related, but the brain areas processing perceptions and cognitions are different. Any serious attempt to relate neurology and psychology calls for carefully differentiating between sensory perception and cognition processes.

The nervous system is predisposed genetically to automatically classify certain types of sensations as pleasurable and others as unpleasurable. Without any presumed action of higher cognitive centres, gross tissue irritation and injury are sensed as something like unpleasure. And habits to avoid the causes of such sensations will be learned. Similarly, stimulation causing low or moderately intense visual, olfactory, gustatory, auditory, and tactile sensations may be perceived as pleasurable and lead to the formation of approach habits. In animals with minimal or no cognitive processing capacity, "pleasure approach" and "pain avoidance" behaviours include both hardwired instincts and habits learned by means of classical and instrumental conditioning. The molecular biology regulating the synaptic changes in sensory and associative neurons that underlie such habits were elucidated first in the sea snail (Kandel & Schwartz, 1982).

Like the early attribution theorists, the psychoanalysts' way of talking about sensation, thought, and feeling is too imprecise for a psychology–neurology integration project. While Brenner's definition of "affect" has the right mix of concepts for explaining mind, my argument begins with the attempt to make his definition more exact, and to expand it:

> Any affect includes (a) sensations of pleasure and unpleasure or a mixture of the two, plus (b) thoughts, memories, wishes, fears—in a word, ideas. Ideas and sensations together constitute an affect as a psychological phenomenon. Whatever the affect, either the pleasure-unpleasure sensations, the ideas, or both, may be wholly or partly unconscious or otherwise warded off …. Pleasure and unpleasure are sensations …. As far as present knowledge goes, the development of affects from infancy to adult life means the development of the ideas that are a part of affects. It is the ideational content that changes and

that accounts for the differences between primitive affects and those that are more mature—between those often called global and those called discrete or differentiated.

(Brenner, 2006, p. 24)

It is important at the start to distinguish clearly between raw sensation and pleasure and pain. "Affect" is used by Brenner to denote both the conscious subjective experience of the person as well as unconscious processes. He also asserts that "pleasure and pain are sensations". While in some informal sense these assertions are not untrue, they both present barriers to effective theorizing.

The relationships between sensation and cognitions are of central importance in understanding the mind–brain. Brenner is trying to get at this idea by indicating how ideas alter sensation. But labelling both the conscious and unconscious processes "affect" is a mistake. The conscious executive processes that control attention during the use and formation of concepts are too different—and too importantly different—from unconscious control processes to not be given their own unique label. Similarly, there is a tremendous difference between raw sensory pleasures and pains that can be experienced without much cognitive input (e.g., pleasant warmth, thermal stress, or tissue injury) and higher pleasures such as a Bach concerto. Saying "pain and pleasure are sensations" does not much help us to understand the subjective experience of the person or the neurological events underlying the experience.

Sensations in the body can be more or less validly conceptualized by the person in terms of their locations, causes, and meaning. Or, the person can have a global, vague sensation such as "impending doom", "headache", or "optimism". The potential range of "differentiation" in Brenner's terms, and the accuracy of conscious interpretations of sensory perceptions, is enormous. One's understanding of sensation can approach the formal conceptualization of a scientist or resemble the beliefs of children or prehistoric people. Operationally, "meaning" is the association of concepts to other concepts. All meaning involves understanding one concept in terms of another (e.g., Bernstein & Burke, 1989).

Consider a child's subjective experience of classical music, renaissance art, or sophisticated foods. Why do they not find them pleasurable but rather "boring"? Most likely, the child's brain is getting the exact same raw sensations as the sophisticated adult who enjoys such stimuli. The pleasure comes from having the cognitive machinery, the concepts, and processing rules that allow the person to enjoy the sensations. Concepts contain and organize sensory perceptions. This is *apperception*—the additional processing of sensory perceptions via concepts. If concepts and the manner in which they operate are valid, they best indicate the meanings of sensations. And, I assume that more complete and accurate conceptual interpretations of sensation have more potential to produce feelings of pleasure than do less complete, distorted concepts. We can think of making valid concepts as *intrinsically rewarding*; and, using them to obtain other reinforcers as *extrinsically rewarding* (e.g. Deci,1971; Ryan & Deci, 2000).

At the most general level, habit-reinforcing feelings are of two kinds: the pleasures of excitement, novelty, and creativity; and the pleasures of quiescence, comfort, and security. This distinction parallels the one that Freud made between Eros and Thanatos. It is not that raw sensation cannot be experienced as pain or pleasure. It is that raw, perceptually driven subjective experiences are unmediated by cognitions. They are the "hardwired" pleasures and pains of the infant or the non-human animal. They are the inherited preferences for patterns of sensation that the Gestaltists called *good figures*. Today evolutionary psychologists would call such proclivities *prepared learning*. Genetic programmes interact with sensation coming from the external and internal bodily environments. Together they form "whole systems" of sensation and behaviour.

Sensory patterns elicit the evolved security and sexual instincts of the non-human and human animal. Very specific sensory arrays, called *releasers* by the ethologists, cause the animal to perform *fixed action patterns*, that is, instinctual behaviour. For example, the first sensory object of geese and ducks becomes *imprinted* in mind and chicks will follow this first object, which is usually but not always, the mother. The ethologists Lorenz and Tinbergen were the first to systematically study these sorts of genetically wired, stimulus-response patterns (e.g., Tinbergen, 1951).

Summary

Neurology, psychophysics, behaviourism, ethology, cognitive-social psychology, and psychoanalysis have made important contributions to our understanding of the mind. But these schools remain mostly un-integrated. Psychoanalytic writers, who had perhaps the greatest potential to connect various schools of psychology, rarely cite work outside of their own literature. But some psychoanalytic writers besides Freud who have made important contributions have used ideas from other areas. Sullivan (1954), Kohut (1977), Winnicott (1960a; 1960b), and Bion (1962) stressed the importance of social psychological variables. Masterson (1978) used ideas from behaviourism. And Jung (1934) postulated the existence of a *collective unconscious* to describe inherited survival strategies or ways of living. For the most part, the contents of the *collective unconscious* are what Freud called *instincts*.

In any case, these authors wrote before the recent explosive growth in neuroscience. Accordingly, they did not have much to say about the brain. The major aspects of psychoanalytic theory that make it hard to integrate with newer knowledge of the mind and brain include:

- Not differentiating sufficiently between raw sensations, feelings, and thoughts.
- Not differentiating sufficiently between conscious and unconscious processes. For example, both are labelled affective processes. This is not wrong, just imprecise.
- Not acknowledging the necessity of a principle of mental functioning other than The Pleasure Principle. A Death Instinct may be problematic, but there is no doubt that repetition is a feature of normal cognitive operations and that excessive repetition is characteristic of most, if not all, mental illness.

CHAPTER TWO

Cognitive and motivational theories

Contemporary clinical psychoanalysis is focused on affect regulation processes (e.g., Fonagy et al., 2004; Schore, 2003; Stern, 1985). Affect regulation theories try to explain how the person controls their feelings. They are interested, as are we, with how thinking and biological processes work to control the mind. The affect regulation school builds their theories to a large extent on attachment theories (e.g., Bowlby, 1973). Attachment theories and research emphasize the utility of social relations for regulating the feelings of infants and adults. For example, the mother–infant studies done by Emde (1980) and Tronick et al. (1978) illuminated how non-verbal communication between mother and infant can work to regulate the child's emotional state. Schore (2003) argues convincingly that the early learning at the hands of the mother works to form the personality and the neural architecture that supports it.

The Object Relations School of writers including Klein (1932) and Winnicott (e.g., 1953; 1960a) had a major influence on the attachment and affect regulation theorists. *Objects* are imagined to be other people or internal, mental representations of other people. Representations of early objects such as the mother are assumed to become the foundation of the infant's mind. The regulatory activities performed

15

by the mother during the preverbal development period and the reactions of the infant are represented and stored in brain and related to subjective experiences of mind. The representations, or *schemas*, include associations between external stimuli and internal tendencies to respond. For example, when the infant perceives the mother's breast, they get excited. Hence, the connection between theories of object relations, affect regulation, and attachment.

And, there is the closely related school of *Ego Psychology*, identified with Anna Freud's *The Ego and the Mechanisms of Defense* (1946). Her book illustrated how various mental defensive maneouvres such as dissociation, regression, and reaction-formation are all more or less extreme attempts to deny some part of reality and thereby avoid pain. That is, to distort or block from awareness valid concepts about reality for the purpose of controlling anxiety or other unpleasant sensations. Psychoanalytic psychotherapy today tends to involve attempts to increase the durability or resilience of executive functioning in the face of anxiety. Structurally speaking this sort of decision-making function is imaged by psychoanalysts to be in an *Ego*. Neurologists would say that decision making is an *executive function*.

Internal representations or *objects* are best considered *concepts*. At bottom, psychoanalytic and all clinical schools of psychology are attempting to understand the relationship between concepts and the regulation of the person's energy. An exception to the idea that relating energy and conceptual operations is central to psychotherapy is the school of Cognitive Therapy (Beck, 1967; 1976). Cognitive Therapy can be a very effective method. It works by remodelling the patient's invalid concepts, which can lead to depression, among other things. For example, the faulty logic of the depressed patient who claims "I am a complete failure" is countered with data that conflicts with this sort of faulty, implicit assumption. For example, "But you did well on your first job assignment".

Cognitive Therapy

Despite the utility of Cognitive Therapy methods, the Cognitive School has some important deficiencies in the theoretical realm. It attempts to do without variables concerning the unconscious and without motivation or energy variables. All mental illness is imagined to be caused by distortions or "mistakes in thinking". No attention is paid to either unconscious or motivational processes. This is in contrast to a form of cognitive therapy developed by Gerald Caplan (1970, Chapter Eight) called *theme interference reduction*.

Caplan understood that while unconscious themes were operating to cause distortions in patients' thinking, treatment did not have to involve analysis of such themes. Rather, he did something very similar to Cognitive Therapy, but he always made a dynamic diagnosis to guide his treatment strategy. For example, he might infer that unconscious, unresolved Oedipal Conflicts were at the bottom of a patient's anxiety in the presence of a sensual colleague. He would then craft comments to the patient that defused the sexual beliefs without analysing them. For example, "I imagine most people would feel that way about a coworker such as yours". This reduces the patient's worry by explaining their symptom as a "normal reaction". "Most everyone would feel that way".

Cognitive treatments involving diagnoses of underlying causes of symptoms or not, are similar to chiropractic treatments. They realign out-of-line structures and can cause quick relief. This often results in renewed movement in the patient's life and the chance to continue development. However, if serious underlying deformities persist in mind or body, problems will recur.

After rejecting "motivational" and "unconscious" factors as causes of mental illness, Beck, Freeman, and Davis (2004) do in fact use such concepts. From a logical point of view it is impossible to try to explain mental processes without motivational concepts. This is because the entire purpose of thinking is to obtain better feelings, sooner or later.

Feelings of increased pleasure and decreased pain are the most important *reinforcers* or causes of thought and behaviour. And, reinforcement is a motivational concept. An illustration of the implicit use of motivational processes by the cognitive therapists is the use of the idea of "compensation" to explain narcissistic personality disorder (Beck et al., 2004). These authors say that narcissistic feelings of superiority and entitlement are part of "the narcissistic compensatory strategy" for underlying feelings of inadequacy (Beck et al., 2004, p. 247). Presumably narcissistic behaviour is reinforced because it makes the person with a feeling of inferiority feel better. Now, "compensation" is a dynamic process, as are all psychobiological processes. That is, they are processes that require energy, in short, motivation.

Beyond the inescapable logic, there is ample empirical validation that both cognitive and motivational processes occur together all the time (e.g., Bernstein, Stephan & Davis, 1979; Davis & Stephan, 1980; Stephan et al., 1979; Stephan & Gollwitzer, 1981). The critical questions involve not cognition *or* motivation but, rather: When are conceptual activities more or less influenced by security concerns? And, when are they more or less influenced by wishes to learn about reality? Or, in psychoanalytic terms, "How do *pleasure principle* and *reality principle* interact?" (See, Bernstein, 1995).

The motives to know and not know

Attribution Theory and research have emphasized the person's motive to know the true causes of events. I assume that "knowing" is potentially very pleasurable. But while the formal scientist may be largely a truth-seeker, the naïve scientist's motive to know is a more complicated matter. This is because the individual wants not only to know and control the objective, external world but also the internal, subjective world of feeling and thought. The motivation to gain control of one's own feeling, thoughts, and behaviours involves conscious and unconscious "habits of thought". Explicit, conscious awareness sits in-between threats and pleasures coming from both the external world and from "the rest of the mind and body", that is, the parts out of awareness. And, sometimes one can control anxiety by "not knowing" the true causes of events.

Often, especially in cases of parental abuse, habits of mind involve denying large portions of what can be horrifying social realities, (e.g., "The person I depend on is dangerous"). This is the "pain avoidance" arm of the pleasure principle applied to pain emanating both from outside in the form of the abusive parent, and from the child's mind itself in the form of anticipatory thoughts and feelings of danger. The abused child is in a constant state of conflict. He or she needs to approach the parent for security and avoid them in order to be protected from abuse.

All tendencies to behave, not just those of an abused child, involve dynamic relationships between forces impelling the person towards and away from people, situations, and thoughts. This is a feature of normal psychological functioning. The relative strengths of approach and avoidance tendencies are affected by many variables. One factor is *defensive need*, the need to not know or to avoid the truth. The need to protect the intrapsychic, conscious space and regulate feeling so that the mind can function is served by "habits of mind".

For example, there is the mental habit of *dissociation* common among abuse and trauma victims (see Ellenberger, 1970; Masterson, 1978). The abused child is aware of security-enhancing attributes of the parent at one time, but at another time thinks only of the security-threatening aspects. At the conscious level of processing, conflict is impossible if there is only one idea in mind. If one "only loves" or "only hates" the other, everything is fine. In psychoanalytic terms this is called *splitting*, a defence against anxiety found commonly in adults who were victims of early childhood abuse. One is conscious at one moment of daddy's loving attributes and unconscious of his hateful attributes. Later, "hate" becomes conscious and "love" is out of awareness.

In contrast to normal types of attentional control such as *thought suppression* (treated extensively in Chapter Eleven), the term *dissociation* is usually reserved for a serial suppression of ideas over time that is not under conscious control; and, that results in a degraded view of reality and troubles in living. Trauma victims often have little tolerance for holding inconsistent attributes of an object in mind at once. Dissociation of ideas over time is what Kohut (1977) called a *vertical split*. This he contrasted with *repression* or a *horizontal split* where an idea is always blocked from conscious awareness.

Clearly, mental operations involving differentiating and integrating information about people and other items in the world are needed to know reality. And, they can be enlisted in attempts to not know reality. The exercise of extreme forms of mental control can have the quality of psychopathology. For example, I treated a Vietnam veteran whose unit had been overrun by the Viet Cong. Each man had been killed or had fled. About ten American soldiers lay in the centre of the battlefield apparently dead. The Viet Cong soldiers tested to see if each man was dead or merely acting dead by sticking a knife in each man's legs. The patient reports that he was able to "not feel the pain", to "lay silent and motionless" and, hence, was able to fool the enemy. He ultimately escaped to tell this tale of an extreme, dissociative security operation.

This extreme ability was not entirely under the patient's conscious control. He was prone to various psychopathic behaviours such as paedophilia which were enabled presumably by his dissociative ability. Specifically, he could disable concepts about morality. In general, the mental manoeuvres needed for reducing awareness of moral standards must be similar to those operating to eliminate other items from consciousness such as intense pain. Such cases illustrate that normal, strong habits to use moral standards to control behaviour when one has an impulse to do something anti-social, may work to inhibit mental operations that might have great utility in abnormal, emergency situations. In any case, biological, psychological, and social factors certainly contribute to the development of dissociative tendencies in general and psychopathic behaviours in particular (e.g., Weber et al., 2008).

Non-motivational biases in thinking

Thinking habits are shaped not only by motives to avoid physical and psychic pain but also so-called "non-motivational reasons". These non-motivation factors which influence thinking are preferred by the Cognitive Therapy School. Non-motivational causes include phenomena such as the Fundamental Attribution Error, also known as the Actor–Observer Difference (Jones & Nisbett, 1971). This is the tendency of the person to see external, environmental factors as the causes of their behaviour. For example, "The social situation caused me to yell at them". Observers, in contrast, tend to attribute actors' behaviours to something about the actor, for example, "Their aggressive personality caused them to yell".

This difference is seen by attribution theorists as caused by a simple difference in what is obvious to actors and observers. That is, the actor sees the environment; the observer sees the actor. Attributions are made to what is attended to. Such an axiom doesn't seem to be "defensive" or self-serving on the face of it. It might best be viewed as an unsophisticated or "naïve" system of attentional control. That is, a system in which the person tends to explain their actions in terms of what is salient to them.

If to know reality is the greatest potential pleasure, then there should be strong motivation to learn to deploy attention on the basis of more than just what is obvious. For formal and *naïve scientists*, advanced control of attention leads to more complete and valid theories of causality. It is probably safe to say that every mental disorder involves some degree of defensive control of attention.

Conceptual security operations

In contrast to the non-motivational biases in attributions are the *defensive attribution theories* such as *Attributional Egotism* (e.g., Snyder, Stephan & Rosenfeld, 1978). Attributional Egotism describes the person's tendency to explain their successes, such as academic exam performance, as caused by the self. For example, "My high score on the exam was due to my high intelligence and hard study". On the other hand, poor performances tend to be attributed to some external agency such as task difficulty ("that was a hard test") and "bad luck". Such a pattern of *self-serving attribution* is motivated by a desire to enhance and protect self-esteem and, in turn, increase positive feelings such as pride and reduce negative feelings such as sadness (e.g., Stephan & Gollwitzer, 1981).

The motivational explanation for why people believe that success is caused by the self, and failure is caused by non-self factors, is different than the cognitive explanation (Miller & Ross, 1975). The Cognitive Theory, also-called the *expectancy confirmation theory*, is that people usually expect and intend to succeed when they attempt a task. And they do so because they believe that they have the necessary ability and have expended the necessary effort. Therefore, when what we intend and expect occurs, we attribute the outcome to ourselves (i.e., our ability and effort which were the bases of our expectation of success). When failure occurs, which is assumed to be unexpected, people naturally imagine that it was due to something outside of the intending and expecting self ("a hard test", "bad luck").

But in a study of university students' expectations and explanations for their exam performance, we illustrated some limits of the Cognitive Theory's assumptions about expectations and attributions (Bernstein, Stephan & Davis, 1979). On the first exam of the academic term, students overestimated their actual score by 10%. On the second exam, expectations were only 4% overly optimistic. By the third and final exam the mean expectation for test scores in the class of over 400 students was almost perfectly accurate (less than one percentage point). Over time and with experience, people learn very well what to expect from themselves and the world.

At first, students engaged in wishful thinking in line with a primitive type of pleasure principle. But with feedback about their real performance, expectations got very accurate. And, expectations came to be based on estimates of effort, that is, extent of study. The overly optimistic expectations for the first exam were based largely on feeling lucky. By the third exam students' expectations were more strongly based on how much they had studied than on judgements of intelligence or luck.

How one thinks about their efforts is perhaps the most important sort of way to learn about oneself. Variations in effort permit the person to estimate the effects of high and low exertion in order to predict and control behaviour and feeling. Cognitive schemas about the world and about the self build up more or less rationally with feedback. In our study, expectations got more accurate as students began to see the affect of study on performance. The more one studies, the better one does in school. Miraculous! Estimates of one's intelligence had little effect on expectations. In other words, when we get feedback about our performance and learn about the situations we are in, the better we understand, predict, and control our real outcomes.

The Non-motivational Theory did predict some of students' explaining behaviour. We divided the class into students whose expectations were confirmed (expected A or B and got it, or expected less than a C and got it); and those whose expectations were disconfirmed (expected A or B and got C or less; or expected C or less and got an A or B). As the Cognitive Theory predicted, exam performance that confirmed expectations either high or low, led to explaining the performance as caused by internal factors, that is, hard study in the case of high performance and lack of study in the case of poor performance.

But the "self-protection and enhancement effect" was much stronger and pervasive. That is, for the most part, exam performance was attributed to the factors that would enhance and protect self-esteem and reduce negative feelings regardless of expectancy confirmation. In statistical terms, the "effect size" or importance of motivated self-esteem protection and enhancement was five times larger than the expectancy confirmation effect.

The point is that both cognitive and motivational factors affect how people think. The self-protection and enhancement motives are always operating. "Protection" and "enhancement" are the two arms of the pleasure principle—harm avoidance and pleasure approach. Over time, people behaved rationally in generating expectations, that is, their predictions became very accurate. They were less rational with their post-test explaining behaviour. From the first exam through the third, students attributed good performance (A or B grade) to the self and bad performance (C or less) to a "hard test" or "bad luck".[1]

Reflective and reflexive systems

Any theory intending to explain the brain and mind must account explicitly for the dynamic, energetic aspects of bio-psychological systems. Motivational Theories including behaviourism and psychoanalysis both use the term *drive* for the energy component. Large amounts of glucose are metabolized during cognition (Gailliot et al., 2007). In the psychoanalytic theoretical system, the *id* is the repository of instinctual energy, while *ego* and *superego*, or *conscience*, are the structural features assumed to regulate *id or libidinous drives for pleasure*. Freud (1923) imagined that ego processes could be more or less conscious. Ego- or Self-Consciousness is a late evolutionary development. The adult human's capacity for self-consciousness differentiates them from infants, animals, and many with autism.

Lieberman and Eisenberger (2004) have made a distinction between what they call *Reflective Brain Systems* and *Reflexive Brain Systems*. Human learning and development depends upon the degree of integration of these two types of brain–mind systems. The Reflective System involves conscious cognition. In psychoanalytic terms it involves *ego functioning*. In neurological terms it involves *executive functioning*.

In contrast, the Reflexive System includes automated, instinctive, unconscious tendencies to behave; and, it includes habits learned by means of repetition that have been reinforced because they have had some instrumental value. That is, it involves the *drive* and *habit* processes of interest to the motivational, animal learning schools. Biologically hardwired, instinctive, self-protective, and self-enhancing tendencies must be included as part of a reflexive system. In psychoanalytic terms a reflexive system is more or less of an *id* system.

Lieberman and Eisenberger locate Reflective Functioning in: Lateral Pre-Frontal Cortex (LPFC); Anterior Cingulate Cortex (ACC); Posterior Parietal Cortex (PPC); and the Medial Temporal Lobes (MTL). Together, these brain areas are assumed to perform conscious "Test-Operate-Test-Exit" functions, or, TOTE functions (Carver & Scheier, 1981).

TOTE involves mental operations that compare the actual state of something (e.g., a nail halfway embedded in wood) to some ideal state (e.g., nail all the way in the wood). This is the "Test" phase. Then one "Operates" by pounding the nail with a hammer until it is flush with the wood. Once the standard has been achieved, one "Exits" the situation. Apparently, operating together, LPCF, ACC, PPC, and MTL can perform these TOTE functions.

TOTE operations are used when a person evaluates some sub-jectively felt impulse in light of standards of correct behaviour. For example, most people would reflect upon the correctness of acting on a murderous wish. They would *Test* the impulse using their standard of correct behaviour; *Operate* somehow to suppress the impulse; *Test* to see that the suppression was sufficient; and, then *Exit* the decision-making process. In contrast, a psychopath manages to be without awareness of a standard for correct action, for example, by dissociation, and, hence, is more likely to act anti-socially.

The neurological structures underlying Lieberman's Reflexive system are: Amygdyla; Basal Ganglia; Ventro-Medial Pre-Frontal Cortex; and Lateral Temporal Cortex. These structures operate together to activate and execute already learned habits and instincts.

The centre of the problem of "mind–brain regulation" is the rela-tionships between these two sorts of systems. The question that must be asked and answered by the person's mind–brain is: "In this situation I am in right now, should I use an Old Habit of responding or should I develop a New Way to behave?"

Of course, the individual has no need to be reflective if an old habit will work perfectly well in a situation. Reflective functions are "higher" functions. Learning or creating a new way of behaving uses more energy in the form of glucose than do habits. Despite its large energy requirement, the evolutionary advantages of a capacity to execute a new behaviour rather than a habit "already on the shelf" should be clear.

Genetic, prewired behavioural tendencies remain in the genome because they somehow promoted survival. But such "on-board instructions" regarding, for example, "what to do in an emergency", do not account for all the specifics of *your current emergency*. They provide general avoidance instructions that work well most of the time (e.g., "Duck!"). And, "most of the time" is what evolution cares about. If the individual enters a novel, dangerous situation in which instincts plus old learned habits won't save them, then they had better come up with a new plan: "You're on your own now pal". (See Chapter Four for a detailed description of such a situation).

Chronic stress caused by dangerous, unstable environments or mental illness causes the individual to rely increasingly on old habits. The brain structures sub-serving new learning atrophy and those supporting old habits become larger with chronic stress (Dias-Ferreira et al., 2009).

Personality and habits of mind

Personality psychologists have studied many traits including: *riskiness* (e.g., Zuckerman & Kuhlman, 2000); *anxiety* (Taylor, 1953); *self-consciousness* (Fenigstein, Scheier & Buss, 1975); *defensive style* (Byrne, Barry & Nelson, 1963); and *empathy* (Davis, 1983). These and many other traits make up what is considered the personality.

But another way to conceive of these stable aspects of the person is to recognize that traits become enacted in behaviours or more specifically, *habitual behaviours*. In our view, studying *the process of* the *enactment* of stable, strong, mental habits is likely to yield the most insight into the mind and brain. The personality is all of the person's strong mental habits.

Habit shapes the person's energy or *drive* (Hull, 1943; Spence, 1956). In behaviourist terms, habits are the structural, controlling elements of mind. The Gestaltists used *tension* as their energy term. Social Psychologists have tended to use *arousal*. And, there are "emotion", "feeling", and "affect" used by formal and naïve scientists to get at some internal state, conscious or unconscious, having the quality of energy. The behaviourists, with *drive* (the energy) and *habit* (the container and shaper of energy), were the most clear at differentiating the force and direction aspects of bio-psychological processes aimed at the achievement of goals. Together *drive* and *habit* constitute a vector, something with force and direction.

Habits are learned behaviours that are reinforced because they have aided the organism in attaining the good feelings associated with food, sex, comfort, safety, money, a promotion, and so on. All *reinforcers* either increase pleasure, decrease pain, or do both. *The Attributional Egotism Effect*, for example, describes habits to explain one's good behaviours as caused by the self and not so good behaviours as caused by something other than the self. These explaining habits are reinforced to the extent that they enhance self-esteem and produce good feelings, and protect self-esteem and, thereby, reduce bad feeling.

An important concept from Hull and Spence is that the mind's structure may be represented as a *habit hierarchy*. Each stimulus situation may be considered as the entire array of sensory stimuli registered in the brain by the situation. This would include all instinctual and learned tendencies to respond to stimuli. And, each stimulus situation has some potential to elicit a behaviour, either an old habit or a new creation.

The strength of a habit determines its place on the habit hierarchy. *Habit Strength* is understood as the likelihood that a *sensory stimulus array* will cause the performance of the habitual behaviour. If the habitual behaviour is strong, low intensities of the stimulus array cause it to be performed. If the habit is weak, high intensity stimuli are needed for it to be enacted. One of the most important concepts from behaviourism is that with general arousal, strong habits become relatively stronger in relation to weak habits. In other words, the habit hierarchy stretches out: the strong get stronger.

This idea should be familiar from addiction medicine. For example, the habit of cigarette smoking is elicited at first perhaps only after eating, then when on the phone, then when anxious and, after a while, virtually any situation can cause the habit to be performed. When a habit moves to the top of a habit hierarchy for a situation it is called the *dominant habit*. Habits with higher thresholds of elicitation, that is, weaker habits, might in the smoking case involve chewing gum, drinking water, or fidgeting. The trick in smoking cessation is to cause a habit other than the addictive one to become dominant. Success in addiction cessation, by definition, is when stimulus situations that formerly caused the addictive behaviour instead cause a less harmful behaviour. A major barrier to changing the relative strength of habits is that anxiety or arousal causes alterations in habit strength. In particular, dominant habits become more dominant when the individual is aroused. This is why smoking, drinking, drug taking, "nervous talking", and all strong habits are more likely to be enacted as the patient's arousal or anxiety increases.

Attention

The biology and psychology of the conscious and unconscious decisions about how to deploy attention have to be very complex. The first important node in the decision tree is: Old Habit or Something New. If option one is chosen, end of game. If option two wins, then a whole set of new decisions need to be made. These involve coming up with new concepts or applying old concepts in a novel way in the new situation. One may have to search memory; compare the costs and benefits of different behavioural strategies; check the time; and on and on. How does one regulate the mind to do these problem-solving tasks?

At some level, the answer is simple. In the subjective experience of the person, perhaps the only effortful or wilful things one can do to regulate mind is to make three decisions: "What to attend to? How long to attend to it? What to look at next?" (cf. Posner & Peterson, 1990).

Because wilful efforts can be made in directing attention, attentional control is the key feature of any mind–brain regulatory system. Snyder and Mitchell (1999) stipulate two general directions of attention: Concepts or Raw Sense Data. Snyder's model can explain in general how attentional focus works to regulate sensation. Activating "sense data containing concepts" regulates the intensity of the sensation and gives rise to thoughts and feelings. Depending on how the sensations are conceptualized, the feelings will be more or less pleasurable or painful. For example, "This water slide is fun"; "This water slide is scary"; or "This water slide is fun and scary".

One can get relief from the constant stream of sense data by thinking about it. Or, one can let the sensations and feelings flow. Clinical disorders involve one or both of the following conditions: (1) Overly contained sensations, thoughts, or feelings; and (2) Under-contained sensation, thoughts, or feelings. From a clinical perspective, the right question is: "How can we increase the competence of the processes and validity of the concepts that control attention in order to enhance the person's ability to achieve his or her goals?"

This is where self-focused attention comes in. "What is in the person's focal awareness?"; "Is it something about self or not self?"; "What controls attention?"; "How might attention work to regulate feelings and thoughts?"; "What are the cognitive and motivational effects of concentrating on a particular object of mind?" And, in turn, "How is direction of attention affected subsequently by feedback from the motivational and cognitive processes it is affecting?"

Self-focused attention

The terms *conscious* and *self-conscious* when used in common parlance have two main types of connotations. One meaning calls up painful experiences and the other connotes something else, something more complex. A focus on the self can be instigated in the person by cues from the social environment. And, the strength of one's habit to be self-conscious (Fenigstein, Scheier & Buss, 1975) interacts with self-focusing stimuli in the social environment. Kurt Lewin is famous for articulating what is now a truism: Behaviour = Person (or personality) × Situation.

The painful sort of self-conscious experience refers to "having made a social mistake" and "being looked at". The other, happier sense of "conscious" enjoyed increased popularity in the 1960s. In that exciting period, consciousness was "raised" by civil rights, woman's rights and anti-war movements, and drugs. These activists challenged others to examine and change long-standing norms of social behaviour.[2,3]

Paying attention to the self is an instance of the more general process of attending to anything. Direction of attention is easily manipulated by the laboratory scientist. Accordingly, theories of the causes and effects of self-directed attention have developed with the aid of many well-designed experiments (e.g., Duval & Wicklund, 1972; Gibbons, 1978; Pryor & Kris, 1977; Scheier & Carver, 1977). Social psychological theories of the self are supported by experimental research in contrast to psychoanalytic theories which have developed largely from clinical observation.[4]

The first social psychological model of self-attention was Objective Self Awareness Theory (Duval & Wicklund, 1972). They assumed that most generally there are only two things a person can attend to: an aspect of the self, or, something else which is "not-self". Duval and Wicklund dubbed the self-focused state, *Objective Self Awareness* (OSA); and the non-self focused state, *Subjective Self Awareness* (SSA). The OSA state is a relatively "stopped" state, in which self-evaluation takes place. The SSA state is a more "flowing" condition where active control of mind and body occurs in the background of the mind. These two states correspond to Lieberman's Reflective and Reflexive modes of operation.

Self-focus has been manipulated in the laboratory by means of seating subjects in front of mirrors or an audience, or playing recordings of their own voice. In other words, things that make us feel self-consciousness in ordinary social life. Duval and Wicklund assumed that the mirrors and audiences work to increase the proportion of time the person spends in the Objective *vs.* the Subjective Self-Aware state. They assumed further that the self-aspect focused upon immediately after the self-focusing cue is introduced, is whatever was salient for the person at that moment.

In particular, self-focus is thought to heighten the person's awareness of some relevant social or internal standard for evaluating their most recent and, therefore, most salient behaviour. In our terms, we would say that the self-focused person is aware of two concepts: "the set of things I should do" and "the set of things I did do". This is thought to lead to a self-evaluation, in which the person measures the size of the discrepancy between Ideal Behaviour and Real Behaviour.

In short, what is focused on in a state of Objective Self Awareness is the gap between some real and some ideal aspect of the self. This is the TOTE processing of Carver and Scheier (1981). If the gap is negative, that is, if one has fallen short of the self's standards, an unpleasant tension state ensues. In Freudian terms, the self-aware person is being regulated by his *superego* or *ego ideal* and can feel anxious and inadequate. On the other hand, if the gap is positive, that is, if one has just met or exceeded an Ideal of the self, the person might seek out mirrors and audiences to enjoy the positive feelings associated with success and pride.

OSA Theory assumes that the person faced with a "gap in the self" can do one of two things: "avoid self-focus" or attempt to "close the gap". The motive in both cases is to rid the self of tension. Being watched by the self or others tends to makes people social or "moral". The pro-social kinds of behaviour promoted by self-consciousness are the opposite of *de-individuated* or wild behaviour which can occur when self-reflection is low, such as in darkness or in intoxicated states (Festinger, Pepitone & Newcomb, 1952; Le Bon, 1896).

The assumptions and implications about the causes and effects of self-focus have been validated from many angles. For example, self-focus: (1) Intensifies negative feeling among students who had cheated on an examination (Archer, Hormuth & Berg, 1979); (2) Increases efforts to conform to self-standards, that is, to close the *real self–ideal self* gap (Carver, 1975); (3) Increases avoidance of self-focusing stimuli in those who feel inadequate (Duval & Wicklund, 1972); (4) Increases consistency between self-reports of behaviour and actual behaviour (Bernstein & Davis, 1982; Fenigstein, Scheier & Buss, 1975; Pryor et al., 1977); and (5) Can lead to the use of substances (e.g., alcohol) to control feelings caused by negative self-evaluation (Hull, 1981; Hull et al., 1986).

On the clinical side, Ingram (1990) notes that almost every form of psychopathology is associated with increases in self-focused attention. This makes sense if attentional processes are called into play by the person to alter old habits of mind when they don't work to make the person feel good or behave effectively. But, knowledge of a person's degree of self-focus is not, by itself, pathognomonic. To begin to describe normal and pathological mental functioning one must consider: attentional variables; conceptual and attributional processing; raw sensation; feelings and expectations of pain and pleasure; and the neurology underlying them all.

It is of central importance for understanding both optimal and pathological mental functioning to learn (1) What factors move the person to avoid focusing attention on the self?; and (2) What factors move them to maintain self-focus, presumably for some functional gain? Since wilfully deployed attention helps regulate the mind, it is very likely that keeping focused can work to help the person achieve goals. Such goals are social and objective, for example, to get a job; and some are psychological and subjective, for example, to experience a pleasant feeling or thought.

The importance of these issues was articulated by Silva and Duval (2001). In particular, they recognized the theoretical importance of understanding the connections between attention, attributions (that is, causal concepts), and expectations. The reason that expectations are so important is that they can set in motion approach and avoidance motives and overt behaviour. In such an instance the self, more or less consciously, is getting in gear. Executive functions are deployed. And, life and death, or at least health and wealth, are always more or less at stake. The person must resolve expectations that imply differing actions.

Mental control

Objective Self Awareness Theory helped to promote the contemporary interest in "mental control". Wegner and Pennebaker (1993, p. 3) note that: "The term 'mental control' does not appear in searches of the psychological literature before 1987 ... [But] the study of mental control has really been occurring for quite some time under other rubrics, only now to surge forward given the spark of a new synthesis".

If a "new synthesis" is emerging it is being driven by advances in cognitive research methods (e.g., semantic priming techniques); psychoanalytic interest in the regulation of emotion; new technologies for imaging neurobiological processes, e.g., functional Magnetic Resoonance Imaging (fMRI); and, advances in neuromolecular biology. Most famously, three Nobel Prizes were earned in 2000 for the elucidation of "signal transduction in the nervous system": Eric Kandel for discovering the molecular basis of Long Term Memory; and Arvid Carlsson and Paul Greengard for their work on the neurotransmitter dopamine.

For any sort of synthesis involving biology and psychology to occur, we need a theoretical framework that is amenable to the diverse sub-fields. Such a framework must recognize the relationships between overt behaviour, the subjective experiences of thought and feeling, and the biological processes that give rise to both molar behaviour and subjective experience. Psychoanalytic theory in its "neo-classical form" (e.g., Brenner, 2006) is inadequate to contain and organize the knowledge from the relevant fields. It is especially handicapped by its dismissal of something like a *repetition compulsion* as a necessary mind–brain process.

Most, if not all, psychopathologies involve ineffectual repetition. "How are thoughts and feelings processed normally?" This question is addressed in Chapters Three through Five. "How and why does normal mind–brain processing turn into pathological, repetitive processing?" These clinical questions are taken up in Chapters Six through Twelve.

Summary

The person's use of concepts is more or less habitual. Concepts that regulate sensation most effectively are reinforced. That is, concepts which work to increase pleasure and decrease pain, such as *attributional egotism*, tend to be used repeatedly. The ideas validated by behaviourists regarding reinforcement, relative habit strength, the effects of arousal, and the difficulty of habit change are applicable to cognitive processing.

Taken together, all the individual's habits of mind, such as tendencies to use certain beliefs to interpret the meaning of sensory perceptions, is more or less equivalent to the personality. And, of course, concept-using habits can be a part of the person's conscious awareness or not.

The interaction between reflexive, habit processes and reflective, self-aware processes are central to understanding the person's behaviour. What is needed is an open theoretic approach that considers both cognitive and motivational variables; recognizes the role of unconscious reflexive and conscious reflective processes; and, is aided by an understanding of the brain. The model, spelled out in the next chapter, attempts to outline the interrelationships between raw sensation, feelings, concepts, expectations, overt behaviour, and conscious awareness.

Notes

1. This difference between preparatory thinking and post-hoc explaining was named the *Basic Antinomy* by Jones and Gerard (1967). *The Basic Antimony* describes the two orientations of conceptual activity: the pleasure of openness and learning; and the comfort of security operations that reinforce existing concepts. The phenomenon of buying a car can illustrate the two aspects of the antinomy. Before buying one does research and compares and contrasts options. After the money has been spent, all the negative aspects of the chosen car cause "post-decisional regret" or the unpleasant arousal called "cognitive dissonance" (Festinger, 1957; Wicklund & Brehm, 1976). In an attempt to reduce the unpleasant feeling caused by all the negative attributes of the purchased car, the person rationalizes: "That squeaking noise is kind of cute, like a bird".

2. The 1960s illustrates the way that advanced concepts and methods from physical, biological, and social science influence the mind and behaviour of the regular guy, the *naïve scientist*. Perhaps most indicative is that 21st-century world economies drive, and are driven by, "knowledge workers". The role of conceptual, scientific understanding in regulating and maintaining our modern societies becomes increasingly immense every year. Both information and space flight technologies grew explosively in the 1960s. Using sophisticated computing machines, and reflecting upon one's own "self-planet" from the Moon, were new experiences for everyone. And, they promoted strong feelings and new thoughts in many people.

3. Also, in the 1960s, there was increased interest in Eastern models of consciousness such as Zen Buddhism. In the East, the environment is seen as more of a causal factor than the self, reversing the trend seen in Western cultures (Miller, 1984). Plus, there was a large increase in the recreational and clinical use of psychoactive drugs. Both the big ideas of the social movements and the pharmacology aimed largely to "alter consciousness". The more recent idea of a "New Age" refers, in large part, to mass attempts to be less "sad", "anxious", and "neurotic"; and, more "high", "happy", or "enlightened".

4. For some laboratory-based investigations of psychoanalytically based hypotheses see Eysenck and Wilson (1973); Bernstein (1984); and, Weston (1999).

CHAPTER THREE

Concepts, feelings, and expectations

The word "concept" comes variously from the Latin *concipere* and *capere*. These mean respectively "to take in" and "to capture". Of course, "concept" is more or less synonymous with "idea". But "to conceptualize" has a "mental process" quality, while "idea" has a "mental structure" connotation. The conceptual process very literally "captures" sensations or perceptions or other concepts. Concepts "take things in". Or, when we remember *apperception*, Wundt's (1874) word for thinking, we might say best that concepts perform an act of re-perceiving sensations so that their meanings or implications can be inferred. Conceptualization has vast potential for regulating the feeling and overt behavioural reactions to sensory perceptions; and, in turn, stimulating and regulating further conceptualization.

The term *schema* has a long history in psychology to denote mental structures that organize and interpret events. Piaget (1928; 1954) used the term to describe what gets developed with learning. Kant (1781) assumed that *schemas* were applied to understand sense data. I use the term *concept* here in similar ways.

Concept is defined as "a collection of attributes". A "cat" for example is a concept that includes various attributes. Some attributes of

35

the typical cat are visually perceivable, such as "tail" and "fur"; some are auditory attributes, such as "meows". And the concept "cat" also involves other concepts about social and appetitive behaviours such as "friendly" and "catches mice". Note that the difference between "a concept" and "an attribute" is not complete. A concept can be an attribute contained in another, higher-order concept.

Since creating concepts involves gathering sensory and conceptual attributes, the level at which objects are assembled can vary. In the case of *splitting*, the defensive operation characteristic of various dissociative disorders, the abusive parent's good attributes may be placed in one conceptual container such as "good mother" and her bad attributes placed in a separate conceptual container such as "bad mother". The lack of integration of the inconsistent attributes causes trouble. These troubles stem from the problem of managing the thoughts, feelings, and behaviours caused by the conflicting impulses to both approach and avoid the mother. Defensive motives work to dissociate the positive and negative attributes of the mother and, hence, they are not all present at once in awareness. Decision making thus becomes "black or white". Such zero-sum thinking is a poor guide for operating in the more complex, "real world" which has many more degrees of freedom for thinking than imagined by one who is *dissociating*.

Similarly, in psychotic thought disorders a concept such as "cat" might be over-populated with attributes, for example, "representative of the devil". Or, one attribute of the cat might become magnified and its other qualities ignored. Take the patient with an obsessional fear of germs who might find that the attribute "touches dirty mice" dominates their awareness.

Following Allen Snyder and John Mitchell (1999), I assume that concepts contain sensory information. That is, they process data coming from the sense organs and the viscera by an act of *apperception* or cognition. Somehow, the brain puts a label on that cat and all the sensory data becomes integrated in the concept of the cat. Instead of seeing disembodied fur and tail and hearing meowing, the cat is imagined to be a whole entity. Conceptualization greatly simplifies the task of living in the world by reducing the number of separate sensory items one is registering consciously. In contrast, Bion (1962a, p. 13) described the difficulty psychotic patients have when sensations are uncontained and are experienced as "splinters" or "smithereens".

Snyder stipulates that when a concept is in awareness, raw sensations of the attributes that make up the concept are not in awareness (Figure 1). In other words, concepts integrate discrete perceptual attributes and turn off awareness of the sensation of any particular attribute. Snyder's model is shown in Figure 1. "Post-concept state" refers to what is in awareness after the concept is turned on. Pre-concept state would be awareness of the sensory attributes themselves.

In the post-concept state only the concept is reported to conscious awareness. The attributes of the object are inhibited, but the inhibition is dynamic and can be switched off and on. A concept is a grouping of object attributes (from Snyder, Bossomaier & Mitchell, 2004, p. 36).

Animals and infants

That concepts and sensations alternate in conscious awareness is a beautiful idea that has numerous and varied types of face valid support. The great sensory acuity of non-human animals—the senses of smell and hearing in dogs; the eye sight of cats and birds—is well known. What is less known is that all new born humans probably possess animal-like sensory sharpness that fades with development (see Snyder, Bossomaier & Mitchell, 2004, p. 33). Independent of

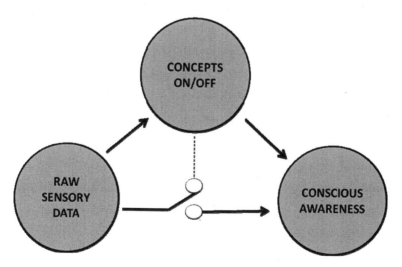

Figure 1.   Model for post-concept state.

special modifications of the sensory organs themselves, such as the reflective nature of the inside of the cat's eye, the reason for high animal and neonate sensory acuity is the same. That is, it is a difference in the nature of the central nervous system. Compared to adult humans, animals and human neonates have rather minimal conceptual systems. Hence, the animal and new born person must be almost entirely aware simply of sensation, unadulterated by conceptual thought.

The world is never as precisely sensed as in infancy. The greater salience in awareness of sensations *vs.* thoughts is consistent with the sense of "nostalgia" experienced by most of us. We somehow remember the early period of life, before a fundamental change occurred in our subjective experience of the world. It was a change that came with learning. The multiple, unfiltered sensations of the tree, flower, sky, water, mother, father, and everything else become more or less contained in our concepts of these things. And, when our concepts are primitive, they are somewhat poor substitutes for the original sensations.

Take the drawings of young children. The stereotypy in drawings made by children of the person, the horse, the tree is remarkable. These are the early containers of sensations—sparse and two-dimensional, poor representations of the underlying sensations. The child draws largely the concept of the horse, not the full sensory array of attributes that are no doubt in their brain. The child's concepts themselves are primitive, leaving out many attributes.

The completeness or validity of concepts themselves is the critical mental structure variable. The critical mental process variable is the individual's competence at turning concepts "on" and "off". Figure 1 indicates that control of this "concept switch" is needed to become aware of the detailed attributes of an object.

We posited earlier that the motive "to know reality" is the strongest motive. Operationally, to know reality with more depth than is revealed by the surface of objects is to use concepts that represent the world with more or less validity. "Validity" is used here in the scientific sense of having a hypothesis that is correct *vs.* incorrect or invalid. It makes sense, too, to keep in mind that we can consider the "amount of validity" of any concept. The drawings of the children are valid as far as they go. But sophisticated artists can do a better job. And sophisticated scientists can build increasingly valid concepts for representing the world.

"Validity" is so important for science that different grades of it have been labeled. An idea can be *Face Valid*, for example, "It is obvious that the rain caused the flood". An idea can have *Predictive Validity*, for example, "The barometer is so low, it is likely to rain".

And, there is *Convergent Validity* when different ideas, perhaps from different schools of thought, make the same prediction. The idea of *displacement* provides an example. Lewin's theory of Topological Psychology (1936), and Ethology, and Behaviourism, and Psychoanalysis all use essentially the same model of *displacement*. In Lewin's terms, if one is striving to attain a goal, a *tension state* will exist in mind. If attainment is frustrated, the energy that was aroused to attain that goal can be *displaced* in the service of achieving an alternate goal. For example, the boss insults an employee, but for fear of losing his job, the employee suppresses his wish to punch the boss in the nose. Instead, he comes home and kicks the dog, or yells at the television newscaster.

Then, there is *Discriminant Validity*. For example, we know that increasing the level of serotonin floating around synapses will likely cause diminishment of *unipolar depression*. But increased serotonin levels alone are not so effective in reducing *bipolar* forms of depression. The predicted effects of serotonin are conditional. We don't say it will cure any form of depression but rather discriminate between the forms of the disorder for which it is effective.

The overall validity of theoretical systems such as psychoanalysis or social psychological theories of motivation (e.g., McClelland et al., 1953), derive from the interlocking of many different concepts that are supported more or less with combinations of *Face, Predictive, Convergent*, and *Discriminant* types of validity.

I think the drive to produce more and more valid concepts is the most general, strong drive. It leads to deeper conceptions of reality. Learning is better than sex, or at least, better as a candidate for "the most general driver" of behaviour. If you take Freud's sex drive and substitute "hunger for knowledge" you have a better theory. In light of practical concerns, that is, that most people are never educated enough to find pure joy in learning, motives that do not depend on too much learning will appear to be dominant. But from a theoretical standpoint, the human is potentially most driven by the wish to learn and create better reality-explaining ideas. This is in the service of generating more precise control of the internal and external worlds. Not to mention that misunderstanding about "what's the most fun" causes all sorts of human misery.

Now, the ability to produce more valid concepts depends primarily on skill at alternating attention between sensation and concept. The most basic process in concept usage and development involves turning concepts "on" and "off". Control of concept activation is "the skill of skills". It is more or less synonymous with the regulation of conscious attention. *A central assumption here is that at the most basic level, the regulation of thought, behaviour, and feeling is determined by the deployment of attentional focus.*

This is because attention brings into awareness either sensory detail or concepts which integrate details. Snyder's model makes it quite clear that there are two general directions of focus: concepts or sensations. And, the sensations can originate from outside the body and be delivered to brain via nerves from the sense organs; or they can emanate from the body and be delivered to the brain via enervations of the viscera.

It is perhaps safe to say that the only way to operate the mind with intentionality and effort is to control the direction of attention. It is something like using a little joy stick to control a giant computer game. There are, of course, methods to increase the competence of the mind to turn concepts "off". For example, there are the art school exercises such as drawing objects upside down, attending to the spaces between objects, and just concentrating very closely to the details of objects when drawing. These sorts of techniques tilt the balance of what is in conscious awareness towards sensory data and away from concepts. On the other hand, we somehow can learn to "call concepts into awareness". For example, when trying to stop smoking the person attempts to switch attention away from craving sensations coming from the body and to activate helpful concepts such as "smoking gives you cancer". At bottom, regulating the mind involves a constant switching of attention from sensation, to more or less valid concepts.

Autists

The work of Allan Snyder and others (e.g., Grandin & Johnson, 2005) makes clear that phenomena seen in autism inform our understanding of normal mental operations. This is because autism might best be considered "a disorder of conceptual processes". Like children and animals, autists have relatively rudimentary conceptual lives. So studying children, animals, and autists can illustrate how the mind operates with few or no concepts. The autistic state differs of course from the animal or child-like mind because it is a neuropathology. Some neurological process affected by genetics and other variables prevents or interferes with the development of conceptual thinking (Bailey et al., 1998; Lamb, Weinberger & DeCuir, 2002). Abnormalities in the amygdyla, hippocampus, and cerebellum have been associated with autism (Courchesne, 1995; Kemper & Bauman, 1998).

Autism is also related to other disorders such as Asperger's Syndrome and Obsessive Compulsive Disorder (OCD). We have seen in practice a wide range of function among those on the so-called "autism spectrum". They can present as children with mental retardation or as neurotic, world-class scientists. The prominence of repetitive behaviours seen in patients on the autism spectrum illustrates that when concepts do not work to contain and channel sensation, sensation and associated behaviours will repeat. This is consistent with the idea that something beyond a pleasure principle operates in mind–brain. Autism is a prototype for a sort of dysrhythmia seen in most mental illness. That is, one has trouble when there is some derangement in the process of switching attention between concepts and sensations. The autist has underlying difficulties with both concept creation and usage.

Two symptoms seen in autism are consistent with the idea that concepts help regulate anxiety. First, the repetitive rocking movements seen in these patients may be understood as a substitute method of self-comforting. That is, the autist uses mostly procedural, muscle movement schemas, and not semantic concepts for comfort. Impairments in the brain's ability to use verbally coded concepts to contain sensation, causes increased reliance on rhythmic rocking of the entire body for self-soothing. That rhythm produces pleasurable feelings is universally known.

Second, autists seem to prefer an unchanging environment. They can become unglued if an object is moved from a familiar place. This makes sense. If conceptualization is inhibited, adjustment to change becomes very difficult. This is because one must change mental representations of the world to "keep up" with any changes that occur.

One gets data about changes from the sensory system. Concept use and development is driven by changes in sensory arrays that originate from outside and inside the body.

A small percentage of people with autism are known as "autistic savants". Sometimes profoundly retarded, these individuals are capable of astounding mental feats. Some of these abilities were exhibited by an autistic character played by Dustin Hoffman in the popular film *Rainman*. He could perform calendar, arithmetic, and memory tasks with great precision. His great anxiety in handling tasks of normal living was also shown; for example, an intense fear of flying.

Snyder postulates that all the mental abilities of savants depend on having conscious access to raw sensory data. This is the kind of data that most of us lost contact with as concepts developed. The autist either doesn't have concepts, or he (*the male to female ratio in autism is* 4:1) isn't able to switch them on. In any case, autistic savants can somehow perceive very raw sensory data.

But Snyder's theory is that such data is not entirely raw. Data coming from the sensory organs undergoes a sort of pre-processing. It is separated into sets of equal numbers of elements. The strong version of this hypothesis is that "equipartitioning" is the basic form of "pre-processing" of all sensory data regardless of modality. In structural terms we might best label the equipartitioned groups of attributes "protoconcepts". Presumably the autistic savant can become conscious of protoconcepts. (It is interesting to note here that having a common method for pre-processing sensory data from all sensory modalities would seem to be a prerequisite for experiences of *Synesthesia*.)

Such ability to be conscious of protoconcepts is consistent with all the savant skills. The typical savant mental feats all involve likely direct and very fast perceptions of equipartitioned visual, auditory, and "arithmetic" sensory attributes. For example, there is the startling story of two twin girls, patients of Oliver Sacks (1985), who, when a box of 111 matches fell to the floor, cried out, "111 and 37, 37, 37". We assume that the girls were seeing each individual match and were apparently chunking them into equipartitioned groups. They were not making an "estimate" of the number of matches. Estimation is what the rest of us would do. Estimates and expectations involve using concepts of some sort to try to discern "How many matches must there have been?" The savants on the other hand are using protoconcepts that minimally, or not at all, distort the "truth" of the data.

The calendar skill of autists is the ability to tell the day of the week of a particular date far back in history. This feat can also be interpreted as depending on the ability to be aware of sensory data at the equipartition stage of processing. Weeks are always seven days, but the length of months is not a constant. Finding a day of the week back through years involves plausibly equipartitioning the entire period of time into equal seven-day groups. Then one counts the number of full, seven-item, protoconceptual containers, and counts any leftover portion of days.

This same process likely operates in identifying prime numbers which, by definition, are those numbers divisible only by themselves or 1. Dividing a prime number by something other than itself or 1 leaves a remainder. It is obvious that access to automatically equipartitioned data about a number would allow very fast and accurate identification of primes. The autistic savant can be considered a "computational expert". He operates with few or no concepts and knows nothing of theories of numbers or mathematics.

The access to protoconcepts also makes savants astonishingly accurate in judging the passage of time, which is clearly a skill involving "grouping units". In the auditory realm they have perfect pitch. Identifying the pitch of a note of course involves grouping auditory frequencies into categories, a skill that would be enhanced by access to the underlying sensory data. They often have astounding memories. And remember, all neonates and non-human mammals likely are aware of sensory data at this detailed level.

Perhaps most remarkable in this story of autism is that Snyder has developed an experimental paradigm to change the mental processing of normal subjects to resemble more that of autistic savants. This is achieved by directing low frequency, Transcranial Magnetic Stimulation (TMS) into the left anterior fronto-temporal lobe, specifically the occipital cortex. The application of TMS at about one pulse per second can inhibit localized regions of the brain (Pascual-Leone, Bartres-Fox & Keeman, 1999). The inhibition lasts for a few minutes.

Snyder et al. (2006) used an experimental analogue of the autistic twins perceiving the falling matches. Between fifty and 150 discrete black dots were displayed on a white background for 1.5 seconds. Subjects were asked after each display to report how many dots had appeared. A key measure was if a subject's report of the number of dots was within plus or minus five of the actual number shown. Results showed that twice as many subjects achieved the accuracy standard in the TMS condition than the control condition. It is assumed that the TMS essentially inhibited concept activation and, hence, improved subjects' awareness of the raw visual sensory input. TMS applied to the same left orbito-frontal region has worked in normal subjects to increase auditory acuity (Bossomaier & Snyder, 2004); and to promote naturalistic drawing styles and improve proof-reading ability (Snyder et al., 2003).

The regulatory function of concepts

It seems plausible that perception of a "leftover portion" of a prime number by an autistic savant causes some sort of arousal. *More generally, we assume that in all people sensory attributes that are not contained adequately by concepts are the primary stimuli for thought.* The more or less chronic agitation of autists is consistent with this idea. While they have very good access to protoconcepts, they have poor ability to make or use more normal, higher-order concepts. This suggests, by the way, that there is no pressing need to think once sensation has been happily organized and packaged. Of course such a state of affairs only occurs in very unchanging external environments and very stable internal, bodily states. In the real world, unresolved conflicts cause sensations, feelings, and expectations of future events to be poorly contained and regulated. The implication is that conceptual agility is a more or less constant requirement of the person.

This last idea is consistent with the intention, I think, of Freud's original idea of the repetition compulsion and its cousin the Death Instinct. The purpose of thinking from my perspective is more or less literally *to kill sensation.* Uncontained sensation is an irritation of sorts. Thinking works to regulate sensation by capturing it and "killing it". Thinking is very much like hunting by this analogy. And one can seek small or big game. The more valid the concepts used to contain the sensation the less need there is to *repeatedly think about it.* Solving a problem, making a good decision, gets rid of repeating sensation. New sensation can then be considered and development may proceed.

Now the sort of arousal caused by the "to be conceptualized" sensation can be experienced in a variety of ways. On the positive side there is curiosity about what this yet to be classified sensation means. Ideally, curiosity promotes enquiry, experimentation, and development of a valid explanation for the sensation, and good decisions about how to cope with it. On the negative side there is anxiety about the novel stimuli. Typically, our responses to unknown sensations are some combination of these reactions. Anxiety is thought to be controlled by *security operations* (Sullivan, 1954); *ego defences* (A. Freud, 1946); *character defences* (Reich, 1933); and *personality styles* (Shapiro, 2000).

How are novel sensory data conceptualized? This is the central determinant of whether a person is mentally ill, more or less normal, or of great mental competence. Conceptualizations can be poor representations of the underlying sensations; "good enough" representations that allow one to get along in normal environments; or very accurate conceptualizations, resembling valid scientific theories. And, of course, the level of the individual's mental competence fluctuates. Very high arousal caused by social, biological, or psychological change can cause regression in anyone and thereby reduce competence. And sometimes an individual will thrive on high levels of stress with improvements in mental performance.

We have outlined the two basic factors that contribute to mental competence: 1) The validity of concepts for interpreting the meaning of sensory data; and 2) Skill at activating and deactivating concepts, in part, to sample sensory data. States of mind that represent less than optimal functioning are caused by problems in one or both of these two sorts of variables. These two sorts of variables—one structural and one processing factor—are central. An additional assumption that works to integrate these cognitive variables with motivational theories is that *concepts are created and used to generate expectations about the potential of a situation, external or intra-psychic, to promote pleasurable feelings or reduce painful feelings, or both. Such expectations sometimes result in overt behaviours.*

Mental processes can result in overt behaviour or not. One might think about having a martini and then decide to order a martini or not. In any case, muscular movements and information about their results is reported back to nervous system. The data will come over internal nervous tracts and it will also eventually be conceptualized. The above assumptions are spelled out in Figure 2.

Figure 2 indicates the relationships between the key structures and processes that determine the individual's mental competence. When everything is working right, the person will develop instrumental, valid concepts. Learning to use more valid concepts has important social, psychological, and biological consequences.

The function of concepts is to represent or describe events inside and outside of the body. Theories are sets of organized concepts. Concepts form the bases of expectations (probabilities) that a situation will result in pain or pleasure in the short and longer term. As in science, it is with the person. The formal scientist and the *naïve scientist*, that is, the typical citizen, use theories to generate predictions or expectations of how situations, characterized in particular ways, will develop over time. They use data to check the validity of their assumptions. In the mind–brain system, sensory data is raw data. Concepts organize such data, in large part, to make predictions (cf. Bar, 2009).

Both valid and less valid, distorted concepts are used to form expectations of a situation's potential to produce pleasure and pain. Taken together, concept validity, the ability to turn concepts "on" and "off" to sample more sensory data and to regulate anxiety, the accuracy of expectations, and the reinforcing effect of feelings, work to establish mental habits that affect overt behaviour and overall mental competence. To the extent that the person decides to act, feedback from overt behaviour comes to the brain from sensory neurons in the muscles; and, via nerves from the specialized sense organs. One can have both kinesthetic and visual sensations of a moving limb. These two sorts of sensory data can then go on to be conceptualized by cortical associative structures and processes. When concepts fail to resolve conflicting expectations, the process will repeat.

The ability to see the long-term pleasure and pain potential of situations increases with development of valid concepts. The better the concepts, the more accurate are the predictions (e.g., Bernstein, Stephan & Davis, 1979). The better the predictions the more effective is the person's behaviour; they know the situations and goals to approach and those to avoid. Finally, the more successful are

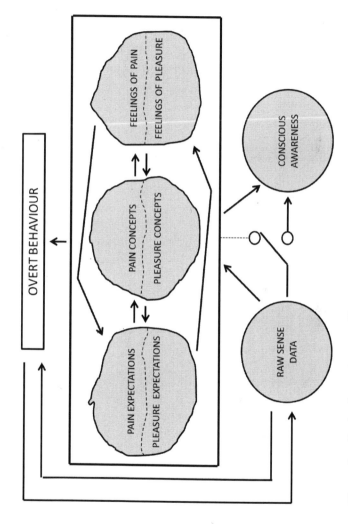

Figure 2.   Basic determinants of human competence.

appetitive and avoidance behaviours, the more feelings of pleasure are maximized and feelings of pain are minimized. The validity of concepts and, hence, the accuracy of the expectations based on the concepts vary within and between people. States of mental illness as well as competent mental functioning can be understood as caused mostly by the interaction of three factors: 1) The validity of concepts underlying expectations of pleasure and pain; 2) The ability to activate such concepts to think; and 3) The ability to deactivate concepts to collect sensory data to think about later.

Everyone is more or less ambivalent about everyone and everything. Brain–mind registers sense data and combines it with concepts that produce feelings, expectations, and sometimes overt behaviour. The whole complex works to resolve more or less satisfactorily competing tendencies to approach and avoid every object in the world and every subjective experience in one's own mind. Reflexive processes are more or less aided or hindered by Reflective processes. Together, instincts and learned habits are integrated with conscious reflective consideration using TOTE processes to produce more or less competent decisions to approach or avoid things. The individual's success in the bio-psycho-social worlds depends on the validity of the concepts used to interpret sense data and other concepts relevant to the situation in which one is called upon to behave overtly. The infant wants to approach the mother to be perfectly touched, feed, stimulated, relaxed—everything. To the extent such wishes are frustrated, avoidance motives develop in conflict with the approach motives.

Roughly speaking, approach motives are stimulated and regulated in large part by adrenergic neurotransmitters and hormones (e.g., norepinephrine, dopamine, and steroids) and glutamate. In subjective states produced by stimulating chemicals one feels active, strong, up, confident, aggressive, and happy. These are the pleasures of "go". The neurotransmitter Gamma-Aminobutyric Acid (GABA), in combination with various ions, promotes the pleasures of down regulation: "stop", "relax", and "be comfortable". The inhibitory effect of GABA can be inhibited itself by *endomorphins*, the endogenous opioid molecules that stimulate pleasure when occupying *mu-opioid receptors* on neurons. These receptors are most prevalent in cortical associative regions of the brain where conceptual activity occurs. This is what makes thinking and learning pleasurable.

> In several systems where neural connectivity has been studied, neurons with *mu-opioid receptors* make synaptic connections with so-called GABAergic neurons.... Thus the activation of *mu-opioids* serves to inhibit these inhibitory neurons ... and so allows local excitation to be propagated with greater intensity to the succeeding stages of information processing.... [Such propagation] may ultimately increase the release of dopamine within the corpus striatum, a structure deep in the brain that is implicated in the control of movement, cognition and habit learning.

> (Biederman & Vessel, 2006, p. 252)

In short, excitatory and inhibitory neurotransmitters are in dynamic relationships. Intense pleasure comes from conceptual activity stimulated by opioids and dopamine. But unmitigated neuronal firing can cause seizures or mania. This tendency is checked by GABA. And, the inhibition itself can be a kind of pleasure.

Feelings are "meaningful sensations"

Earlier, I stated that integration of theories of mind and brain phenomena calls for finer distinctions between the many terms that have been used to describe subjective states. We must differentiate between raw sensations, minimally processed protoconcepts, concepts proper, and expectations. And then there is what has been called "feeling", "emotion", "affect", "intuition", "arousal", and so on. Figure 2 gives an outline of the states and processes we need to explain. The words used are somewhat arbitrary. The theoretical requirement is that the terms help to differentiate as unambiguously as possible important aspects of brain–mind phenomena.

What should be clear is that there are subjective states caused by very raw sensory data. Ulric Neisser made a similar point in *Cognition and Reality* (1976). Raw sense data must be given some structure by the brain–mind. It is likely minimally processed and organized by something like equipartition. Bion (1962b, p. 311) too saw the need to distinguish between "preconceptions" and more complete concepts. What have been called *percepts* or *perceptions* are more or less what I am calling *protoconcepts*. So the processing sequence is: raw sense data→protoconcepts→concepts.

Sensory attributes that cannot be contained by equipartition (e.g., prime numbers), can trigger instinctual responses in the body and mind. The Gestaltists would say that *tension states* are always produced by incomplete or "bad" perceptual figures. And, instinctual tendencies are automatically activated to make bad figures good. This sort of activation in response to sensorial tension can bring conceptualization processes on board. Conceptual activity is called for at the point that unconscious, automatic, and instinctual processes are insufficient to handle or regulate sensation.

The assumption is that "sensation" turns into "feeling" when concepts are brought to bear to interpret the meaning of raw sensation (see Figure 2). Feelings can be conscious or unconscious. This means that the person can be more or less aware of the underlying system of concepts or assumptions they are using to interpret sensations. By our definition, feelings are always "meaningful sensations" regardless of the level of awareness of the interpretive system. What the person is always aware of at some level when "having a feeling" is the effect of the conceptual interpretation of raw sensation on the subjective experience of more or less intense pleasure or pain or both.

Of course, sensation can cause overt behaviour by means of simple reflex action, unmediated by semantic concepts. This is indicated in figure 2 by the causal arrow from sensation to overt behaviour.

When in explicit awareness, concepts are represented most usually as words. *The Semantic Differential* of Osgood, Succi, and Tannenbaum (1957) is very relevant here. They were interested in the meaning of meaning. That is, "What are the general dimensions of meaning that all words convey?" Their conclusion, after extensive research, is that there are three general dimensions of semantic meaning: Evaluation; Potency; and Activity. These three dimensions indicate, respectively, that any object represented by a word can be assessed as to whether it is "Good or Bad"; "Weak or Strong"; and "Active or Passive". The Evaluative Component accounts for the most meaning as assessed by factor analytic methods—about 70 percent. Potency accounts for about 20 percent and Activity about 10 percent.

These "dimensions of meaning" are exactly what one would like to know about the potential of an object or stimulus to create feelings of pleasure and pain. Is the thing good (pleasure) or bad (pain)? Is it of high or low potency or intensity? Is it something that can move towards or away from me, or is it relatively immobile and passive?

The semantic meanings of concepts are the main determinants of the expectations we develop in regard to situations. Our concepts or theories of the meaning of situations determine what we expect from them. Or, more exactly, what we expect from the stimulus arrays in the brain that represent situations. At bottom, all concepts and the expectations we generate have a deep root in the process of deciding consciously and unconsciously whether to approach a pleasure, and whether to avoid a pain. The process can be fast and raw, involving immediately pleasurable or threatening stimuli, such as a looming predator. Or it may concern more considered, subtle forms of feelings of pleasure and pain that occupy all our waking social and vocational pursuits.

The meaning of concepts, along with some physiological arousal, works to produce subjective feeling states. This approach is in the tradition of Schachter and Singer (1962). Their *Two Part Theory of Emotion* is that emotion is comprised of a label or concept, plus an arousal component. Both the arousal and cognitive component were deemed necessary for a person to have an emotion. In their research, subjects received injections of epinephrine or saline. Both injections were described as a "vitamin" with no indication that the drug would cause physiological arousal. They then placed subjects in a waiting room in which a confederate of the experimenters acted either angry or euphoric.

As predicted, subjects searched the environment for a cause of their raw sensation of arousal. In the "angry confederate condition", subjects who had gotten the epinephrine reported feeling angry. Subjects seeing the same angry confederate who had received saline did not report feeling angry. The same sort of effect was observed in the "euphoric condition". Subjects injected with epinephrine seeing the happy confederate reported feeling happy. Those getting the saline placebo did not report being happy. When subjects in another condition were told that they were receiving a stimulating chemical, they did not interpret their subjective state of arousal on the basis of observating the confederate's angry or humorous actions. Instead, they used the label provided by the experimenter for the cause of their arousal, that is, the norepinephrine and did not report much emotion.

I am using the word "feelings" to signify *meaningful sensation*. It is probably prudent to assume that all meaning is connected at some level with feelings of pleasure and pain. Pleasure and pain are the two basic underlying categories of "meaningful sensation" or "feeling". Feelings are what reinforce concepts and behaviours. The need to label global sensation, that is, capture it in a concept in order to produce feeling, is what Schachter and Singer were getting at. They emphasized that the person typically searches the external environment to know the meaning of sensation. That is, they exposed aroused or non-aroused subjects to social cues that the subjects used to label their own internal subjective state.

Social cues can and do influence how we understand our internal state. But here we want to stress the importance of sensations that originate within one's own mind and brain as cues that the person uses to understand sensation. This of course is necessary when developing a theory that must explain many normal and pathological states in which the person is having feelings not because anything has happened in the social or physical environment, but because something has changed internally in the body and mind.

The characterization of *feelings as meaningful sensations* works to differentiate *feelings* from *affect*. Patients with certain lesions in the brain due to stroke, multiple sclerosis, and other conditions may suddenly, without any obvious cause, begin a short spell of crying, laughing, or rage (e.g., *pseudo-bulbar affect*). When asked how they are feeling they often report that they feel nothing in particular, just normal. In contrast, a feeling involves some sort of attribution that gives meaning to the experience. Performing gestures usually associated with a feeling may be without any particular psychological significance. While *affect regulation* is certainly a problem for a person with some types of brain damage, *feeling regulation* is more of the issue for people with functional psychopathology.

The key tasks for the person interpreting sensation are to: (1) Correctly identify the location of the stimulus for the sensation; and (2) Generate accurate expectations of the potential of the stimulus situation to cause pleasure and pain. In other words, mind–brain must answer two questions: "Does this sensation originate from a change in the environment external to the body, or does it originate in my own body?" And, "What are the implications of this sensation for future sensations, feelings, concepts, and behaviour?"

Awareness and compromise

Figure 2 specifies that concepts, expectations, and feeling can exist in and out of awareness. Just as items sitting on a computer's hard drive can exist without evidence of their operation appearing on the computer screen, concepts out of focal attention can operate and affect other conscious and unconscious processes. This has always been an assumption of psychoanalysis. But the nature of this unconscious action has never been specified clearly by psychoanalysts or others. Following Snyder and Mitchell (1999), I imagine that concepts, expectations, and feelings come into awareness when raw sensation goes out of awareness. How brain–mind structures and processes operate differently in and out of focal awareness is a key question.

Obviously, mental contents out of awareness must be stored in memory. The ability to encode, store, and retrieve items in long-term memory is central to thinking. And, problems with one or another of these memory processes are of central importance in understanding both normal and pathological psychological functioning.

Brenner (2006) and other psychoanalysts consider conscious experience, or *what we can be aware of*, a *compromise formation*. The recent affect regulation writing is based more or less on a compromise formation idea. From a psychoanalytic point of view, the content of consciousness is always a compromise between what we think is true and what we would like to be true. These compromises are imagined to be security operations motivated by a wish to control thoughts, feelings, and sensations. The mind's eye is constricted and dilated variously to regulate the contents of consciousness and, in turn, the intensity of feeling. One needs to be aware of enough "reality" to function, but also needs to restrict ideas that might stimulate overwhelming feelings. Somewhere in the mind, an agency "makes a decision" about where limits should be placed on awareness. How does the person develop habits of mind to regulate the permeability of consciousness to unconscious contents?

Brenner's theory of the "compromise" leaves out an important determinant of what can be in awareness. We would say that consciousness can contain valid and invalid concepts or raw sensation and feelings. When the person is lacking a valid concept that might help explain a situation, what can be in consciousness but a "compromise"? Consciousness, at least focal awareness, always misses part of reality. Valid concepts can be out of awareness for cognitive reasons (e.g., span of attention is limited); for motivational reasons (e.g., awareness causes anxiety); and for reasons of ignorance (the person never learned the concept).

The psychoanalytic idea of "compromise formation" does not make explicit that ignorance of valid concepts is the largest cause of compromise formations. This idea is more a "cognitive" than a motivational explanation of the nature of consciousness at any one moment. This is an important consideration if we are to have a more balanced assessment of how both cognitive and motivational factors affect the person. And, it has the implication that psychotherapy might best work as an educational experience in which people learn concepts for controlling their minds (Bernstein, 2001).

If we look at what people used and still use instead of science to explain the world, (e.g., alchemy, fundamentalist religions), it is obvious that a lot of what has been, and will be, in people's minds are invalid concepts. Invalid beliefs, if not known to be invalid, work to "make sense of the world" and to contain emotion. However, they are inferior to valid beliefs for forming accurate expectations and for controlling events other than the believer's own emotions.

Until recently, physicians came to patients with texts full of invalid theories. But they did at least give the sick hope and a perception of control. The perception of control is central to regulating emotion (see Glass and Singer, 1972). The power of belief, for example, the placebo effect, is real and strong. But holding valid beliefs that might confer real control is preferable to placebo beliefs. This, of course, is why the motive to learn about reality is so strong. The alternatives, denial or avoiding reality, lead in the long run to less control and pleasure, and more pain.

Self-awareness

What about self-awareness? Is it a special form of consciousness, distinct from awareness of sensations, feelings, concepts, and expectations? We assume that when a person becomes aware of anything—sensation, feeling, concept, or expectation—the contents of consciousness are labelled by brain–mind in one of two ways. What is in focal awareness is either about the self or not about the self. In other words, the mind's entire contents must have been labelled in this fashion. Of course, we might conceive of this distinction as more graded, that is, having to do with estimates of distance from the self ranging from "close" to "far". Either way—continuous or categorical—I assume that some process of discrimination is activated in mind–brain to assess the self-relevance of each object in awareness.[1]

That mental objects are labelled as more or less *self* is an important feature of various psychoanalytic traditions. Kohut (1977) reserved his label *selfobject* for anything that had a self-soothing or calming effect on the person. Winnicott (1954) used the term *transitional objects* to describe how teddy bears and blankets function like the mother's breast until the person's own mind could perform the soothing function.

Jung's notion of self is perhaps most germane for our argument. In its simplest, least arcane sense, Jung's idea was that the self is the most central concept in the person's mind. It is sort of the king of concepts. Compared to any other of the person's ideas, the self-concepts have the most power to organize all of the others.

Jung's "Self" should not be confused with the "Ego" in the Freudian sense. Jung's central idea was that something like a Freudian Ego was the executive of the mind's cognitive processes. The Self, on the other hand, is a larger structure that the Ego must manage. It is the repository of what Jung called *archetypes* and Freud called the *instincts* that promote survival and reproduction.

As executive functions mature, these self-instincts become, ideally, more conscious and linked to verbal concepts. In other words, the Reflexive and Reflective systems become more aligned. For example, an ego regulates the self's aspirations so that they might be achievable in light of validly conceptualized reality. Without such a connection to reality, the person's goals and plans can resemble more childish fantasy or manic grandiosity than plausible strategies for living. What people think of as God is, in Jung's view, essentially a projection of the self-concept. This sort of projection undoubtedly works to keep many people functioning psychologically (e.g., Jung, 1940).

Jung's thinking is consistent with my assumption that every object in the mind is subject to some sort of "self-test". If the self organizes everything else, then every concept's relationship to the self-concept must be taken into account. How else would we remember something except by giving it an address within a larger system of coordinate concepts? More or less of this process might be conscious. And, of course, psychoanalysis of every type (Freudian, Jungian, Kohutian, etc.) puts a premium on making such organizing habits of mind conscious. Ideally, one develops an ability to reflect upon the self itself.[2]

Kohut's Self Psychoanalytic School puts a great emphasis on *mirroring*, or the caregiver's and the therapist's ability to accurately reflect the internal experiences of the infant or patient. In the way they regard the child, the early caregivers demonstrate "how to regard the self". Depending upon the caregivers' empathic competence (Davis, 1994), the child develops a more or less durable self-regulatory function (e.g., Emde, 1980; Schore, 2003; Tronick et al., 1978). I think of this sort of management function, as did Jung, as the province of an agency more like a Freudian *Ego* that performs *executive functions*, than a Jungian *Self*. *Executive functions* manage the conceptual universe of the mind–brain. Hence, The Executive must arbitrate when the person's expectations, feelings, and tendencies to behave, or other concepts, are in conflict.

How is conflict resolved in the mind and brain? Well, it can be resolved out of, or in, awareness. If the process is conscious, resolution must involve some consideration of the elements of the conflict. Then, an attempt is made to change one of the elements to be consistent with the first and, hence, reduce conflict (the TOTE idea) and anxiety or *cognitive dissonance*.

Cognitive Dissonance Theory (Festinger, 1957) says that the person's subjective state is *dissonant* (uncomfortable, anxious) when a cognition about a behaviour is inconsistent with some other concept. For example, dissonance might occur when someone who holds the belief, "I hate fish", eats fish. The cognitions that are dissonant here involve a behaviour (e.g., "I just ate fish"), and a privately held belief ("I hate fish"). Festinger predicted that the person can reduce discomfort by changing one of the cognitions. Usually the private preference changes, not the cognition about the behaviour. The person revises his concept of what he likes to eat, for example, the attribute "fish" in now contained in the concept "what I like to eat". He does not deny that he actually ate a fish. This works out well, of course, since outright denial of publically observable aspects of reality can cause trouble for everyone.[3] Aronson (1969) added the idea that dissonance is not aroused unless the concept that is inconsistent with the cognition about a concrete behaviour is a *self-cognition*. In this case, a cognition about what one likes to eat and, hence, should logically eat or not eat.

But how much of conflict resolution involves conscious deliberation? How durable are the person's executive functions under conflict and anxiety? Can the person keep conflicting objects in mind, and think logically about them in order to make the best decisions? At what point do they opt for short-term anxiety reduction, over the potential benefits of a decision that takes longer term consequences into account?

Pleasure principle and repetition compulsion

We assume, as did Freud (1920), that two general factors determine mental functioning: the pleasure principle and a tendency to repeat unresolved conflicts. Specifically, if a conflict is not resolved so that pleasure–pain trade-offs are in some sense "favourable" for the person, the brain–mind will reprocess the problem. If the new concepts that are needed to make a better decision are not developed or used, the process repeats unchanged. When a conflict is "stuck" in repetitive cycling, a new, better concept is needed to resolve it. If no new idea can be imagined, raw sensations are no better contained, expectations are no more accurate, and overt behaviour is no more effective. Sooner or later, fruitless repetition causes anxiety, confusion, and hopelessness.

Summary

The model (Figure 2) includes six sorts of variables and the interactions between them: (1) Sensory Data; (2) Concepts (e.g., words for collections of sensory attributes); (3) Executive functions such as Attentional Control (i.e., the switch for turning concepts "on" and "off"); (4) Feelings; (5) Expectations of pain and pleasure; and (6) Overt Behaviour. This may be the fewest number of concepts needed for a theory to have robust validity and meaningful implications for applied clinicians and basic neuroscientists. The processing of sensory data into thoughts, feelings, and expectations can work to produce more or less logical decisions; and more or less effective overt behaviour. Decisions based on relatively "invalid concepts" of the world and the self, are poor decisions. If old habits are not adequate to cope with a current problem, the sensations driving thinking, feeling, and behaving will repeat.

The brain–mind developed to make decisions in real time. All thinking involves decision making associated with more or less conflict. In Chapter Four we ask, "What is the subjective experience of emergency decision making?" and "What role does time play in decision making occurring at high levels of threat to life and limb?"

Notes

1. Both the immune system and nervous system have a capacity for memory and recognition. Both function in part by making *self vs. not-self* distinctions. The potential of Psycho-Immunology to enrich the discussion of mind–brain theoretical integration is great. The self's membranes are biological, psychological, and social. And the separate systems are part of a whole.

2. Kierkegaard's (1849) definition captures something of this idea: "The self is a relation that relates itself to itself".

3. Tulving's (1972; 2002) distinction between episodic and semantic memory is relevant here. Perhaps, the discussion of which aspects of the mind are most malleable should consider the relative ease of altering a semantic lexicon *vs.* a log of episodes. Clearly either can be altered with different costs and benefits to the person. An "episode reviser" is likely to be considered a "liar"; while the one who alters the conceptual lexicon itself is a "theorist".

   Are ideas or feelings "deeper" aspects of mind? If one thinks of feelings as "meaningful sensations", then the whole argument becomes pointless. A better question might be: "Are concepts that are held relatively dispassionately and objectively, deeper than feelings, which are concepts full of intense, subjective sensation?" But one needn't think that a rise in objectivity is always associated with a fall in subjectivity. That is, thinking and feeling are part of a system with many degrees of freedom; hence, thinking and feeling, and objectivity and subjectivity, are not necessarily involved in simple, zero-sum relationships.

   This type of argument is related to the Jones and Gerard (1967) *Basic Antimony* idea which assumes that rational, objective processes of mind are inherently different from subjective processes. Another way to think of the same thing is to ask, "Are objectivity and subjectivity always in a zero-sum relationship to each other?" If indeed there is a "basic antinomy", then at some level, perhaps at the boundaries of the body and mind, objectivity and subjectivity are in a zero-sum arrangement.

CHAPTER FOUR

Decisions and time

Brain–mind is a decision-making system. Decisions, by definition, involve choosing between alternatives. Hence, at some level, decision making is always "conflict resolution". The central importance of conflict in human psychology has been recognized by psychoanalysts since Freud, and by social and neuroscientists (e.g., Deutsch, 1977; Lieberman & Eisenberger, 2004). In this chapter we describe decision making under emergency conditions. In such situations there is not usually conflict about "ends", that is, the clear goal is to avoid the danger. Emergency decision making involves choosing between "means" or methods of life saving. "What is the best way to avoid the danger?" Since the stakes are high, emergency operations ideally consider alternative interpretations of a dangerous situation; and, alternative predictions about the outcome of different "avoidance strategies". At the same time, danger induces strong feelings that must be controlled in order to effectively think and act. Recollections of a real emergency decision-making situation are described below.[1]

A driver had given a ride to a young man touring Northumberland. The tourist was heading to Newcastle but the driver was going to turn off at the outskirts of the city. The hitchhiker would need to find another ride into the city proper. Since the driver was a local citizen, the hitchhiker assumed that he was knowledgeable about the traffic situation. The poor rider had no expectation that he was about to face a serious threat to his safety.

He was let out at the top of a five-story, spiralling, three lane ramp that descended to the city streets below. The ramp had no sidewalk, but a six-inch-high curb of about a foot in width. The curb supported a four-foot-high, iron fence with horizontal cross bars, separated by about two feet. A fleet of loud, smoking lorries were coming down the ramp ceaselessly in all three lanes at about twenty miles per hour. The spiral of the ramp was so tight that drivers had to be constantly looking in the direction of the turn.

The young tourist was perched barely on the six-inch curb, his back to the fence. The street lay seventy feet below. A large lorry was bearing down on him from about ten yards. The driver was completely unaware or indifferent to the tourist's waving and shouting. And, as the driver curved down to where the tourist was standing, the cargo-carrying part of the lorry was swinging out over the fence clearing it by inches!

What was the subjective experience? The hitchhiker reports that he had "intense arousal". This included "hair on end", "heart pounding", and "a sense of dread". The objective, scientific assessment of the situation was not in doubt. He knew he would be hit by the truck in about three seconds if he could not devise and execute an effective avoidance plan. We can also assume that "instinctual" tendencies were activated in parallel with the conscious concepts, predictions, and feelings. Moreover, we assume that there is extensive, neurological, and psychological cross-talk between the instinctual and conceptual systems, especially in emergencies.

Emergency responses

"Looming objects" such as predators (and large trucks) activate instinctual, "prepared" avoidance behaviours in all animals. It is so advantageous to have an inborn, automatically activated sensory and motor system to avoid collisions and predators that we can safely assume its universality. Researchers have studied looming and "collision avoidance" at neuronal and molar behaviour levels of the organism. Subjects have included humans (Dubreuil et al., 1998); monkeys (Schiff, Caviness & Gibson, 1962); and insects (Rind,

Santer & Wright, 2008). The fearful hitchhiking experience can be taken as a prototype of reactions to conflict. We assume it is descriptive generally of decision making. That is, decision making occurring at low and moderate stress levels too.

The brain–mind is driven and regulated by two general types of systems that work to keep the individual safe: (1) An evolved, instinctive, neuro-endocrine-muscular system that produces fast, global "flight or fight behaviour"; and (2) A higher level, partly conscious, cognitive system. This is the "concept-expectation-feeling system" in Figure 2. Its function is to augment the "decisions" made by the evolved instincts.

An advantage of the instinct system is that it is fast. Neuronal circuits are "pre-wired" to respond to general gestalts of stimuli that may indicate danger, for example, a fast moving shadow associated with a stalking predator. The sensory system is wired to muscular reflexes to produce avoidance behaviours. How well the stimuli match a stored, mental representation determines if the avoidance actions will be triggered.

The advantage of the conscious system is that it can be much more differentiated. The instinct system produces global and stereotypic avoidance reactions such as "crouching" or "covering up" to minimize profile; and, generalized sympathetic arousal to provide energy and defence against injury (e.g., vascular changes). But the conscious executive system can channel and refine the individual's avoidance behaviour for a particular, more or less unique, danger situation.

Our model assumes that sensation, consciousness, concepts, expectations, feelings, and behaviour all have bidirectional causal effects on each other (Figure 2). We also assume a lot of parallel operations, and both feedback and feed-forward information links. Neuroscience today, due to advances in technologies, does not shy away from attempting to specify what we know must be tremendous complexity.

Compromise

Cognitive capacity varies phylogenetically. Having more rather than less capacity comes in handy when avoidance reflexes and rudimentary ideas are inadequate to protect the individual. The thinking system functions in real time to embellish instinctual responses. One can "think on their feet" to generate very specific and very effective predictions and decisions.

Of course, the benefits of conscious deliberation may induce very high anxiety, especially in real emergencies. In psychoanalytic theory, the anxiety-reducing function is served by coming to a "compromise formation". It does the person little good to be so scared out of their wits that they can't generate any avoidance response at all and merely freeze or panic.

So, although more truth accounted for consciously may be useful for making the best decisions, "compromises" that generate "good enough decisions" are the norm. Selective evolutionary pressures establish minimum and maximum limits on cognitive capacity. If the depth of decision making is "good enough" to promote survival and reproduction, the genes and cultural institutions that produced the decision making tendencies are reinforced. Perhaps the most important situational variable working to limit analysis and deliberation and working to promote "good enough" or "compromise" solutions, is time.

Cognitive processing and time

Time is at a premium in fast changing, dangerous situations. The brain does its processing fast, but not infinitely fast. Neural events occur in real time on the order of milliseconds. The way the brain–mind adjusts to meet the demands of life-threatening emergencies is to increase its processing capacity. This brings us back to the Newcastle adventure.

We left our hitchhiker seventy feet up, three seconds from being run over by a lorry and experiencing: "arousal", "sense of dread", "hair on end", "racing heart". His memory for the event is that he immediately "made a decision to make a decision". He was conscious of the wish to deny that "this was happening". He was not in conflict beyond this brief moment in which he rejected a "wishful thinking approach". He reports also an "aggressive feeling". The "decision to decide" involved crushing the wish to deny reality. This sort of explicit, tight regulation of the pleasure principle does not occur in normal day-to-day situations.[2]

After deciding to be decisive, the hitchhiker remembers being "very analytic" and "very sharp". He went to work considering the possible options. Waving and screaming had already failed to halt the driver. That left two plans: (1) Climb over the fence and "hang" on the outside of it; or (2) Find a way to avoid the truck while "staying inside" the fence. He chose to focus attention on analysing the "stay inside plan". He recalls that this decision was influenced by a sense of aversion to "hanging" seventy feet above ground. Although not especially afraid of heights, the general, human instinct to be wary of heights clearly influenced his decision-making process.

So, now he had to discern a space inside the fence to avoid the truck. He decided that the space underneath the cargo section of the lorry, down by the wheels, was ample. To be most sure, he needed to calculate: (1) the size of the space between the wheels and fence; and (2) the width of himself plus the rucksack on his back. He had to compare the two quantities. His body plus his rucksack was smaller than the space so the plan should work. Now to execute! He put his body horizontally against the fence and pulled on the fence rails to minimize his profile. Happily, this plan worked. The lorry passed by without causing injury!

These decisions are all examples of the TOTE operations characteristic of Reflective thinking. Genetic instincts and previously learned habits cannot prefigure the exact quantities of space, time, and speed relevant for creating an optimally effective avoidance response in a very specific threat situation. A novel response needs to be created by means of Reflective processes. The hitchhiker had to run the TOTE operations in his mind and make estimates of the probabilities of success of alternative plans.

This is not to say that no old habits were used in this situation. The Reflexive habits that sub-served his Reflexive processes were "problem-solving habits". These were learned in the past and reinforced because they had been instrumental in solving previous— albeit less life-threatening—problems. Problem-solving habits involve knowledge of logic, cause, and effect, measurement, and other "scientific methods". The Reflexive habits about how to solve problems formed a critical foundation for his real-time TOTE operations.

During his calculations the tourist felt as if time was dilated. This was itself comforting. There was hope and a certain floating, thrilling sensation. Similar feelings can be induced reliably by skydiving, race driving, skiing, rugby, and American football. A common feature of these sports is that they all activate perceptions of looming and collision. These stimulus arrays, in turn, stimulate powerful mind-brain states suited for interpreting quickly sensory data to make life saving decisions. And, as noted in Chapter 3, interpreting sensory data to make decisions is the greatest pleasure (Biederman & Vessel, 2006).

I have seen more than a few patients who use very fast motorcycle driving as a way to treat their attention deficit disorders. The perceptual arrays caused by speedy transit through the physical world enhance cognitive control as do amphetamines. Both sorts of "speed treatments" cause a subjective sense of time dilation.

Basic and advanced processing

Allan Snyder says that, at bottom, brains are arithmetic calculators. We are always "counting". Lightning-fast counting is necessary to minimally organize sensory data. Snyder calls this organization process "equipartitioning". One also may imagine a structural aspect to the system. I use the term "protoconcept" for the structures containing equipartitioned sense data. The assumption is that protoconcepts are data used to make concepts proper.

By "concepts proper" I mean that the data about the sensory attributes that are organized by the concept can be put in semantic form. Categories need addresses or names so that they can be recalled and used. At a level higher than individual concepts are *metaconcepts*. These act as nodes for similar concepts. The priming literature (e.g., Hines et al., 1986; Marcel, 1980; Meyer & Schvaneveldt, 1971; Najmi & Wegner, 2008) and the evidence for *spreading activation* of concepts (Collins & Loftus, 1975) strongly support the assumption that concepts are arranged in mental networks and corresponding neural networks.[3]

Equipartition and *protoconcepts* are very nice ideas. They represent a good "compromise solution" to the brain–mind's information requirements. One requirement is for clean, non-distorted, unadulterated, minimally pre-processed data. Theoretically, this allows the executive functions maximal, although not infinite, degrees of freedom to process data into valid concepts. Conscious thinking about data involves executive access to concepts, feelings, and expectations. The other general information requirement of brain–mind is the need to not be swamped with data. Conscious awareness and executive functions may be "overwhelmed" by too much data. Thinking can also be disabled by seemingly incomprehensible data. Overload can cause anxiety and panic.

So, a compromise allows consciousness to do its work and also be protected from disabling anxiety. In contrast to the psychoanalytic idea of "compromise formation", our notion of compromise recognizes the cognitive factor explicitly. That is, the person's ability to be conscious of some aspect of their sensory and cognitive worlds is not only a function of a wish to deny anxiety-causing mentation; it may also be due to a lack of relevant concepts to interpret certain data, that is, it may be an educational or developmental problem.

The potential to be aware of something depends proximally on the state of the conceptual system. The conceptual system of today includes what was learned yesterday. This establishes more or less of a "readiness to learn". Readiness is also powerfully influenced by what have been called *instincts, prepared learning,* and *epigenetic rules.* We are prepared, in part, to learn about the very world in which we evolved (see Wilson, 1999). The degree of integration of bio-instinctual systems and psychological systems is a key to development.

Synchronization

There are many clock-like nodes in the brain that are "counting" or "oscillating". The person's subjective experience, their feelings and thoughts, are important determinants of the ability to learn. If our assumptions are correct, we can add the idea that a person is most prepared for learning when brain–mind is in some theoretically optimal rhythm. In common parlance, sometimes the person is really "in the swing of things". Certainly, interest in music has become prominent in neurology (e.g., Sacks, 2007). Types of rhythms seem to be related systematically to types of subjective states. Music is a form of energy that affects the way we feel. Fast music is arousing. Slow music is relaxing. And, less subtlety, electric energy applied directly to the brain will affect the mind.

There is no commonly accepted explanation for how ECT works to lessen depression and psychotic states (Grover, Mattoo & Gupta, 2005). But we might speculate that it works for the same reason that turning your computer on and off will often improve its functionality. That is, ECT likely shuts down momentarily the activity of various neural nuclei and in effect "resets" them to time zero. Now they will start-up together and so increase the likelihood of synchronous action. The brain–mind and the computer will usually work better after being re-started. They will stay synchronized more or less depending on whether regulatory forces, less extreme than ECT, are functioning effectively. There are various well-known ways that bio-psycho-rhythms can become "reset" or restarted. These include sleep, exercise, orgasm, drugs, electric and hypoglycemic shock and thermal stressors. Any sudden, intense stimulus seems capable of resetting a person's clock. At least in old movies, slapping an hysterical person always worked to calm them down.

Time sensation and estimation

We all develop more or less accurate expectations about the number of things that happen in a unit of time. These "countable things" happen in the external world (e.g., number of times the boss comes out of their office per minute); and the internal world (e.g., number of heart beats per minute).[4] The dilation of time felt during emergencies is probably a result of applying one's usual "events to time ratio" in a situation where rates are much increased. This view is consistent with Boring, Langfeld, and Weld (1948); and, with the newer, brain-based work of Craig (2009).

Most obviously, the number of calculations the Newcastle hitchhiker was making was higher than usual. We would say to the Cognitive School: "He was very motivated to think in order to make a life-saving choice". As a result, his time sense was distorted. Time was sensed, felt, and thought to be passing more slowly than usual. As measured by a clock, time was moving at its own pace. Subjectively, and relative to the number of mental events taking place in a more typical situation, time seemed extended.[5,6] This is consistent with the well-known reports of emergencies that "time seems to stop"; "thinking is sharp"; "feelings are intense". And, the emergency body-mind has many enhanced competencies such as increased muscular and cognitive powers.

Emotional calm is produced by the idea that one has "ample time". The feeling state can, in turn, lead to better decision making. The subjective thinking and feeling states induced by increased rates of mental processing have plausibly increased the survival chances of individuals in emergencies and, hence, have been selected in evolution of the mind–brain.

Another extraordinary aspect of the hitchhiker's experience was a vivid sense of details. The task of measuring the distances involved in the problem was done fast and his judgements seemed to him to be exactly accurate. That the estimates were accurate is of course consistent with the positive outcome of his plan.

The hitchhiker was experiencing integrated, competent functioning of mind and brain. He seemed to have access to very raw data about space and objects and movement. This is the sort of access to raw data seen in autists, infants, and animals. Yet, his full calculating mind including concepts, feelings, and expectations were operable too, so he could devise an avoidance-strategy specific for his particular emergency. He had to be shifting attention smoothly between raw sensory data and conceptual processes in order to devise an ultimately effective plan.

There was a subjective experience of great mental power. We know his enhanced processing state was stimulated by a great surge of energy supplied by neuroendorcrine, sympathetic arousal systems. *These emergency systems were activated by both "looming instincts" and an explicit awareness of a strong expectation of immanent extreme pain and injury.* Perhaps the instinctual process is activated sooner, and/or moves faster. Certainly, the processes can operate more or less independently. And, they can organize into more and less differentiated, integrated, and functional forms.

Harm-avoidance situations illustrate how quickly one can "get more" out of the brain–mind system. This is only possible because brain–mind processes have been rearranged. The re-organization involves changes in rates of processing and changes in the mutual excitatory and inhibitory relations of brain–mind sub-systems. Such changes in somatic and psychic equilibriums are associated with many varied subjective states.

Of course, more chronic states too are supported by some "brain–mind system configuration". Psychopathological states have their characteristic subjective correlates. The demented person feels "confused". The obsessive feels anxious. Hypomania causes "high" feelings and rapid thinking. The depressive feels sad, often anxious, and "slowed down" physically and mentally.

How can one regulate one's own mind? As noted previously, about the only thing we can "try" to do with the mind is to decide what to attend to. If the self is defined as the system which operates the rest of the mind and brain, then self-focused attention has to be an early and continuous feature of any "self-change" exercise. What role is played by self-focused attention in normal and pathological conditions?

Time, death, and self-esteem

Having a negative feeling, thought, or sensation of "too little time" can be caused by either actually not having enough time to complete a critical task, or merely imagining that one does not have sufficient time. In either case, collecting data, analysing it, making predictions regarding the effectiveness of various options, deciding on and executing a plan, all this takes some time.[5]

Various schools of psychology have vied to name "the biggest fear". Freud (1926) called it *castration anxiety*; Kohut used *disintegration anxiety* (1977); Earnest Becker (1973) and Solomon, Greenberg and Pyszczynski (1991) emphasize that the worst anxiety is a form of *terror* derived from a fear of death. Roosevelt said it was "fear itself". In any case, I assume that "too little time" is a most basic form of anxiety. This is because time is often the most precious quantity in an emergency.

Now for someone in excruciating pain, the greatest fear might be "too much time". But at that point the damage to the wish to live has been done. We want to consider more common states of mind; those characterized by more chronic and relatively less extreme levels of anxiety or utter despair.

Roosevelt's theory is psychologically perceptive and clinicians often talk of "fear of fear" in anxiety disorders. If "everything is sex" as Freud (1905) seemed to think early on, then being castrated is an equivalent of death. But castration fear is literally more a fear of an injury and pain than death of the entire organism. It starts to get at the fear of the demise of the mind in particular. Castration is symbolically injurious to the mind in the sense of losing power, competence, and so on. Kohut's idea that *self-disintegration* is the biggest fear adds the idea of the *coherence of self-consciousness* into the equation. Disintegration of a coherent consciousness is "the death of mental control". In the end, maybe "death" is the greatest fear. But how does the brain–mind "operationalize" the concept of death? That is, "How does the 'death fear' play out in time and space in life?"

From a theory-building perspective, we are more likely to understand deep psychological processes if we pay attention to what are arguably the two deepest mysteries of all: Time and Space. What are the causes and effects of different subjective experiences of time and space on brain and mind functioning? What are the relations between objectively measurable spatial and temporal locations of the person and other objects in the world, and their subjective experience of the locations? For example, "What are the spatial and temporal relationships between my body and that lorry?" Such inferences are based on more or less valid self and non-self concepts.

In any case, there is a saying from management consulting that goes, "You can't increase productivity by trying to increase productivity". For our current purposes we can modify the idea to say, "You can't understand fear by studying fear". Instead, we will have more luck studying the way that sensations of objects in time and space operate as causes and effects of conceptual, emotional, and overt behavioural processes.

Our hitchhiker remembers that he did not think of death at his moment of greatest vulnerability. Rather, he immersed himself in the problem of devising a way to avoid death. The more proximal fear was about having enough time to devise and execute a life-saving plan. This makes sense if the person is to function effectively. The evolutionary requirement is to devise and enact an effective response. One does not have the luxury of being neurotic about it like a *Woody Allen Character* with low self-esteem.

A sense of "time urgency" has survival value. But thinking about "death" or "castration" or "self-disintegration" is not especially helpful in an emergency. Terror Management is assumed to be a non-conscious process that works to prevent conscious experience of negative emotions that would otherwise reduce one's ability to think competently (Rosenblatt et al., 1989). Rosenblatt et al., assume that thinking of oneself as a good or moral person, that is, keeping one's *self-esteem* high, works to reduce anxiety about death. Operationally this must involve attempts to conform to one's *ego ideal* or, at least, to imagine that one has behaved ideally.

Any psychoanalyst would agree that anxiety regulation is a partly unconscious process. And, it seems plausible that mechanisms which enhance and protect self-esteem, such as *attributional egotism*, can work to lower anxiety on a day-to-day basis. But *attributional egotism* is a bias in how people explain events in the past. Defensively biased, post-hoc explaining does not interfere necessarily with a person's ability to develop valid predictions about upcoming events (Bernstein et al., 1979). It seems that biased thinking and more objective assessments of reality occur in parallel most of the time. But distorted thinking is a liability under extreme threat conditions.

Self-esteem is preserved largely by telling oneself a story about the past. Why not engage in some self-delusion about the past if it doesn't damage the ability to cope with the future? Terror Management is a theory about dealing with a fear of the future by assuring oneself that one has been a good boy or girl yesterday. Maybe Terror Management Theory was never intended to explain behaviour in the face of real threats to life. It certainly doesn't explain defensive operations that repeatedly work to lower self-esteem. Self-esteem is probably not a great predictor of how one might behave when life is actually threatened. That is, the self-loving citizen may be no more likely to devise an effective plan to evade an urgent threat than a self-hater. Studying the causes and effects of self-esteem without also measuring the extent to which a person actually achieves their ideals of safety and creativity is of rather limited utility.

Self-esteem is of great importance to the Cognitive Therapy School which has explicitly forbid examination of depth, unconscious processes, or motivation. There is ample evidence that cognitive treatments can increase self-esteem and reduce anxiety, at least in the short term. But people do not live to have high self-esteem. Self-esteem is a cause and an effect of many social and psychological phenomena. But psychotherapy of all forms takes time because many patients persist in maintaining self-concepts that are self-esteem lowering and self-defeating. Such invalid concepts in turn expose patients to real, increased risks of injury and death. This is illustrated in the case study of Mr. K (Chapters Six through Nine).

Efforts to increase self-esteem and manage terror may be fine treatments for a child. But they are not enough for an adult interested in psychological depth. It makes sense to assume that people want to learn about reality, whatever it entails—including the exact features of a pressing threat to life—because learning and using valid concepts about the self leads to more security and more exquisite feelings than simple self-esteem repair.

Summary

The brain, managed by instinct and learned habits, is prepared to add to its repertoire of competencies by learning. In the case presented here, learning had to be fast in order for the person to avoid harm. Special mechanisms increase the capacity of the mind–brain to help us devise plans to live when confronted with an emergency. We assume that a concern with "not having enough time" is a basic fear. This is because devising plans and executing them takes time. The rates of processing of sensory data, concepts, and feelings increase during emergencies. Also, time seems to go very slowly. This is adaptive. Perhaps it reduces fear of losing time and, hence, removes thoughts and feelings that might not help in conflict resolution. We might describe the brain–mind system as something of a "collection of clocks" or "oscillating functions". These processes can be more or less synchronized. The normal biorhythms of life are altered in emergencies and in mental illness.

Notes

1. This is an actual experience I had years ago during a tour of Northumberland. Oddly, while researching this section, the first reference I found regarding *looming instincts* was the paper by Rind, Santer & Wright (2008). This group is stationed at Newcastle University, in the city where the event took place. Is it Jungian *Synchronicity*?
2. The utility of aggression for decision making is illustrated by the Newcastle story. The hitchhiker's report is consistent with Fiedler's (1964) Contingency Theory of Leadership. Fiedler found that the most socially attuned leaders did best when conditions were moderate or more normal. On the other hand, tough, task-oriented leaders produced the best results when a group's situation was either very poor, that is, an emergency, or when the situation was particularly good. Presumably, when things are normal, life or death decisions rarely come up. One can gossip with the gregarious boss at the water cooler. But, in an emergency, it is best to have a decisive, aggressive manager.

3. Semantic Priming involves exposing subjects to a word (the prime), for example "hand", for 200 milliseconds. The area where the word is displayed is then *masked* with visual noise (e.g., #%#%). The masking works to suppress any conscious awareness of having seen the prime. Then, words either related to the prime or not related to the prime are displayed. The key measure is how fast the subjects recognize the post-priming word. For example, if subjects had been primed with "hand" they recognize "palm" more quickly than "moon". Recently, the method has been used to study thought suppression (e.g., Najmi & Wegner, 2008).

4. The number of conscious cognitive processes could function as a good marker of "perceived time". The notion of *Field Dependence* is relevant here (Witkin & Goodenough, 1981). The Field Independent person has more differentiated internal processes and structures than the Field Dependent person. The less differentiated mind sees the perceptual field as a whole, processes information globally, and is not attentive to detail. The more differentiated mind is analytical, detail-oriented, and can "think for itself".

5. From the evolutionary perspective, more time is necessary in order to more completely solve every problem. Death is the "executive" in evolutionary processes. If the competence of the animal is inadequate, it dies. On the scale of an individual life, correction of invalid concepts is the executive function of the mind. In a real sense, the "killing off" of bad ideas is the method of the individual's psychic development, while the killing of the entire organism is evolution's method.

6. Feeling "bored" appears to be the opposite of feeling a shortage of time. All the bored person has is time. Boredom is best considered to be a sort of anxiety. Boredom is often a co-morbid feature in anxiety disorders. From our perspective, it can be best conceived as "time without awareness of pressing goals or objects". Outright anxiety, in contrast, results from implicit or explicit expectations that "one lacks sufficient time to attain goals or avoid objects".

CHAPTER FIVE

Approach–avoidance conflict

The Newcastle case represents a clear emergency. There was no ambivalence about goals. The decisions were about means not ends. In contrast, most of modern life takes place in less extreme conditions. With threats to safety not urgent, motives to "feel better" instead of merely "not feeling worse" come into play. One thinks about "getting ahead" and "development", not just about "not losing" and "being safe". There are complex relationships between Pain Avoiding and Pleasure Approaching mind–brain systems. Of course, this is an understatement. All animal life is busy, all the time, with the relationships between pleasure and pain. And, we are especially vexed when a situation has aspects that we wish to both approach and avoid.

Starting in the 1930s, the relationships between approach and avoidance forces were illuminated by Kurt Lewin (1931; 1936), Neil Miller (1944), and their colleagues. The related dynamics of frustration and aggression was of central interest to this group (e.g., Dollard, Doob, Miller, Mower & Sears, 1939). The entire "Motivational" or "Conflict School" was influenced strongly by Hull–Spence Drive Theory. But Lewin and Miller were less attached to a strict version of Behaviourism than Hull (1943) and Spence (1956). They recognized that social needs and goals as well as physiological needs could drive behaviour, and did not scorn psychoanalytic theory as the doctrinaire Behaviourists did.

In this mid-twentieth-century period, psychoanalysis was dominant in psychiatry. Schools of academic psychology always had a weird distain for psychoanalytic theory. I saw this first hand as an undergraduate and graduate student in the 1970s. Psychoanalytic writers have not helped because they rarely cite anyone outside of their own literature. This stupid Balkanization has somehow continued to the present. As Whittle (1999) perceptively described it, most normal citizens would be surprised to learn that psychology is not one discipline but rather composed of fractious schools.

But all psychological schools, except perhaps the Cognitive Therapy School, recognize that understanding conflict is of central importance. Conflict is involved in all efforts to cause human change, for example, psychotherapy, organization development, negotiating, bargaining, politics, economics, and so on.

Kurt Lewin (1935) differentiated between four basic types of conflict: Approach–Avoidance; Approach–Approach; Avoidance–Avoidance; and Double Approach–Avoidance. The Newcastle hitchhiker's report suggests that his mind and brain were full of Double Approach–Avoidance Conflicts. These are situations in which there are two or more options, each of which has both positive and negative features. For example, he had to decide between two plans: "over the fence" or "stay on the road". Each had both attractive and repelling attributes. "Over the fence" was sure to allow him to avoid the lorry, but it exposed him to a risk of falling. Staying on the road was attractive because it eliminated death from falling, but it called for doing many more cognitive tasks than the "over the fence" plan. He had to get a measure of the distance between the truck wheels and the curb. He had to get a measure of the thickness of his body plus rucksack. He had to compare the relations between the variables, that is, subtract the two distances.

Now, while he estimated each of these operations to be relatively simple, he had first to estimate if he had enough time to carry them out. So an estimate of "time to impact" was a critical node in the decision-tree. Did he have time to pull off the more elaborate plan? He would have to predict the time for each task and once again do a subtraction of the "total task time" minus the estimated "time to impact". Such predictions likely derive from both conceptual reasoning and a more instinctive sense of timing. In any case, the complexity of all these tasks and the need for "timing" indicates that the brain–mind is doing some sort of "parallel processing" or "multi-tasking". In an emergency, when time is short, one has to do more than one thing at a time.

The die was cast once he decided "time is adequate". His actions would all have to be performed within the conceptual container—"between now and then". "Objective Time", with units agreed upon socially, was ticking. And, we have his subjective report that he sensed, thought, and felt that time had slowed. He had no control over the truck or its speed. But he could, potentially, in part, control the speed and accuracy of his mind in creating an effective plan that he could execute before impact.

Asymmetry of approach and avoidance motives

Animals have been important subjects for conflict researchers. In the Dollard and Miller tradition, for example, a hungry mouse is placed at the top of a runway and a cheese meal is put at the other end. This is repeated a few times and the mouse quickly develops a habit to run down the ramp and (happily) eat the cheese. Then, the section of the ramp right in front of the cheese is connected to electric cables. When the mouse steps on this section of ramp a painful shock is administered to their feet. This procedure induces a strong approach–avoidance conflict in the mouse. It has learned that the trip down the ramp evokes both the pleasure of eating and yet the pain to the feet, with its attendant irritation and anxiety.

The central finding from both animal and human studies is that approach and avoidance tendencies change differently with distance from goals. When a creature is far from an attractive goal region, the approach motive begins to be activated. In comparison, when a creature is in close proximity to a feared object, then avoidance motives are activated. Also, the slopes of the strengths of the approach and avoidance tendencies are different. Avoidance gradients have a much faster rise with decreasing distance to an object than approach gradients.

The mouse set-up allows us to disentangle the approach and avoidance tendencies and allow for quantitative measures of both. Figure 3 shows that approach motives activate at a great distance from the ambivalently charged goal region. But the avoidance tendency

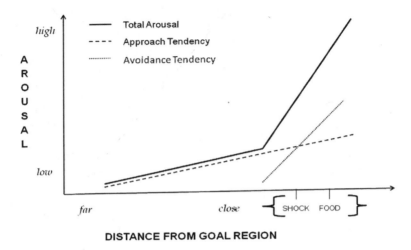

DISTANCE FROM GOAL REGION

Figure 3. Approach and avoidance of an ambivalent region.

is stimulated closer to the area. And, once the avoidance gradient is stimulated, it increases much more quickly than the approach motive as the conflict area is neared. A critical point is reached at which the relative strength of the two motives changes. Approach motives dominate at far distance. Avoidance motives are stronger at closer distance. For example, one may fantasize all night about punching the boss in the nose but then lose the nerve to do so on actually seeing them at the office in the morning.

In Miller's lab, the mouse begins running in earnest when at the far end of the ramp. As it gets closer to the ambivalently charged region, it starts to slow. Now depending on its hunger, the amplitude of past shocks, the tastiness of the food, and so on, the mouse may stop, run back up the ramp, or decide to take the pain to get the pleasure. Miller and Dollard (1941) found that mice were very fast at learning and applying methods to avoid shock (e.g., they learned to turn a small wheel to escape shocks).

The purpose of brain–mind is to represent the external world with precision and, hence, promote competent decisions and behaviour. The human has more mental hardware and software than the mouse. In particular, the Reflective Learning functions of the person are greater than that of the mouse. Both species of course have Reflexive systems. In all animals approach and avoidance motives are related in a similar fashion.

The asymmetry in approach and avoidance dynamics makes sense in terms of conserving biological energy, preserving safety, and learning about the world (see Brehm, Wright, Solomon, Silka & Greenberg, 1983). "Why worry if the danger is far away or generally unlikely to occur?" On the other hand, if danger is near, one needs to avoid it quickly. If danger is far away, "Why not take an amble over there and see what's up?" The psychology of approach should be dominant in any low risk situation. Healthy psychological functioning should involve curiosity and interest in the environment. Pathological functioning imagines a danger behind every tree, even after logical proofs have been offered to the contrary.

Conflict in the human

The psychology of approach–avoidance motivation is applicable to "objects in mind" as well as objects in the external environment. Thinking replaces "overt movement in the world" as a method of getting feedback about the validity of one's latest theory. Figure 4 spells out the likely results of combinations of pain and pleasure expectations. When the individual expects high pleasure and low pain from a person, situation or idea, approach is likely. In the opposite case, an expectation of low pleasure and high pain, avoidance should occur. If both types of expectations are high, there is conflict. If neither pain nor pleasure is expected, no movement should ensue.

For example, the person, or mouse, may deliberate privately about whether to make a pass at an attractive female in the library. We assume that the mouse's behaviour is determined in large part by instinct. But a mouse can learn to make new associations

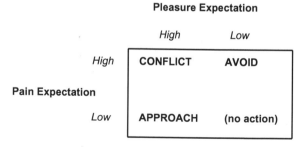

Figure 4. Likely results of pleasure and pain expectation combinations.

between causes and effects by trial and error. This calls for a form of conceptual learning. But the mental competence of the mouse is limited compared to that of people. Any particular human pickup-artist will have more or less valid concepts about other people, their own attractiveness, social customs, and so forth. The level of conceptual competence, in turn, will produce more or less accurate predictions of what the female will do. If the pickup-artist is sophisticated, they understand the situation as somewhat complex. They may be more or less aware of optimistic, pleasurable feelings and thoughts of intimacy that support the approach. And, as they consider interrupting the poor girl's studying, they may be more or less aware of pessimistic thoughts of emotionally painful rejection (see Carver, 2006).

Approaching what we want may expose us to threats. In nature, the most desirable sex partners, sources of protein, breeding grounds, and nesting areas are sought by others. After fighting off competitors, reaching the most physically attractive person exposes the person to rejection and hurt feelings. Compared to others, the physically attractive are assumed to be more successful, likable, happy, and intelligent (e.g., Byrne, Ervin & Lamberth, 1970; Clifford & Walster, 1973; Dion, Berschied & Walster, 1973). Hence, being rejected by an attractive "wonderful person" poses more risks than rejection by a more typical person. For all the same reasons that one wants to be with an attractive person, rejection might be particularly painful.

The problem for the person in the library is, "How can I achieve my goal of meeting the attractive girl and minimize the risk of personal rejection?" In terms of Figure 3, their problem is, "How to reduce the avoidance gradient?" This is the same sort of dilemma faced by anyone with an approach–avoidance problem, "How to maximize pleasure and minimize injury and pain?" Solutions are actively sought by Research & Development (R&D) workers in many fields often involving some sort of "stealth technology".

The military asks, "How can we drop our bombs but not be killed doing it?" Bombers have radar-evading shapes and soldiers wear camouflage clothing. The research pharmacologist asks, "How can we design a drug to get to its target before being metabolized?" Stalevo is a clever combination of agents for increasing dopamine levels in the brains of Parkinson's patients. It contains levodopa that is converted into dopamine; carbidopa that cannot cross the blood-brain barrier and works to inhibit the conversion of levadopa into dopamine in the body; and entacapone that inhibits the breakdown of dopamine in the brain.

In the tradition of Lewin and Miller, we have studied approach and avoidance behaviour in humans under various "conceptual conditions" (e.g., Bernstein, Stephenson, Snyder & Wicklund, 1983; Snyder, Kleck, Strenta & Mentzer, 1979; Snyder & Wicklund, 1981). Bernstein et al. (1983) invited 104 male college students, one at a time, to what was said to be a "movie rating exercise". As each male subject entered the lab, he could see a female sitting in front of a blank TV screen a few yards away. There were two seats in front of the screen, one empty. And, the male subject could also see that there were two empty seats in front of another TV that was separated by a wooden partition from where the female was sitting.

In one condition the subject was told, "We will be showing two different movies today. 'Movie A', which features W.C. Fields, will play on screen one. 'Movie B', with Buster Keaton, will be played on screen two". This is called the *Low Pain Expectation/High Conceptual Ambiguity Condition*. In the other condition males were told, "Normally we have two different movies for people to rate, but because of an equipment malfunction, the same movie will be playing on both screens". This is called the *High Pain Expectation/ Low Conceptual Ambiguity Condition*. The experimenter's speech in both conditions was delivered so that the female sitting a few feet away could obviously hear it. Then, the male subject was instructed to take a seat in front of whichever screen he wished. The simple dependent variable was "Where did he sit?" Figure 5 shows the key results from this study.

Pleasure Expectation (female's attractiveness)

	High	Moderate	Low	
High/Low	33%	9%	13%	17%
Low/High	72%	41%	24%	46%
	54%	23%	19%	

Pain Expectation/Ambiguity

Figure 5. Proportions of males approaching females as a function of her attractiveness and conceptual ambiguity.

The figure indicates that in the *High Conceptual Ambiguity Condition*, approach is a direct linear function of the attractiveness of the female. In contrast, in the *Low Conceptual Ambiguity Condition*, approach is largely suppressed. "Ambiguity" in this situation refers to the presence of either one plausible causal concept to explain the males behaviour (Low Ambiguity); or two plausible concepts (High Ambiguity).

In the *High Ambiguity Condition* the subject knows that there are two plausible concepts that could explain his seating choice: "I want the girl" and "I want to see a particular film". He also knows that the girl knows there are two causal concepts at play. With ambiguity about the causes of his behaviour, the chance of a painful rejection is lowered and, accordingly, his expectation of pain is lowered. The girl can't so easily rebuff the fellow if she is uncertain about his motivation.

Similarly, the boy himself can use the ambiguity. He might really have a preference for W.C. Fields or Buster Keaton. (We controlled for any real film preferences by counterbalancing the film titles over all the trials.) In any case, the subject can construe his behaviour as something other than his interest in the girl and, hence, lower his expectation of receiving a painful rejection. Overt behaviour in the *High Ambiguity* situation reflects an un-conflicted approach motive. The pain avoidance motive has been neutralized by the conceptual camouflage and behaviour is a simple function of the approach motive, which varies with the attractiveness of the girl.

Should the boy sit next to the girl in the *Low Conceptual Ambiguity Condition*, both of them must attribute his behaviour to his attraction to her. In effect, he will be making a direct approach with no cover or subtlety about it. Expectations of being rejected and hurt should therefore be higher in the *Low Ambiguity* than in the *High Ambiguity Condition*. The overt behavioural results are consistent with these assumptions. With no way to reduce the risks of rejection, the avoidance motive stays high in the *Low Ambiguity* situations and the subject avoids the female even if she is attractive.

Now this sort of exploitation of conceptual ambiguity is used all the time in social life. We decline a dinner invitation and offer an alternative cause for it, for example, "My car is in the shop". Ambiguity lubricates social life. Rarely do we hurt other's feelings gratuitously, for example, "I won't be attending because I think you are a moron".

The socially competent citizen takes it as their responsibility, in part, to regulate the emotions of others. But most relevant to the present argument is that self-manipulation of the conceptual apparatus is central to the regulation of our own feelings, expectations, and behaviours. One can use the model of mind in Figure 2 to trace the mental and behavioural events in this experiment:

1. The appearance of the woman activates in the male's brain an array of sense data. In this situation visual data is most important. By means of something like *spreading activation*, the sense data potentiates or readies instinctual motoric action patterns. The more attractive the woman, the more the instinctual approach responses are potentiated. This is what is selected for in evolution, that is, the neurological tendencies to respond to specific arrays of sense data. And, of course, the arrays themselves are given a selective advantage. Seeing a woman with attractive, secondary sexual characteristics works to stimulate males' reflexive, overt, approach behaviours.

   It is worth noting here that Freud used the term *instincts* for what ethologists term *fixed action patterns*. Such actions are only stimulated and enacted when precise stimulating signals or, in ethology terms, a *releaser* is present. Notable examples of *releasers* other than secondary sexual attributes are the beak movements of newborn birds, which stimulate the mother's regurgitating process to feed her offspring (Tinbergen, 1951).

2. In parallel with the activation of motor pathways linked to the releasing action of sexual sensory stimuli, the minimally processed visual sense data (protoconcepts) travel to conceptual processing areas of the brain.

3. Semantic concepts in conscious awareness interpret the data as indicating that the woman is more or less attractive.

4. The more attractive the woman, the more the male may alternate attention between the raw data and the concept of the woman. This process can be more or less pleasurable. The immediate activation of a strong "approach pleasure tendency" is also accompanied by the activation of an "avoid pain tendency". This is because memories of past similar situations are part of some common neural network that is activated by the sensory array of the woman. Since no one wins all the time, memories

of rejection are activated. The male is also using, more or less explicitly, general, non-self concepts of social life to assess the nature of this social situation. He generates expectations of success/pleasure and expectations of pain/failure from his sensations, concepts, and feelings. "What are the odds of making a successful approach and not getting hurt?"

5a. In the *High Ambiguity Condition* where there are two social explanations for approaching (the female; the movie), the male subject can *lower his expectation of a painful rejection*. If the woman is attractive he can approach under the cover of the woman's and his own ambiguity about why it is that he is doing what he is doing. Sensation, concepts, expectations, and feelings are all aligned and he makes an overt behavioural approach.

5b. In the *Low Ambiguity Condition* the same sensory and conceptual processes are operating, but the outcome is different. In this situation, the risks of a direct approach are high. Pain expectations cannot be reduced by means of ambiguity, and the typical, overt behaviour in this condition is avoidance. When the woman is very attractive, avoidance must be due to fear of rejection and social pain. When the woman is less attractive, the low rates of approach are due to low approach motivation.

* * *

In the next chapter, we begin to use the assumptions we have made so far to describe a prototypical case of psychopathology. The patient—Mr. K—suffered from an *anxiety disorder*, that is, one of the most commonly seen sorts of DSM-IV diagnoses. Understanding of the mind–brain processes illustrated in this case is informed by our understanding of the emergency processes described in Chapter Four. But typical psychopathology does not involve pressing threats to life. Nonetheless the person feels afraid. Mr. K was anxious because he thought he was in danger. He had the legitimate health concerns of a Sixty Five year-old man. But he exaggerated the seriousness and urgency of the usual threats to health, that is, he *kvetched* about his symptoms.

CHAPTER SIX

Developmental sources
of psychopathology

T he red line separating pathological from normal anxiety is the presence or absence of serious threats to security inside the body, in the external environment, or both. In mental illness, the nature of threats and/or their severity are misjudged. This is not to say that very similar instinctual biopsychological mechanisms are not brought into play in the case of both correctly and incorrectly understood threats. A central survival-enhancing function of the brain–mind apparatus is to make decisions about the seriousness of threats. Mental competence involves *the ability to make accurate assessments of conditions in and outside the body*.

Compared to the biological and social environments in which humans evolved, most of us live in very safe places. Cultural institutions have developed to the point that biological threats to security such as animal predators, famine, and disease have been reduced. Our security systems are supported economically by governments, private capital, laws, and technology. We have temperature-controlled buildings, waterways, highways, hospitals, and manufacturing facilities. Success in reducing many immediate threats to biological security has generated excess resources (and unintended threats like pollution). Increases in our material and social security allow us to allocate time and effort for the development of science, art, education, and various entertaining diversions. Yet, many people become anxious, depressed, or "out of touch with reality" despite living in materially safe environments. A small percentage of such troubled people seek psychological treatment.

A patient of mine, Mr. K, has been a help in developing some of the ideas presented in this book. His story includes examples of both competent and incompetent mental functioning. He is capable of considerable self-awareness and self-control. But his troubles stem from holding various invalid concepts about himself, and from difficulty in suspending the habitual use of such concepts to regulate his subjective states and his overt behaviour.

Mr. K is sixty five. He is an avid sportsman who continues to play competitive squash. He loves music and art of all kinds. He is very fond of his wife of many years, and most of the time they have had satisfactory sexual relations. He is actively and appropriately involved in the lives of his two adult children. Both children obtained college degrees and became married parents. He is intelligent and curious about individuals and the social world at large.

As a younger man Mr. K had obtained an advanced degree. A few years before our first meeting, he had retired from a long, successful career as an administrator of inner city schools. The job involved breaking-up fights that occurred between unruly students. These pupils were not small children but adolescents. As might be expected, playing such a role at work caused anxiety. He used the minor tranquilizer Lorazepam for the first time eighteen years ago in this school context and it had been very effective.

He is very anxious about his health. He has consulted various specialists about aches and pains in his stomach and muscles. He has had insomnia, gastric reflux, skin allergies, and kidney stones. All sixty five year-old men should be somewhat concerned about caring for their health. However, the reports from his various treating physicians indicated that he was in good overall health. In short, he had, in addition to his non-serious physical conditions, hypochondriasis.

Descriptive diagnosis and pharmacological treatment

He comes in with a friendly smile. His movements and posture suggest that he is in good health. His visage communicates some anxiety. He speaks somewhat hesitantly and seems ashamed when complaining about his symptoms, but he is fluent when on other topics. He has used Lorazepam, 1 to 2 milligrams per night, for the last eighteen years. He has developed dependence and tolerance. He has been using 20 milligrams per day of Paroxetine for his anxiety with moderate effect for about two years. Paroxetine is a Selective Serotonin Reuptake Inhibitor (SSRI) anti-depressant. He complains about the sexual side effects of the SSRI. He has had morning dysphoria for the last two months, accompanied by anxiety. The symptom picture indicates an undertreated depression and obsessive anxiety about health. He qualified for DSM diagnoses of: Depressive Disorder, Obsessive/Compulsive Disorder (OCD), Somatoform Disorder (i.e., Hypochondriasis), Benzodiazepine Dependence, and Insomnia.

The immediate treatment involved replacing the Lorazepam at bed with one half a milligram of Clonazepam. Changing to a different benzodiazepine often works, at least in the short term, to get more effective relief from insomnia and anxiety. The subjective effects on anxiety of Clonazepam start and stop more gradually than do those of Lorazepam. Addiction is best understood as a form of classical conditioning. Agents with fast onset and fast offset create the strongest associations in the mind between the drug and some desired subjective state. Strong habits to use such drugs are developed quickly. Alprazolam, sometimes useful when fast relief is called for in panic attacks, is the "fastest on" and "fastest off" of the benzodiazepines. It is hence the most problematic in its class and should be avoided if possible.

Use of Clonazepam for Mr. K sets the stage for moving him to "as needed" use of benzodiazepines after two or three months. We switched SSRIs from 20 milligrams of Paroxetine to 10 milligrams of Escitalopram. This dose of Escitalopram represents an increase in anti-depressant potency over his Paroxetine dose. Plus, Escitalopram usually causes fewer sexual and other side effects. Psychotherapy was offered as an additional treatment and he accepted.

Object relations

He has one brother, seven years older, whom the patient describes as a "bully" who teased the patient for being a "daydreamer". Mr. K reports three traumatic events from childhood: (1) At age five, he was hospitalized for two weeks with pneumonia, and got "200 penicillin shots". He says that "the doctors and nurses were very nice to me", but "it was very scary". He adds that "my parents were upset that I was upset"; (2) Later the same year he began school. He was told maliciously by the brother that the teachers would beat him. This frightened him so much that he vomited each day on the way to school for two weeks; (3) He says that his mother made two suicide attempts. The second incident occurred when the patient was thirteen years old. He found her unconscious from an overdose. The mother's psychiatrist told him at that point that these suicide attempts were her way of manipulating others. He reports "liking when mother took care of me when I was sick" but that this pleasure lessened after his realization about the mother's manipulativeness.

He used a favourite blanket as a security object for sleep until he was seven years of age. As an adult he is often "afraid to be alone" and anxious when his wife is away. He had a close, comforting attachment to a housekeeper who worked for his family. He says, "She was like a sister or mother". When his parents would fight he would go to her and ask anxiously, "Will they break up"?

He describes his father with somewhat contradictory attributes: "gentleman", "bad sport", and "caring". He also reports that his father "understood him better than anyone else in his family"; and that he and his father shared the habit of "worrying". The father was quite religious and sent Mr. K to a Hebrew High School. He reports being much less religious than his father.

The mother is described as "the centre of attention", "a fighter", "supportive", and a "trouble maker". He says that his mother was "somewhat understanding but insecure" (i.e., a vulnerable helper). The mother "used illness" to influence the others. She "pitted me and my brother against each other" and apparently was jealous of her sons' relations with their wives. Asked to describe the mother's physical attractiveness he said she was "very pretty", and then added, his father was "very handsome". The mother is diagnosable as a Histrionic Personality.

The first three months of treatment

Meetings with the patient were initially taken up with complaints of physical symptoms and questions about the medications.

The frequency of visits was about every other week. These early meetings would be classed "medication management and counselling procedures" in insurance company lingo. He appreciated explanations of the biology underlying his symptoms, and of the presumed pharmacological mechanisms by which he might be relieved. He was reassured by such talk and this seemed to be the reason he came to our meetings.

Psychoanalysis includes two elements: reassurance and analysis (Strachey, 1934). We were not "analysing" Mr. K's neurotic obsessions at first; we were talking about his symptoms, something that was comforting and gratifying for him. My explicit intentions were to manage his psychopharmacological regime and to collect data in order to make a model of his mental operating system. His explicit intentions were to get help with medicines and to be comforted by me. He was consciously aware that coming to see me made him feel better.

Most patients believe, not entirely incorrectly, that if the doctor is to comfort them it would be best if the patient was liked. Accordingly, Mr. K maintained a mostly friendly demeanour and attempted to be a "good patient". He attended sessions reliably and punctually. And, we maintained a friendly, overtly cooperative connection.

After three weeks his anxiety lessened and his sleep improved. Now his most pressing concern was that it was almost impossible for him to have an orgasm. He worried that this was awfully disappointing to his wife, even though she had tried to disabuse him of this. I suggested for the anorgasmia that he use before sex Bupropion, an adrenergic reuptake inhibitor. At the fourth meeting he offered that he was afraid to use the Buproprion and was worried that the other drugs "will stop working if I take them too much".

The next week he reports that Buproprion taken before sex with his wife did not promote orgasm, but that he was able to climax by means of masturbation. I suggested to him that anxiety could explain the results of his "orgasm experiments". That is, his anorgasmia was due, in part, to the conditions surrounding his sexual behaviour (i.e., alone or not). This social variable works to affect his anxiety level. After two months of talk and drug therapy he is able to have an orgasm while having sex with his wife; and, his depression and anxiety are much reduced.[1]

At three months symptoms reoccurred. He reports "feeling crappy" for about thirty minutes after waking in the morning; decreases in ejaculatory competence; and obsessive focus on both symptoms. Somewhat paradoxically, he asks at this point if he "really needs to continue in psychotherapy if the medicines are working?" I indicated that if he wished to learn more about himself and perhaps get better control of anxiety he should continue in therapy. He says that he does want to learn more about himself. The treatment now continues on a more regular, one time per week basis.

A mind regulation habit of Mr. K

When more regular psychotherapy began, Mr. K related that as a young man he learned that "by acting happy, I can feel happy". This type of mental control attempt should be recognized at once as a version of a "simple suppression" operation. Attempting "to not think about x" works to some extent; "acting happy" when one is not happy can also be effective. This was illustrated convincingly by results from John Lanzetta's laboratory at Dartmouth (see Smith, McHugo & Kappas, 2005). They studied the role of facial expression in the self-regulation of feelings. Configuring the mouth into a smile can make one feel happier, less afraid, and more resistant to pain (e.g., Lanzetta & Orr, 1986).

That behaviour affects feelings and thoughts must be known, at least implicitly, by everyone. Sensations of motor actions are contained in thoughts and feelings; and subjective experiences of thoughts, expectations and feelings can stimulate overt behaviour (See Figure 2).

Adopting various physical gestures and postures influences not only one's own subjective experience, it also affects the experience of observers (e.g., Bernstein, 2001; McHugo & Smith, 1996). In the mother–infant dyad, the mind–brain regulatory systems of both individuals are intimately related (e.g., Schore, 2003). Ideally, non-verbal gestures of the infant are accurately sensed and then accurately interpreted by the mother. Then she is in a position to generate a competent, contingent reply that can regulate the internal state of the relatively ill-equipped child (Tronick et al., 1978). Besides lacking muscular mass and coordination, newborns lack valid concepts to allow them to operate autonomously in the world. These they learn from the family. The person comes to regard himself/herself, in large part, as they were regarded by early caregivers.

The infant research and common experience shows that one can help the child regulate their internal state by, for example, smiling at them. Neurologically, this might involve *mirror neurons* (e.g., Decety & Jackson, 2004; Gallesse, 2001). Mirror neurons are stimulated when an animal observes another animal act and when the animal performs the observed action themselves (e.g., Rizzolatti & Craighero, 2004). These types of cells have been directly observed in primates, and most likely exist in pre-motor and inferior parietal cortical regions of the human brain (Iacoboni et al., 1999).

Taken together, the Lanzetta and the *mirror neuron* findings give us a neurological hypothesis for how social interactions work to regulate brains. If smiling, for example, makes one feel better, seeing another smile causes one to feel better too. This is especially noticeable and well studied in parent–child interactions. But socially mediated regulation of mind and brain no doubt occur at many levels in animals at all stages of development.

The belief that the comfort lies in the mother or teddy bear exemplifies the primitive nature of the young child's self-regulatory methods. The attachment to external objects, living or stuffed, which function to regulate subjective experience, is the hallmark of primitive thinking. Comfort comes originally from the outside, from the mother. But the caring functions of the mother can be internalized and improved upon. The self is not particularly salient early on as the central operator of the mind. In a Jungian sense it is like a latent force pressing for expression. And, clinical experience suggests that it is in dreams that the self expresses itself most forcefully. Probably no one ever realizes all their self-potential. But the range of *self-actualization* is very wide (Maslow, 1954). What inhibits and promotes self-knowledge and development?

Difficulties regulating sensations, concepts, feelings, expectations, and behaviour are at the bottom of most mental illness. Concepts, feelings, and expectations come from memory and are also stimulated in current situations by incoming sense data. The person's inability to make use of the new sense data to develop new, more valid concepts is at the core of their illness. Fast activation and repetitive enactment of old thinking, feeling, and behavioural habits cause anxiety, mood, and thought disturbances.

Diagnoses based only on easily observable symptoms, for example, DSM diagnoses, are helpful for deciding on psychopharmacological regimes. And Cognitive Therapy which focuses on thoughts that the patient can easily observe in himself/herself can be effective. It is especially effective for Panic Disorder (e.g., Bruce, Spiegel & Hegel, 1999). This is because the cognitions of the panic patient are so salient and so distorted (e.g., "I am having a heart attack right now"), that even a little reality can have a large effect.

A patient such as Mr. K already knows that "acting happy" is of some utility in regulating his subjective states. But it still represents a denial of how he is feeling right now. Of course, "if ignorance is bliss 'tis folly to be wise". But denying reality is a bad habit for an adult. If underlying distortions of self-concepts and deficiencies in using concepts are not diagnosed in some way, symptoms will recur and self-development will remain inhibited.

Learning new, valid concepts is necessary but not always sufficient to cause fundamental change in patients. Learning does not do away with old habits. It builds new concepts "on top" of the old ones. New habits are less strong and more easily disrupted by high levels of stress than are old habits. Psychoanalytic theory is an excellent diagnostic tool. But most psychoanalytic treatment methods are not so great at attaching new concepts about the person to the rest of mind–brain so that they are functional. Insight-building psychoanalytic psychotherapy is sometimes very effective, but most often it is only partially effective. And, like all treatment methods, psychoanalysis sometimes fails entirely.

Infantile sexuality and self-development

Infantile sexuality, Freud's (1905) most sensational and "scandalous discovery", describes the exquisite sensitivity of all parts of the infant's body to the regulatory attempts of those who touch and "talk" to them. Care-giving includes both calming and exciting touches, sounds, and facial displays. Pleasure can come from the "down regulation" of arousal, that is, feelings, thoughts, and behaviours associated with relaxation, quiescence, and sleep. And, pleasure can come from the "up regulation" of arousal, that is, feelings, thoughts, and behaviours associated with curiosity, creativity, and novelty.

The optimal caretaker regulates the infant's arousal up and down to keep them in a "comfort zone". And, the parent works to enlarge the range of situations in which the infant can feel comfortable by means of *optimal empathic failures* (Kohut, 1977). For example, the mother may delay rewarding the infant with a smile until he attains some goal, such as grasping a spoon.

From a *Gestalt* perspective, unattained goals cause psychological *tension*. Attainment of goals results in a lowering of tension and a good feeling which is *intrinsically rewarding*. The mother's feedback to the infant in the form of a good touch or smile upon his achievement of his goal is an extra, *extrinsic reward* (see Ryan & Deci, 2000). To a large degree, the parent regulates the infant's subjective experience of *tension* by manipulating the salience, number, difficulty and relationships between goals (e.g., congruent or conflicting).

The preverbal, conceptless infant, like the autist, is aware only of minimally processed sense data, that is, protoconcepts. Remember that these are packets of equipartitioned sensory attributes. The infant must have some inborn competence to differentiate between "good" *vs.* "bad" stimulus arrays. Good stimuli are "whole", "complete", and "symmetrical". "Bad" sensory data is that which cannot be easily equipartitioned; it is "incomplete", or "asymmetrical", or in some way "bad form".

Preferences for "good gestalts" are genetically determined. They represent the "aesthetic sensibility" of the infant and, at some level, they underlie the aesthetic preferences of all adults (e.g., Köhler, 1917; Lewin, 1936; Wertheimer, 1923). The "most comforting other" understands these Gestalt ideas intuitively at least, and stays in contingent communication with the infant (e.g., Emde, 1980).

The mother's stroking of the infant's skin produces a positive state if it is a rhythmic motion of moderate intensity. It should be repetitive, rhythmic, easy to predict, and easy to package completely in a "protoconcept". Alternatively, if touch, sound, or facial expressions come unexpectedly, at the wrong time with no predictable rhythms, the subjective state of the infant will be negative. These sorts of sensory stimuli provided by the mother are not easily contained in "whole" equipartitioned units or protoconcepts. The leftover, uncontained sensations cause *tension*, maybe anxiety and ideally, curiosity and the development of "sensation-containing concepts".

The signal developmental achievement for the infant is to differentiate its own internal experience from that of the mother. Before this moment, "there is no infant" (Winnicott, 1960a). Mother and baby are one. An early executive function is to make concepts for *self* that are separate from *not-self*, which in the beginning are more or less equivalent to *mother*. *But what are the first attributes of the first self-concepts?* I assume they have to do with *agency* rather than *existence*. That is, I think it likely that the self's foundational attributes concern being a causal agent—*one who can do x*—rather than *one who is x*. This is because self-concepts become durable by means of activity.

The first, fragile self-concepts are made more robust by means of repeated tactile, visual, and proprioceptive sense data produced in interaction with *transitional objects*. This idea is consistent with Piaget's (1928, 1954) theory that concepts develop in mind–brain by means of repetitive sensorimotor interactions with objects. Playing with a teddy bear allows the infant to experience by trial and error the effects of various self-generated actions on their subjective experiences. For example, rocking back and forth rhythmically with teddy may cause a comfortable feeling. And, in time, some sort of semantic concept will be formed (*rocking contains the attribute "feels good"*). All of this depends of course on having a concept to represent the self as a distinct causal agent.

The early teachers, good or not so good, provide the templates upon which the infant forms self-concepts. The early caregivers' competence to regulate and expand the infant's self-concepts works to promote the development of the child's nascent mental structures and processes. Over time, self-regulating operations are learned, remembered, and deployed autonomously.

Autonomous regulation involves self-reflective capacity. Self-reflection is impossible without at least one self-concept. Before the first concept develops, instinctive, reflexive preferences for stimulus arrays with "wholeness" and "symmetry" are manipulated more or less competently by the caregivers. No parent can perfectly please the little baby. Breaks in *holding* occur. If the breaks are traumatic and repeated, the person will have problems developing and using valid self-concepts to control subjective experience and overt behaviour.

The only way to renovate such a self-system is to teach the person new concepts and habits of mind. But classic psychoanalytic methods of treatment are not entirely effective for many cases.

This is often not because the person can't learn and understand the new concepts at some level. Rather, it is because the new concepts are not "realized" in the brain; they are not "activated" to take over control from the old habits.

Mr. K's object relations history includes some trauma suffered at the hands of his histrionic mother and his bullying older brother. That is, people that he depended on to comfort him were also sources of danger. His father was inconsistently empathic. In a testament to the durability of the mind and brain, these relationships left him with core self-concepts that were "good enough". He was able to regulate his feelings and thoughts enough to graduate from college, work effectively, marry, raise functional children, and even enjoy some aspects of life including films, sports, and sex. But his self-concepts are nonetheless partly invalid. They are relatively poor "compromise formations" that sometimes collapse under high stress.

The "whistling a happy tune" method was helpful for him in regulating small to moderate levels of fear. When treated with drugs that reduce anxiety, his defences sometimes became functional. At higher levels of stress, defensive habits of denial such as "acting happy" are insufficient regulators of his subjective states. Instead, obsessional thinking about somatic symptoms and sexual performance increased. And, actual physical health and sexual performance became worse.

A central self-concept of Mr. K

As therapy continued, the compromise formations at the centre of Mr. K's personality became clear. The reader will recall that his job at a rough school called for him to frequently break up fights. This required him to mobilize and control high levels of aggression and, in turn, caused him anxiety. His main conceptual security operation was an attribute of the self that can best be labelled "I am one who only uses aggression in the service of the law".

He told me in the fourth month of therapy that his favourite movie was *High Noon*. He identified with the character played by Gary Cooper, a sheriff in a small Western town who had to single-handedly protect the town's citizens from a band of criminals. In other words, as long as he is on the side of the law and doing the morally right thing, he is free to express aggression. He said he liked the idea of "being up against something and having to do your job even if you are afraid". He also reported each week on his successes on the squash court. He had a compulsive need to play three or four times per week, and did so even after injuring his shoulder and being advised by his physician to avoid playing for a few weeks.

Two weeks later he reported a dream. "I was a boxer in the ring, fighting. It felt neat, a controlled sporting event. Then, from the audience a spear-wielding savage jumped into the ring. I woke up terrified". It became apparent that Mr. K had developed a system of self-concepts that allowed him to regulate his aggressive instincts quite effectively. He was able to transform his frightening feelings into effective aggression as long as it was in the service of his job as leader and peacemaker at a school filled with often violent students. But his dream indicates that he had made an "uneasy compromise". It is one he made as a small child without the benefits conferred by knowledge of formal logic or a durable set of self-concepts. It was developed in the specific, social environment of his family. It is really quite remarkable the defensive schemes that people devise as young children with minimal logical competence or formal learning of any kind.

For Mr. K, and for everyone else, the concepts regulating instinc- tive motives to use aggression are linked more or less strictly to con- cepts associated with morality. This is the self-concept "I am a man who only uses force in the service of the law". This concept contains both the attributes of "aggression" and "moral". It allowed him to experience the pleasure of aggression while at the same time reduc- ing his tendency to punish himself for it (see Figure 4). Aggression was permissible if consistent with an *ego ideal*. In Dissonance The- ory terms, the conflict he experiences is between the concepts "I am moral" and "I want to use aggression". The dissonance-reducing cog- nitions might include "the other deserved it". Dissonance-reducing cognitions or *rationalizations* are concepts that contain, explain, and resolve otherwise unpleasant conflict between self-concepts.

This habit to use a higher order concept to contain two incon- sistent cognitions was no doubt cooked-up early on. Mr. K's early aggressive feelings were experienced intensely in his relationship with his older, bullying brother. If he got a conscious whiff of sensations, thoughts, or feelings associated with aggression, Mr. K would become first aroused and then anxious. Then he could use anxiety containing and reducing concepts. The social context of sports is especially useful for Mr. K and others because active, aggressive behaviour is regulated by the commonly known "rules of the game". This lets the sportsman worry less about self-regulation than he would outside the boundary lines of a sports field.

But Mr. K was unconscious of all this. Instead, he was conscious of constant anxiety and obsessional fears of dying from this or that disease which he did not really have. Despite being constantly worried about his health, he ignored his doctor's orders to not play squash until his shoulder healed. This was consistent with his other counter-phobic operations in which "he approached what he feared" and "smiled when sad". And, while his most prominent conflicts involved fear about aggression, Mr. K also had anxiety about sex with his wife that caused anorgasmia on occasions.

Self-concepts and other concepts

The first concept marks the creation of a boundary between the infant and the mother. So, really the first self-concept is born at the same time that the concept "mother" or, at least, "other", is born. Before the creation of the two-concept system, the infant exists in a sensorial matrix contained in some sort of reflexive, instinctive apparatus. The first concept is also the first self-concept (Winnicott, 1960a).

Having just two potential causes for everything is a boon to the baby as it is a very simple theoretical system, a "toy system" if you will. The simplicity of operation of a simple causal system is why paranoid defences are so effective. A two-concept system is a zero-sum system in which "if it wasn't me, it was mummy". Melanie Klein who invented child psychoanalysis called the normal, two-concept state, the *paranoid position* (e.g., Klein, 1946).

Everything is magic to the "two-concept infant". The subjective experience or *phantasy* in infancy is what Klein was so good at understanding. She imagined that for the infant, *good breast-good mother-good feeling* were equated with the *present mother* (Klein, 1940). In our terms, the infant would have a meaningful sensation (a good feeling) when the sensory attributes learned to belong to the concept "mother" are streaming into mind. Klein assumed that the infant characterized the *bad breast* as the *absent mother*.

With the mother absent both sensorially and socially (i.e., not there to regulate the baby's internal state), the self needs to support itself.

The early lack of mental differentiation makes it impossible to distinguish between realistic expectations and fanciful wishes. Hence, what might it mean for the neonate to "support itself"? Primitive awareness of sensations indicating bodily needs become reinforcing in themselves if caretakers are reasonably reliable in discerning and meeting the infant's desires (Winnicott, 1970). This is because a sense of deprivation becomes associated with a sense of satisfaction. So, the first attempts at self-support involve merely paying attention to sensations of deprivation coming from the body and imagining fulfilment. This is the idea of *the omnipotence of thought* (Freud, 1912b). This mode of operating is what Winnicott (1960b) called the *true self*. And, he named the inability to experience this state *the false self*.

In normal development the *depressive position* (Klein, 1940) supersedes the *paranoid position*. In our terms, the increasing durability of the causal concept "I affect mummy" underlies the attainment of the *depressive position*. Logically, both a concept of the self as a causal agent and standards of correct behaviour are necessary to feel guilt. According to Klein, the infant starts to feel guilty at some point for hurting the breast/mother by biting and so on, and then feels depressed.

Conflict always involves inconsistency between at least two items. But it is inconsistency concerning important *self-concepts* which arouses the most dissonance (Aronson, 1969). This is a sensible evolutionary feature of mind–brain. If conflicts within the central regulatory agency of mind are chronic, energy is spent on repetitive cycling of the elements of the conflict either in consciousness, out of consciousness, or both. In other words, there are bio-energetic factors promoting self-conflict resolution. The bad feelings we get from unresolved conflict are a more or less urgent signal that the self-system needs work.

What many writers have called *self-concepts* may be thought of best as the concepts that have the most importance for the regulation of sensations, other concepts, expectations, feelings, and overt behaviour. These are *metaconcepts* that can contain or "make sense of" other concepts that seem inconsistent (see Snyder, 2009). *Metaconcepts* function to organize many other, lower-order concepts. For example, a concept representing a career choice (e.g., "I am a chef") is a higher order concept that has more potential to organize and regulate other concepts, feelings, and expectations than would a concept about food preferences such as "I like chocolate". The difference between *metaconcepts* and other concepts is a structural difference. *Self-concepts* occupy the highest nodes in lexical networks. It is important to recognize that TOTE processes can be used for comparing all sorts of concepts, low and high level, to their corresponding standards.

There has to be some "cut-off" point, some standard used more or less implicitly by the person to make the decision about what concepts comprise *the self* and which do not. A rule used for deciding what is self can be over-inclusive or under-inclusive, and either extremity can lead to psychopathology. *Paranoia* can be defined operationally as a condition caused by some sort of over-estimate of the relevance to the self of events occurring in the world.

Mr. K's early object relationships left him with functional but somewhat distorted concepts to explain who he was. His self-regulation system included obsessive thinking and hypochondria. He was more effective than most men at work and love. But obsessional, repetitive thinking was a "default option" that came on-line when "acting happy operations" failed. Obsessions bind anxiety but do not produce much happiness. They clearly represent a "holding action" in which invalid concepts are recycled repeatedly.[2]

Distortions in foundational self-concepts work to complicate the subsequent development of concepts needed to accomplish the two major tasks for the adult: maintaining security and being creative. We are born with genetically determined, reflexive security and sexual systems. Both systems can regulate overt behaviour without too much input from conscious, self-reflective conceptual processes. Instinctive security operations include the affiliative, attachment behaviours necessary for the infant to survive, and the "fight and flight" behaviours needed to protect the security of the adult. Instinctive sexual operations include tendencies to respond with stereotypic behaviours to specific sensory attributes of individuals of the opposite gender.

Instinctive sex and security systems come on-line much more intensively with hormonal changes at puberty. The self-concepts developed to that point will be strained as never before to contain sense data and behavioural impulses. Defects in self-concepts forged earlier will cause functional problems at this developmental stage.

Updating the model

At this point we should revise the model in Figure 2 to include some of the assumptions we have added since Chapter Three. This updated model appears in Figure 6. The figure indicates that self-concepts are differentiated in mind–brain from concepts that do not define the self. For example, the concept "chair" is not likely to define the self but, of course, it exists in mind. The concept "generous", on the other hand, might be used by the individual as a description of him or herself. We assume that concepts about the *real self* and the *ideal self* are contained in the *self-concept* area of the model (e.g., "how generous one is" and "how generous one would like to be"). Self-evaluation and regulation involve TOTE assessments of differences between concepts containing attributes of one's *actual* behaviour and concepts containing attributes of *ideal* behaviour.

Figure 6 makes explicit the difference between expectations one has of the self, and expectations about other people and events in the world. For example, I expect myself to do x in a certain situation, but expect mummy to do y. While expectations of the self and other people are generated by more or less *naïve* concepts of social psychology, non-self expectations are generated by more or less *naïve* concepts of physics (e.g., "This wind is likely to blow that tree down").

I am assuming still that all concepts, self or not self, are pain and pleasure concepts. For example, the concept" chair" like all other concepts finds its place in mind-brain because of its utility in explaining and predicting sensations of pleasure (e.g., the relaxation of sitting); and pain (e.g., one can smash a toe into a chair).

The model has been altered to illustrate the idea that feelings can be located or associated with the self or not. In some sense, all feelings "belong" to the self. But empathy involves feelings or thoughts we have in reaction to observing another (Davis, 1983, 1992). At the beginning of life, before self-concepts are differentiated, the difference between one's subjective state and their caregiver's state is not too easy to discern. Operationally, adult psychological competence depends on some ability to differentiate the operation of a

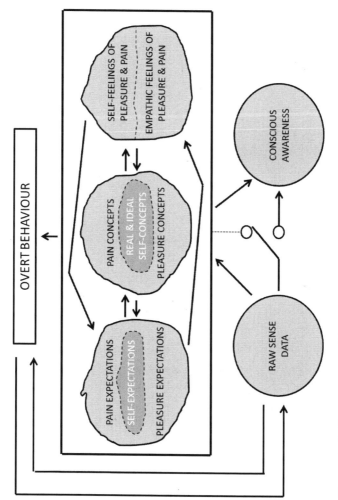

Figure 6. Self-concepts and human competence.

mirror neuron system in which observations of others automatically stimulate feelings, from feelings arising from one's own system of semantic *self-concepts*. For example, a competent individual can distinguish feelings resulting from TOTE operations indicating that one has fallen short of one's own ideals, from feelings stimulated in them by a disappointed expression on another's face who has witnessed their failure.

People are more or less able to do this. Some become overwhelmed by the behaviours and feelings of other people, for example, fainting at the sight of another's injury. And, some are indifferent to the feelings of others. Plausibly, the ability to *dissociate* from awareness concepts for ideal standards of behaviour underlies the behaviour of psychopaths.

Self-concept development occurs "on top of" the early, foundational self-concepts. Adult self-concepts are needed to enjoy and regulate sexual and aggressive feelings and behaviours. Snyder et al., elaborate the point:

> Concept building continues throughout life with the formation of metaconcepts, groupings of concepts, which comprise complex cognitive operations. These in turn confer expertise. Once a metaconcept is in place, the concepts that comprise the metaconcept are suppressed from conscious awareness. Everyone has experienced how the details of complex operations can become automatic and nonconscious, such as driving a car.
>
> (Snyder et al., 2004, p. 34)

The flexibility of the person to switch attention back and forth between higher- and lower-order concepts is a critical mental competence. In psychopathological conditions the person may become "stuck" and unable to bring concepts into awareness as needed due to some defensive prohibition.

* * *

The next chapter examines ideas from Object Relations and Oedipal Conflict theories and their implications for the development of self-concepts that regulate sensations, feelings, expectations, other concepts, and overt behaviour.

Notes

1. This case clearly illustrates the interaction of physical and psychological variables. There is no doubt that SSRIs increase serotonin in the sexual apparatus which in turn does something to delay orgasm. But anxiety also affects the performance of these organs. For Mr. K, ability to have an orgasm was a function of: 1) serotonin levels in the sex organs; 2) an increase in dopamine and norepinephrine levels in brain due to Buproprion; 3) the state of serotonin receptors in brain altered by 5-HT levels; 4) his anxiety about his relationship with his wife; and 5) countless other neurological variables of differing importance. Mr. K did an experiment to vary one of the factors—anxiety. When he was in the "masturbation-low anxiety condition" he could have an orgasm. In the "intercourse-high anxiety condition" he could not.

2. Obsessive, repetitive rituals can be effective at reducing anxiety and can produce a charming sort of pleasure. Our entire "organized culture" depends to an important extent on repetitive checking behaviours. Scientists, physicians, surgeons, pilots, and anyone performing exacting tasks tends to benefit from some type of obsessional thinking and/or compulsive behaviour. However, the effectiveness of obsessive rituals and any "magical thrills" associated with them, (e.g., the idea of *the omnipotence of thought*) usually starts to fade at puberty. At extreme levels, obsessive-compulsive defences operate as barriers to knowing reality; become ineffective for controlling anxiety; start to cause anxiety themselves; and can transform into psychotic operations.

CHAPTER SEVEN

Sex and aggression

Sexual and aggressive instincts have developed to create and preserve life. Overt sexual and aggressive behaviours need to be regulated in order to promote individual and social security. What we are calling *the self* is the integrated mental and neurological system with the primary function of guiding and directing mental processes occurring at various levels of awareness. The self executes its regulatory functions by containing and explaining: sensation; self- and non-self-concepts; and self- and non-self-expectations. It also helps if the person can differentiate between self-feelings and empathic reactions. The self-regulatory system (or personality) can be more or less effective and efficient. The level of self-competence determines, in large part, whether the person will realize few or many of their aspirations in love and work (see Figure 6).

Sex

Genes that promote the performance of particular adult sexual behaviours are kept in the genome if they increase the odds of producing viable offspring.[1] The highly pleasurable feelings and thoughts that can precede, and result from, infantile and adult sexual behaviour are important features of the evolved sexual apparatus of animals. Feelings, or what we have called "meaningful sensations", are the proximal reinforcers of sexual and all biologically critical (and trivial) behaviours. If one remembers what sex feels like, one may have high expectations of getting the good feeling again when approaching an attractive member of the opposite sex. Inborn tendencies and learned concepts in memory are activated upon receipt of sense data (e.g., olfactory, tactile, visual) emanating from arousing goal objects. These perceptions produce expectations of pleasure and overt sexual approach behaviour (see Chapter Five).

But physical closeness to another can be fraught with danger. The classic example is the black widow spider that eats her mate after sexual intercourse. Mere physical closeness to individuals of one's own or another species can stimulate two mind–brain systems. One system promotes sexual behaviours, and the other stimulates fighting and fleeing behaviours. Fight–flight tendencies must be somehow contained, co-opted, suppressed, or integrated with affiliative or sexual tendencies if one is to get in, and stay in, a position to have social or sexual intercourse. Sex and security systems are closely related in the brain and in our subjective mental experiences.

One spends half of their life trying to avoid being hurt by other people and the other half trying to get close enough to have sexual or other connections with them. Often sexiness and danger are embodied in one person, for example, *the femme fatal, the bad boy*. When we locate pleasure and pain potential in the same situation or other person, brain–mind will have to resolve the conflict with more or less help from conscious, reflective functions. By definition, with less reflective information processing, decisions will be based more on reflex and habit.

It is probably safe to assume that the typical citizen today is conscious of more concepts concerning sex than their counterpart of One Hundred years ago. This is due in no small part to Psychoanalysis itself. Freud's (1904) ideas about *slips* in which unconscious thoughts are expressed seemingly by accident in speech and other overt behaviours are now widely known. Other commonly recognized psychoanalytic ideas include the Oedipus Complex; and ideas stemming from the psychoanalytic theory of psychosexual development and fixation. For example, *naïve psychologists* may describe others as having "oral" or "anal" personalities.

The latency period and puberty

By about the third or fourth year the child should be equipped with a somewhat durable notion of self. They have experienced some very good feelings of "infantile sexuality", and also paranoia, guilt, and some kind of depression. They are now ready to start resolving Oedipal Conflicts. Typically, foundational "Oedipal resolution concepts" are formed by about age six. Then the pleasant latency period ensues and lasts until puberty. Self- and non-self-concepts about nature (plants, insects, dogs, cats, the sky) and human nature are developed, to a large extent, in *play*. *Latency* is a time for acting, for trying out concepts in games. The child does *role play* and learns social skills when, playing, for example, "soldiers", "house", "doctor", or baseball. "Who shall be the leader?" "What is my role?" The body is still in a pre-pubescent state, but the mind–brain is practicing for adulthood.

When sex and growth hormone levels rise in puberty, secondary sexual characteristics and dreams of sex begin. The self-concepts tested in play during latency will need to be durable enough to stand the stresses of more serious, adult sexual and aggressive sensations, feelings, thoughts, and behaviours. For the rest of the person's life, self-regulatory systems that were formed in the pre-Oedipal and Oedipal resolution stage (from the fourth to sixth years), will work more or less well to control the mind and body in order to attain pleasure and avoid unnecessary pain and injury.

The foundations of the personality will remain strong shapers of the psyche and brain throughout life. We assume that the development of self-concepts will occur beyond childhood to varying degrees in everyone. But explicit, conscious analysis of underlying self-concepts can greatly facilitate development. People have engaged in self-analysis since the beginning of written history. Psychoanalytic psychotherapies, a relatively recent invention, function to involve more people in purposeful study of the self. Usually, of course, painful mental and/or physical symptoms bring the person to therapy. But the processes of self-development are similar whether one starts the project with a clinically diagnosable psychopathology or not.

Sex is more or less anxiety-provoking for adults. With the development of self-concepts based more on reality than wishful thinking, sexuality is transformed from its infantile beginnings. Freud (1924) felt that anxiety about sex usually results from a less than ideal resolution of the Oedipus Complex. In general, Freud and psychoanalytic theory is better at understanding the child, the neurotic, and the male, than the mother, the normal person, and the female. But Freud's theory of adult male sexual development illuminates general mental processes occurring in both genders involved in approaching pleasure and avoiding pain.

Oedipus

At the centre of Freud's system (e.g., 1930) was the idea that feeling guilty, even if one had not really broken any laws, was the most common psychopathology of the 20th century. To feel guilty one must be able to compare concepts about behaviour, thoughts, and feelings against standards of correct behaviours, thoughts, and feelings (see Chapter Six). Such standards are learned early on. The mental comparison processes for comparing the *real* and *ideal self* are Test-Operate-Test-Exit processes described by Carver and Scheier (1981). Development of functional self-concepts and regulatory processes work to contain anxiety and guilt that ensue when one falls short of standards; and, they work to regulate the excitement that occurs upon exceeding standards. Too much guilt and anxiety, or too little, can be a problem.

Freud (1912a) reported on a prototypical example of guilty conscience. Many male patients reported to him that they could maintain erections and ejaculate only if they were having sex with a prostitute, or if they imagined the woman they were with was no good. If they had loving feelings for the woman they would be impotent sexually. Freud (1912a, p. 179) called this *psychical impotence* and "the most prevalent from of degradation in erotic life". The more popular label is *Madonna–Whore Syndrome*. A severely afflicted man may function sexually only when he feels no tender, loving feelings for the other.

Freud assumed that if loving feelings became conscious during sex, a man can became anxious and guilty because the feelings were too similar to those he felt as an infant for his mother. The fear is that one is violating one of the deepest taboos in our culture—the prohibition of incest. If the woman is imagined to be the farthest thing from one's own presumably virtuous mother, such as "a whore", anxiety can be reduced and sexual functioning enhanced.

Although guilt about incestuous feelings is universal, its strength varies between individuals depending on basic biological and social variables. Nature is parsimonious with energy. Ideally, guilt needs to be just strong enough to prevent taboo behaviour. Denial of taboo wishes is proportional to the wish to perform the taboo behaviour. The variables that predict the strength of sexual approach tendencies operate in the human too. The physical attractiveness of the mother; her youthfulness (which is, in part, a proxy for fertility); the strength of the son's sexual drive (operationalized by sexual deprivation); and social intimacy with the mother are the key predictors of the magnitude of a son's denial of incestuous wishes (Bernstein, 1981, 1984).

Fear and antipathy towards the father is the other component of the Oedipal narrative. The full Oedipal Complex, derived from Sophocles' *Oedipus Rex*, involves sexual desire for the mother; fear that the father will frustrate such desires and castrate the son; and aggressive, murderous wishes towards the frustrating father. Freud wrote that psychical impotence is due to an incomplete resolution of the conflicts inherent in the Oedipal Complex. He felt that the normal resolution of this conflict involves identification with the father or *identification with the aggressor* (Freud, 1924).

The man who cannot have sex with a woman he loves is most likely using a concept very like "my mother" to contain relatively raw olfactory, tactile, and visual sensations aroused by sex or physical closeness with a woman who resembles the mother. In severe cases, *any* woman the patient is with is somehow taken to be the mother. Hence, sex with any woman is the subjective equivalent of actually violating the incest taboo.

Uniting with the father, that is, developing a self-concept containing the attributes "me" and "dad", works to reduce conflicts the lad may have about sexual impulses towards the mother and aggressive impulses towards the father. That is, a concept such as "the best guys in the world", contains the attributes "me" and "dad". This sort of self-concept resolves problems with the father and to some degree the mother. But identification with the father does not rid the mind of memories of real sexual feelings the man may have had about his mother. In a very real sense, at the deepest level of the psyche is a zero-sum conceptual relationship between some sexual impulses (the taboo feelings about mother) and the renunciation of the impulses by means of identification with the father.

Civilization is made possible, in part, because "bad thoughts" may precede "bad behaviour". Rather than a police officer on every corner, we have the controlling agent in the mind–brain of each individual. Citizens have, by and large, internalized taboos prohibiting murder and incest. Because these subjects are often not talked about, most people's original concepts of the taboos remain in a relatively primitive state in memory. The most intense taboos regarding the body and its functions are learned early on and processes working to inhibit taboo thoughts and behaviours are mostly unconscious.

Depending on their level of sophistication, the parents themselves may not be able to think competently about these frightening subjects. A child of such parents will be handicapped similarly and may, therefore, come to more or less equate "bad thoughts" with "bad acts". As an adult, the person who has not differentiated adequately between thoughts and overt behaviours may feel guilty and anxious during frankly sexual activity, or any other sort of potentially pleasurable activity, such as thinking.

In the mental network of concepts, some ideas lie closer to the foundational self-concepts. And, the most foundational self-concepts concern taboo behaviours, the most central standards of correctness. These are variously called *values* or *morals*, and become associated more or less with other concepts and processes used to control sensations, expectations, other concepts, feelings, and behaviours.

Since most people are not even conscious of impulses to violate taboos, concepts and processes that are associated with the taboo concepts, not the taboos themselves, operate as the proximal regulators of behaviour (see Chapter Ten, the case of Mr. C). These are called *derivatives* by psychoanalysts (Freud, 1915, 1926). The conceptless, guiltless baby is able to enjoy just about anything to do with the body, that is, *polymorphous perversity* (Freud, 1905). It is a giant, complicated task to regulate strong impulses under a constraint that one may not be aware of their underlying causes. From this perspective, most mental structures and processes used to regulate subjective experience and overt behaviour can be considered derivatives. This is the logic underlying the assumption that most cultural creations are driven by sexual motives.

The nature of passionate sexual pleasure

In general, the processes that regulate repetition, pleasure seeking and pain avoidance are different at different levels of physiological arousal. For example, we know that habit strength changes with arousal levels (See Chapter 2). High arousal levels are often reached during sex. How are control processes altered in sex? What changes in regulatory processes promote pleasure in sex?

There is some sort of common wisdom that the capacity to enjoy sex or other things depends on being able to be more aware of sensations than concepts (see Figure 1). But we have maintained that thinking about sense data, not merely being passively aware of it, is the greatest pleasure (See Chapter 3).

With all the theoretical disarray in psychoanalysis between Freudians and Jungians, and between theorists that focus on pre-Oedipal *vs.* Oedipal causes of psychopathology, there is a surprising sort of agreement about what makes good sex good. In short, the best sex is something like incest. The very Freudian Kernberg says so, and so does Jung.

> Sexual intercourse [after "normal" resolution of the Oedipus complex] represents the crossing of the boundaries that separate a man from a woman, an act of defiance which secretively ruptures unconscious oedipal prohibitions. Overcoming oedipal prohibitions is a profound source of sexual excitement and passionate love. Here, the love for the oedipal object and the triumph over the oedipal rival, the erotic excitement of sexual intimacy linked with the aggressive gratification of overcoming the secret, unavailable and forbidden sexual barriers that separated the oedipal objects replay the condensation of love, eroticism and aggression ... at the level of polymorphous perverse infantile sexuality.
>
> (Kernberg, 1988, p. 67)

> Although the union of close blood-relatives is everywhere taboo, it is yet the prerogative of kings (witness the incestuous marriages of the Pharaohs, etc.). Incest symbolizes union with one's own being, it means individuation or becoming a self, and, because this is so vitally important, it exerts an unholy

fascination—not, perhaps, as a crude reality, but certainly as a psychic processes controlled by the unconscious, a fact well known to anybody who is familiar with psychopathology. It is for this reason, and not because of the occasional cases of human incest, that the first gods were believed to propagate their kind incestuously. Incest is simply the union of like with like, which is the next stage in the development of the primitive idea of self-fertilization.

(Jung, 1946)

So, it seems that great sex depends, in part, on acting inconsistently with the deepest, foundational ideals of the self. This requires durable and flexible conceptual competencies that can resist collapse under high conflict and arousal. Perhaps the greatest pleasures depend on doing without distant derivatives for representing conflicts while one is symbolically violating deep moral standards. Derivatives, by definition, permit the person to be unaware of foundational conflicts and the feelings that they arouse.

The competent management of such non-conformist activity promises to be highly rewarding in sex and the rest of life. It represents a commitment to self-development at the risk of detachment from the security of the group. The means of management are durable, valid self-concepts that work to contain and make meaningful one's own sexual and aggressive sensations. Failing such development, zero-sum conceptual systems such as the Madonna–Whore system operate to cause an inability to love a sexual partner, or have sex with a loved partner.

Sexual behaviour can be enormously creative if self-concepts are valid and durable and if the processes for the activation of such concepts are flexible. One common sort of sexual creativity involves more or less extreme play at bondage, discipline, sadism, and masochism (BDSM). It is plausible to assume that combining the neurobiological systems underlying social behaviours of attachment, tenderness, and love, with those regulating aggression and hate, works to *increase* the intensity of sensations available during sex. To make this sensory data available to consciousness, a man, for example, might need to consider the sexual partner as both the Madonna and the Whore.

But one must maintain a degree of differentiation between the concepts of love and hate, sex and aggression, and self and other, to enjoy anything. Otherwise, the person may experience a break with reality, or at least may fear such a break. In the midst of fantasy sex play where partners are vulnerable, being able to make critical differentiations is essential for safety. Without such competence there will be reluctance to play, *or tendencies to behave psychopathically.*

A particular patient of mine was happy for the most part playing these sorts of BDSM sex games. Then, he met a woman who asked him to adopt a role of a "dominating older brother" while she played "the helpless sister". This involved her speaking in a child-like voice. Given this scenario, he experienced Erectile Dysfunction.

It turns out he had two older sisters. The younger of the two was an unhappy girl. The patient said, "I'm most like her, the weakest, unhappy one". So, we can assume that his foundational self-concepts were modelled to an important degree on the concept containing the attribute "weak little sister". Behaviours that might be associated, even in play, with hurting this already wounded aspect of self, caused the sexual play space and his erection to collapse. The case illustrates how specific and individualized the self-concepts regulating sex and aggression can be.

Of course, society is counting on every citizen having internalized a rule that says something like: "Adults are forbidden from having sex with children". This man was facing Double Talion Dread due to the violation of two strong taboos—incest and paedophilia. No wonder he couldn't play the game. But why was he driven to play it in the first place?

Let's assume with Kernberg and Jung that symbolic violation of foundational self-concepts is necessary in order to generate dynamic forces that can be converted into passionate sexual pleasure. It follows that violating two taboos might result in more passionate pleasure than violating one taboo. Maybe an expectation of very great pleasure in line with this assumption motivated the patient's attempt to play his girlfriend's game. But it was beyond his competence. He did not make repeated attempts to comply with her request. If he had, his prognosis would have been worse than it was. Every self-regulatory system has its limits. Inability to recognize and act in accord with such limits leads to repeated self-defeating behaviour.

Development beyond Oedipus

Psychobiological life is more or less filled with injury. The mind–brain system, like all other body systems, will suffer acute and then more chronic conditions over the life span. Conceptual processes of mind–brain become less efficient due to aging. Important causes of the adult's mind–brain dysfunctions are: old severe traumas (e.g., outright child abuse); an accumulation of old, mild to moderate empathic mistakes of good-enough caregivers; trauma suffered as an adult; and underlying decrease in brain functions with aging.

Cases in which the personality had functioned well enough in youth often present in psychotherapy at late middle-age, after some small decrement in brain function starts to make a difference in conscious, subjective experiences. Stress from the social environment starts to increase at mid-life. Mortality looms larger. A mind–brain that was able to use distorted self-concepts in youth starts to develop symptoms. "Who am I?" the person asks. "What am I living for?" "Why am I depressed and anxious?"

An urgency to develop the self often is felt at mid-life—*the midlife crisis*. In a very real sense, the loss of efficiency of the mind–brain system motivates this wish for change. Think of the pitcher who can throw a fast-ball at 100 mph at age nineteen. At age thirty nine, his fastest pitch is only 80 mph. How can he still get people out? There is no doubt he has become smarter. He has learned to be more efficient and to do more with less. In a very real sense, there is no need to get smarter if one can compensate for regulatory inefficiencies with raw power. This power diminishes with wear and tear occurring over time.

Ideally, one's life experiences operate to enhance the pleasure of experience in sex, baseball, and everything else. But if one or both participants in sex have distorted self-concepts there will be some trouble in sex per se and all other areas of life, especially when underlying brain functions become less efficient and effective.

Standards of correctness and Mr. K's aggression

Mr. K had occasional sexual functioning problems but he enjoyed sex with his wife. The regulation of aggressive feelings and behaviours was more of a clinical issue for him. So, we assume that

Mr. K lacked some valid self-concepts, regulatory processes, or both, regarding aggression. Early on, he had made a typical regulatory compromise. He was only permitted to use aggression if the other had violated legal or moral standards of society. This compromise and his hypochondria were derivates of the underlying conflict.

But hadn't Mr. K been wronged egregiously and repeatedly by his older brother? When a young child is frustrated by those he is attached to, instinctive aggressive reactions are aroused. Aggression in response to frustration is instrumental for the most part in helping the individual overcome barriers to goal attainment. But a poignant conflict is aroused in the young child who is "not understood" or "teased" by an older brother; and manipulated by a histrionic mother. These are the very same figures that he depends on for security. Since the self is not too well differentiated from caregivers early on, anger or rage directed at frustrating others are more or less equivalent to threats to the self itself (see Stark, 1994).

In therapy, Mr. K recalls a particular day when at age seventeen he was playing basketball with his older brother. The brother was, as usual, harassing Mr. K verbally and physically. In response, Mr. K threw a basketball at the brother's head, hurting him slightly. He remembers that the incident caused anxiety but also a sort of pride. The story speaks in favour of Mr. K's psychological health and indicates that he was capable of acting against the brother in self-defence without collapsing in anxiety. Tellingly, the event occurred on a basketball court, a social context associated with "rules" and ideas of fairness. This sort of external, social structure works to regulate feelings and behaviours. It is especially helpful when the individual has less than optimal internal control systems.

Mr. K maintained a stable but uneasy relationship with his older brother until a final break occurred after the death of the father. These sorts of breaks are common in distressed families. Avoiding contact is often attributed, as in this case, to something about the inheritance of money. But a more fundamental reason that family members avoid each other after a father's death, is an unconscious fear that violence will break out (see Freud, 1921). Mr. K and his brother were consciously aware of their mutual antipathy even if they were not aware of the fundamental causes of it. They decided to avoid each other after their father's death.

The self-regulatory system keeps grandiose, forbidden sexual and aggressive impulses in check by means of a fear that the family will collapse if such impulses are not suppressed. Later on, especially in neurotics, there is a fear that the self will disintegrate (Kohut, 1977). The adult version of the mechanism is essentially modelled on the child's fear about the parents dying or divorcing. Remember Mr. K used to go to the family housekeeper asking her to reassure him that the parents would not get a divorce.

Mr. K's self-concepts, and the self-concepts of all people in families and organizations, are part of social psychological meaning systems or systems of beliefs that are partly explicit and partly implicit (Bernstein & Burke, 1989). That is, the mind–brains of all group members operate simultaneously on the basis of both explicit and implicit assumptions about reality.

Bion (1961) considered the explicit, rational assumptions of group members a property of a work group mentality, and different from the unconscious basic assumptions of group members. Bion described three common types of unconscious *basic assumptions* made by groups: *Dependency, Fight-Flight, and Pairing*. Observations of many types of work groups tend to validate Bion's theory that otherwise rational, business-like groups often behave as if they had met in order to depend on a leader; fight or flee from an enemy; or get two people in the group to pair-up and give birth to a solution for the group's problems.

Habits to activate newly learned concepts are relatively weak compared to older habits that have been reinforced over time. Sensations, coming from the actual object the concept is meant to represent, work to support fragile mind–brain structures. For example, we write a phone number down and refer to it before it becomes a durable memory. This is also why psychoanalysts sometimes sit where the patient on the couch cannot see them. "With the analyst out of sight, the analysand's self becomes relatively deprived of stimuli that evoke self-sustaining object experiences ... resulting in a weakening of the self's structure" (Wolf, 1995).

One thing leads to another

If sensations give rise to instinctual or learned tendencies to behave sexually or aggressively in ways which are inconsistent with standards of correctness, signal anxiety is aroused (Freud, 1926). Then compromise concepts, different from but related to the underlying cause of the anxiety, are quickly activated to contain and explain the anxiety. By definition, sensations of signal anxiety are not accompanied in awareness with concepts indicating the cause of the anxiety. Accordingly, people exploit the ambiguity about causes in the service of defence (Snyder & Wicklund, 1981).

Theoretically, ambiguity about the cause of signal anxiety should decrease automatically over time if no barriers to free association are in place. This is because there is an automatic tendency for the thresholds of activation of concepts associated with a recently primed concept to decrease, that is, spreading activation (Collins & Loftus, 1975). Since derivatives are, by definition, associated with foundational self-concepts in conflict, activation of any node in the network of the defended against concept becomes more likely when associates of the foundation concept are stimulated. This is what makes the repressed *return*. The sequence is: stimulation of taboo tendencies- → signal anxiety → activation of defensive concept to explain and contain anxiety → spreading activation → additional defensive operations to block activation of underlying conflict.

When defences fail to stem anxiety, as they are certain to do on occasions, the person can repeat the activation of the defensive operation, for example, obsessing about health in Mr. K's case. If this fails, there is a regression to more primitive sorts of defences, such as acting out or even loss of consciousness. Cases of sexual assault are so problematic and may lead to Post Traumatic symptoms because victims often use *regression in the service of the ego* and other dissociative operations to "not be present" during an attack. But in the regressed state one risks uncovering memories of old traumas, small and large. That is, old traumas can become unrepressed during the attempt to defend against the current trauma.

In PTSD, we imagine that associative processes, uncontrolled by regressed executive functioning, permit memoires of old and new injuries to combine. The new, more extensive network of painful memories then repeats in consciousness. In PTSD, mind–brain is demanding that conscious attention be focused on the injury. Ideally, this can lead to important growth via re-conceptualization of self-attributes: "I was a victim; I am no longer a victim".

Safe areas

When consciousness is focused on concepts relatively distant from problematic core self-concepts, anxiety goes down. All people have areas of their minds where they feel comfortable. These conceptual areas are well defended against *spreading activation* in the psychological and neurological senses. For example, the typical male enjoys watching football on Sunday on television. Aggression is observed taking place within a defined field, within "rules of the game" administered by neutral judges or referees. The rules are cleverly adjusted so that violence is barely in check and excellent feats of physical prowess occur. People were and are hunters who tracked, killed, and ate their prey. Observing aggression, the hunt, love, and sex via television, cinema, and reading stimulate aspects of the mind and can create deep pleasures. For many, vicarious pleasures work, in part, to lower the drive to act in ways that might expose the person to physical, social, or legal dangers.

This is what Jung (e.g., 1904) was getting at with his Word Association Test. He noted how subjects responded to words and assessed the latency of the responses. If responses were slow or odd, he assumed some discomfort or conflict had been aroused by the stimulus word. These he labelled defensive *complexes*. In our terms, *complexes* are areas of the network of semantic concepts that somehow do not adequately contain sensations or other concepts. These un-integrated items behave something like a pebble in one's shoe. They are at least an irritant, and more importantly can inhibit movement to attain desired objects and goals. The Word Association Test is an efficient way to identify resistances to thinking about anxiety-provoking concepts. It allows observation of the type of difficulties that people have when attempting to follow the basic rule of psychoanalysis, that is, "to free associate".

Just as sexual sensations experienced with a woman who is not one's mother might be wrongly contained in the concept *my mother*, aggressive sensations are subject to the same sorts of conceptual mistakes. For example, one might have "problems with authority" such as "being afraid of police officers". Or, the problem might manifest in behaviour, that is, the person is seemingly always engaged in arguments with authority figures such as police officers, bosses, and teachers. A psychoanalyst would likely connect these problems with the person's difficulty regulating fear and aggression concerning his father. The person's old unresolved, uncontained fears and hates are projected onto others in positions of authority. It is a rule of thumb in psychoanalysis that uncontained ideas will be projected more or less all the time. This is why the most extremely dysfunctional people are the easiest to diagnose. Their unconscious is on public display. But they are sometimes very hard to treat effectively.

Psychoanalysts call habitual tendencies to project self-aspects onto others *transferences*. In our terms, projections represent errors in identifying the source of feeling, thoughts, or expectations. In terms of the model in Figure 6, there is a habitual tendency to decide that aspects of the self are really attributes of the other. Of course, sometimes projections are correct in that the other person is indeed having the feeling that the self is experiencing unconsciously. Empathic reactions and projections are often confused by naïve scientists, psychotherapists, and formal scientists (see Bernstein & Davis, 1982).

A central insight of Freud was that patients typically perform their dominant transference habit with the analyst. This provides excellent, real-time data about the patient's mental operations. Psychoanalysis was designed to "analyse the transference". This is done first by pointing it out, making it conscious. The hope of psychoanalysis is that some revision of the patient's self-concepts will result in improved mental competence.

Summary

Oedipus for naïve and formal scientists

The social and psychological prohibitions of incest and murder are the foundations of the individual's mind in large part because they are the foundations of society itself. Before exogamy became the social norm, the person was a member of essentially one group—the blood group, the more or less extended biologic family. The incest taboo forced individuals to mate outside the boundaries of the family. Subsequently, diverse reasons for affiliating with people other than biological relatedness became encouraged. The complex social and technological cultures we live in today are the result of the process beginning with enforced exogamy. That is, the differentiation of people into groups on the basis other than blood relations. At that point, cultural and social psychological factors, not only biological factors, can drive development.

Cultural or cognitive-social means of processing and transmitting information operate at a much faster rate than genetic processes. This is part of what Dawkins (1976) was expressing in his invention of the term *memes*. *Memes* are concepts. Concepts can be transmitted to other people in a manner analogous to the transmission of genes encoded in Deoxyribonucleic Acid (DNA). The competencies of the human brain to use semantic concepts make cultural development possible.

Freud (e.g., 1912b) realized that the story of *Oedipus Rex* illustrated something general and important about the psychological development of all people. But if psychological theory is to advance, it is better to imagine the story of Oedipus as an example of a more general process of how self-concept development and conflict between concepts can work to promote and inhibit growth of the self. Psychoanalysts in the *Drive* or *Id Schools* have focused on the motivational aspects of the Oedipus conflict to explain psychopathology. Analysts from *Self* and *Object Relations Schools* tend to focus on the pre-Oedipal period to find causes of adult psychopathology.

The theoretical debates inside psychoanalysis are somewhat similar to the ones inside social psychology, but they are less productive. As noted in Chapter Two, experimental social psychologists argue about whether cognitive *or* motivational factors should be used to explain psychological phenomena. This sort of "cognitive *or* motivational explanation argument" is sometimes useful to design research to identify the conditions under which different causal factors operate (e.g., Bernstein et al., 1979). But certain assumptions are beyond doubt: all mental phenomena are biological phenomena; brain activity to accomplish any task uses energy; thinking is an energetic phenomenon regulated dynamically by mind–brain self-systems; and mental processes take place in and outside of awareness.

The task is to account for the cognitive *and* motivational, the biological *and* social psychological variables affecting thinking, feeling, and behaving. If the theorist does not take the preceding statement as axiomatic, theoretical integration attempts are very difficult. For example, Greenberg and Mitchell (1983) attempted to integrate Psychoanalytic Drive and Object Relations Schools. The effort was admirable. But because they didn't have a more general theory to contain the ideas in Drive and Object Relations theories, they had to build many awkward theoretic scaffolds to make connections between the schools' ideas. It is better to begin theorizing at a level that is general enough to avoid getting involved at once in the conflicting, zero-sum assumptions of two warring theoretical schools. Also, Greenberg and Mitchell do not consider neurobiology. It turns out that studying the brain makes it easier to understand the mind.

Integration between biological and social psychological views of the person is important for many reasons. One reason is that the treatments preferred in psychiatry today are psychopharmacology and Cognitive Therapy. This is due in part to the explosion of knowledge in psychopharmacology and the availability of effective agents. It is also due to the trend towards *evidence-based medicine*. There is more research validating the effectiveness of Cognitive Therapy than there is validating other sorts of talking therapies.

There is no doubt that cognitive therapies can be effective. However, an abundance of empirical support for it relative to other treatment methods exists because: (1) It is harder to study "deeper" processes; (2) Psychodynamic, depth therapies work for a smaller group of diagnoses and patient types than do cognitive therapies; (3) Most psychoanalysts are not trained experimental scientists; and (4) Cognitive psychologists are more experienced with research methods than psychoanalysts and psychiatrists, and they tend to have negative attitudes towards psychoanalysis.

The most curious aspect of today's Biological Psychiatry School is that it seems to have forgotten about its old fellow traveller, *Mr. Id, the Biology Kid*! We understand why the Cognitive School isn't interested in the *id*. The whole school was formed to leave it out! The Affect Regulation School is now the carrier of psychoanalytic theory. Their interests in mentalization, reflective processes, and neuroscience (e.g., Fonagy et al., 2004) are also our interests. If the need is to integrate psychoanalytic, cognitive, and biological theories, one must consider Oedipus, sex, aggression, and conflict.

Development of the system of self-concepts

The infant must learn to differentiate its body and mind from its physical and social environments. For this purpose the child needs to mentally represent themselves; a process in which a concept of "other", very likely "mother", is also formed. After the "self" and "mother" concepts are created, the child must conceptualize other objects that are salient in the sensory field. The father is a likely candidate for early representation depending on how much he is around. The family's dogs and cats are probably provided early with representational concepts.

Development depends on adding concepts to the self-system as well as the not-self system. And, development has to include some learning about "how to operate the mind". The child needs more concepts to contain the attributes of more people and things. This helps to regulate the mind in more situations. Also, the child adds attributes to existing concepts. The ability to activate concepts as needed to represent social objects such as the *self* and *others*, as well as *non-social, non-self objects* (e.g., an aeroplane) is a key mental competence that, by definition, is lacking to some degree in mental illness. The person must learn to regulate attentional focus in order to think competently.

The child loves and wants to approach the mother and is sometimes frustrated by and wants to avoid the father. And, of course, the child is sometimes frustrated by the mother and more or less loves the father. Social rules about how they may go about expressing love and aggression are learned, and help to regulate adult behaviour. These are truisms. In other words, the child is faced with approach and avoidance conflicts in regard to both the mother and father. The self-system develops by means of more or less satisfactory compromises to the conflicts. Compromises based on invalid concepts that either over- or under-control a child's instincts will cause problems at subsequent developmental stages.

Sorting out conflicting thoughts about, feelings for, and expectations of the self, and of other people, is central to the formation of self-regulatory structures and processes. *Signal anxiety* is stimulated when sensations identified as part of one's *real-self* conflict with *ideal-self* standards. In other words, at some level of mind, a TOTE process has found a gap between the *real* and *ideal-self* functioning. This, in turn, generates expectations of painful punishments. The worst taboos—incest and murder—define the central fears and, of course, they represent primitive wishes too. Why prohibit something so strongly if no one ever thought about or actually did it? (Frazer, 1910).

Mind–brain must decide constantly between using old and creating new methods to minimize pain and maximize pleasure.

The processes occur both in and out of focal awareness. The strong habit of all members of social groups is to conform to *societal standards of correctness*. The self must be able to perform TOTE processes to compare self-concepts of actually intended and performed behaviours to self-concepts of ideal behaviours.

Freud focused on *Oedipus Rex* because it is about intense, universal fears and wishes that shape human psychological development. But Oedipus' father Laius, as drawn by Sophocles, was a brutal, murderous person who attempted to kill Oedipus by hanging him by his foot in the desert (*Oedipus* means swollen foot in Greek). Most children are not cursed with murderous, scheming parents. But all infants do need to separate from their parents by making concepts that represent the self, other people and everything else in the external and internal worlds. Separation always involves aggression to a degree. In thought and overt behaviour, separating or differentiating entails creating a boundary that "cuts-off" one thing from another. Resolving Oedipal conflicts prepares the person for a life of differentiating and integrating ideas.

Self-concept making is regulated by the pleasure principle and the tendency to reprocess sensory data that is inadequately conceptualized on the first pass (or first hundred passes) through the mind. A major incentive for developing concepts to integrate conflicting sexual and aggressive tendencies is to experience the most intense sexual and loving feelings. Compared to others, competent mothers and fathers are more likely to help children develop durable self-structures and conceptualization processes.

Note

1. The survival of social animals with big brains is promoted by behaviours that are related to, but peripheral to, the sexual act that produces offspring. For example, homosexual behaviour among juvenile, male dolphins promotes attachment bonds that strengthen their effectiveness as a fighting unit that defends the entire group against predators. Because the homosexual behaviour enhances group survival, the genes promoting homosexual behaviours are retained in the genome. Other individuals and the male fighters themselves will live longer and, hence, have more heterosexual interactions which increase the viability of the group (see Bagemihl, 1999).

CHAPTER EIGHT

Guilt, dread, and heroism

The relative dynamics of approach and avoidance tendencies illustrate nature's method for promoting both the security and development of animals (see Figure 3). That is, avoidance tendencies are activated more quickly, and increase more sharply with decreasing distance from areas expected to be injurious, than are tendencies to approach areas of expected pleasure. This system puts "safety first in an emergency", helping the individual quickly avoid close, looming threats. And, it promotes healthy curiosity, aroused at distances from which situations and objects are unlikely to be injurious or deadly. Self-concepts and executive functions work more or less competently at all levels of stress to prevent conscious awareness from being overwhelmed by anxiety (see Chapter Four).

The impact on consciousness of both intense pain and high fear of intense pain is considerable. Pain and fear are maximal in situations such as intentional torture performed on a person by another. In mental illness, the self more or less tortures itself for experiencing sensations, thoughts, and feelings that are associated with cultural taboos. An insightful description of terrible pain comes from a

New York Times reporter who had endured many serious medical conditions and surgeries:

> I think I can safely state that pain falls into two broad categories: the kind you can articulate, and pain that is beyond words ... All the worst pain does is reduce us to our most primal animal. We want it to stop. We want to survive. It short-circuits any sense of self, diminishes us to a bundle of biological reflexes.

(Jennings, 2009, p. D5)

Differentiating pain into two general types, the worst type being "beyond words", is consistent with the idea that the self is made up of semantic concepts. When our ability to process words is destroyed, consciousness is subject to pain different from that of "regular pain". By our definition and this author's description, pain that disables semantic conceptual processes needed to regulate pleasure and pain sensations, reduces the person to a pre-human state. That is, at a certain point, pain creates a state of mind that is unprotected by security-promoting, sensation-containing, conceptual defences.

All of us had negative (and positive) sensations of different intensities before we could use semantic concepts. The nature of memory for experiences in the preverbal state is open to question (see Kihlstrom et al., 1992). Freud (1905) proposed two explanations for the almost universal *infantile amnesia* for events occurring before about three years. One explanation is that the amnesia is due to a motive to *repress* or block painful memories from awareness. The other ascribes it to a *selective reconstruction* of mind. That is, to a disjunction between the earliest and later modes of processing information (Pillemer & White, 1989). Of course, motivational scholars champion a pleasure principle or pain avoidance explanation; and cognitive theorists prefer information-processing explanations such as selective *reconstruction* of the brain.

In any case, for our argument the important thing is that all people likely have some episodic memories of *pain that could not be modified by thinking*. If the pain was severe, becoming conscious of pain memories might be terrifying. Anticipating such a state makes time seem too short. Being in such a state makes time seem much too long.

Anxiety and other symptoms are poorly regulated in mental illness. Most generally, dysregulation of subjective experience, including the management of memory, is due to: (1) Structural problems involving invalid self-concepts (e.g., "I am no good at all"); and, in cases of very poor education or low IQ, a lack of valid, non-self concepts (e.g., "can't tell a hawk from a handsaw"); and (2) Information Processing Habits, for example, endlessly activating memories of past negative events, or generating negative expectations about the future.

Mr. K, an otherwise reasonable fellow, cannot stop worrying about being ill after he has been provided with numerous, competent medical opinions to the contrary. I tell Mr. K, "But reality is your friend in this situation". Why is it so difficult for the person to grasp reality? In particular, "Why do people cling to false expectations of pain when adopting more accurate expectations would make them less anxious?" Psychoanalysis describes this as *resistance*. Cognitive Therapy is very good for people whose problem is mostly the implicit use of negative self-concepts. It is not so good at dealing with resistance to changing habits of negative thinking that, on the face of it, everyone should desire.

Resistances are powerful, in large part, because of a fear that refraining from using some current habitual defensive operation will cause a terrible calamity. Such expectations are generated by the use of invalid self-concepts that have been reinforced because they worked to reduce anxiety in childhood. The invalid self-concepts generate inaccurate expectations of catastrophe. These feelings heighten arousal and anxiety (see Figure 6).

Instead of altering the underlying invalid concepts, the patient repeats the defensive operation, for example, obsessing about being seriously ill. Constant obsession about non-existent threats often leads, naturally, to a feeling of unreality.[1] In panic disorder the patient says "I am having a heart attack" or "I am losing my mind". As noted before, panic disorders are corrected very effectively by Cognitive Therapy. Of course, these patients have unconscious conflicts and anxiety that are not corrected in Cognitive Therapy. But the immediate effect of reality on these patients is marked and results in improvements in their state of mind.

Mr. K's anxiety varies from moderate to panic levels a few times a week. He obsesses about his health and worries that things will get worse. There is always an implicit fear of catastrophe underlying resistances to altering invalid self-concepts. Since arousal strengthens already strong habits, it is especially hard to switch to other, healthier habits when anxiety is high.

Kohut's term *disintegration anxiety* rightly describes this implicit fear of what will happen if one stops their usual defensive operations. That is, the collapse of executive functions and the inability to manage the mind. Freud imagined the catastrophe to be castration. From our perspective, understanding *what* the person fears is less important than understanding *how* the person fears. We assume that when invalid, foundational self-concepts are working to contain primitive sexual and aggressive sensations, signal anxiety may be high. The important thing is that whatever is feared is imagined to signal horrible pain and impending doom.

The naïve scientist infers that large causes should have large effects (cf. Kelly, 1967). That is, most people assume that the sizes of causes and effects are proportional. A little anxiety means a little danger; a lot of anxiety means a lot of danger. If the person senses *signal anxiety* of a large magnitude, they infer that something "big and bad" is coming. Additionally, people tend to believe in *A Just World* where sinners get what they deserve (Lerner, Miller & Holmes, 1976).

Standards of correctness deter anti-social behaviour because people apply something like *just world* thinking to themselves. That is, "If I violate this rule I deserve to be punished". This is the Law of *Talion*. *Talion Dread* is the fear of the application of the *Law of Talion* (e.g., "an eye for an eye") to the self. When one has a taboo impulse, signal anxiety is large because the imagined punishment is death or some horrible pain. Freud assumed that incestuous and murderous wishes are at the bottom of very high signal anxiety. The anxiety alerts the person to expect a severe punishment by castration, death, mental disintegration, and so forth. The underlying mental processing is largely out of awareness. What is in awareness are derivatives of the process including global anxiety, obsessional thinking, psychosomatic symptoms, and so on. I assumed that Mr. K's resistance to accepting a "happy reality" and his clinging to hypochondrical obsessions was due to something like Talion Dread, that was inadequately suppressed by defensive compromises made early in the formation of the self.

Although psychoanalytic methods and theory can lead to very accurate diagnostic formulations of a patient's mental processes, diagnosis is not a treatment. Diagnoses should guide treatment decisions. Psychoanalytic interpretations are essentially communications to the patient in real time of "diagnoses" or characterizations of how the mind is working. If provided with an accurate reflection of their mental habits, the patient may be able to change them. There is also a feeling response to being accurately understood that is itself pleasurable and works to reinforce the whole process of analysis. But despite any dual action of accurate interpretations, it is partly wishful thinking to assume that interpretations can cause real change in all, or even most, patients.

When change does occur in psychoanalysis it is often due to some aspect of the treatment situation besides interpretations. Compared to the traditional "couch method" of psychoanalysis, therapists from more modern psychoanalytic schools may express more empathy (Kohut, 1977), or interact more authentically with patients by being more open and relaxed (Sullivan, 1954). When patients are asked to identify the moments in treatment that changed them the most, they almost always point to an instance of close interaction with the therapist that is unlike the more usual, neutral patient–therapist interaction (Aruffo, 1995).

Mr. K responded partially to both drug therapy and talk therapy that included cognitive and psychodynamic features. But the changes he experienced in anxiety levels resulted largely from the *reassurance* aspect of our relationship (see Strachey, 1934). He was able to use his in place, generally competent, system of social functioning to allow others to regulate his subjective experience. This was not a transformation of the self. Rather, his experience in psychotherapy represented getting the most out of the self-system he came in with. He was getting as much of a feeling of security from another person as any adult can rightly expect. After seven months of drug therapy and four months of once-a-week talking, he was better but not entirely well. He had been reassured but not especially enlightened about how to better regulate his mind and body.

Mr. K "acts out"

When once-a-week meetings began, Mr. K reported his habit of "acting happy" in order to regulate his mood. That is, he denied feeling anxious and sad. And, it became clear that he used a self-regulatory concept that permitted him to act on aggressive tendencies only if his behaviour was in the service of, or consistent with, rules or morality and law (see Chapter Six). In this, he is similar to most other people. After two months of once weekly meetings, Mr. K said that he wanted to revert to once-a-month meetings. He remained on the serotonin reuptake inhibitor Escitalopram at 10 milligrams per day.

On the second, once-monthly meeting, he comes in complaining that he had hurt his shoulder playing squash. He reports obsessing about the shoulder. He worries that people won't want to socialize with him now that he can't play. His doctor advises him to avoid playing squash until his shoulder injury had healed and to get physical therapy. The next month the shoulder still bothers him and he continues in physical therapy.

A month later he reports that he has been waking with panicky feelings. This is an old symptom that has been associated with a worsening of his condition. Everyone's symptoms have a periodic aspect; they get better, worse, better, and so on. This is consistent with the notion that mind–brain function involves more or less rhythmic oscillations of its various component processes (see Chapter Four). Diurnal variation in mood, especially worse in the morning and improving in the evening, is a cardinal symptom of so-called *vegetative depressions*. Some writers have characterized mood disorders as essentially *circadian rhythm* disturbances (see Murray, 2007). Mr. K's rhythms were off. His level of stress had increased due proximally to his shoulder injury and worry about the injury. Stress was also increased by the restrictions placed on him by his doctor's advice to avoid activities he enjoyed a great deal.

At this same meeting, Mr. K mentions that he has been forgetting to take his SSRI anti-depressant. He then reports the following story:

> Last week I was at the squash courts and there was a guy there who everybody hates. He seems to gloat over beating people. He hits people in the body with hard shots when he has a chance. And he is one of the best players at the club. Turns out he needed someone to play the other day. I got excited about the chance to play and beat him. I gave it as much effort as I could and I won! But the next day I had terrible pain in my shoulder. It is still hurting worse than ever and I have been worrying about it all the time. My doctor told me not to play at all, let alone a match like this.

So! We have Mr. K experiencing morning depression; forgetting to take his anti-depressant; ignoring his doctor's advice to avoid playing squash; creating injury, pain, and anxiety; and engaging in obsessive regret and self-recrimination.

It seems clear that the nasty, sadistic fellow at the squash club activated Mr. K's partly unconscious concepts of his older sadistic brother. And, the man likely stimulated some concepts of his father whom Mr. K had described as a "bad sport", albeit a "gentleman" (see Chapter Six). People on whom we project old concepts, formed initially to contain sensations emanating from people in our past, always resemble to some degree the original people. We say "projections must have a hook". This is why it is difficult to disentangle one's projections about a person from who the person really is. But that a *brother transference* was involved here is really beyond doubt. The chance to vanquish this stand-in for his own sadistic brother was too good for Mr. K to pass up. He felt he was Gary Cooper in *High Noon*, representing an entire town (or squash club) and defeating the villain. Despite warnings from both the doctor and his own body to not exercise the shoulder, Mr. K fought the bully. He won the match but he reinjured himself.

Playing this match was in the service of his aspirations to be a hero who uses "aggression in the service of the law or morality" to save the town's people from a villain. His ability to act on such impulses had served him well to a large degree in life. As a younger man he broke up fights to keep order in a school. He was then and in this case too, fulfilling a deep, self-story of survival and heroism. His history with his brother shaped and gave meaning to his life. And, his mental competence was "good enough" to regulate his overt behaviour so that he had achieved some important things for himself and the children at the schools where he worked. But of course, his actions resulted in injury to himself and constant complaining and obsessional worry, for example, "I'll never be able to play again". His injury and his reaction to it were entirely predictable.

Deep explanations involve distal causes

How might Mr. K strive to achieve his heroic ideals without injuring himself? Or, at least, not complain so much afterwards about his pain? In order to start answering such questions we need to understand the multiple causes of his behaviour. Some causes may be considered deeper than others. Perhaps the best way to think about the *depth of explanations* is in terms of the position of variables in the causal chain of events leading to behaviour. We can consider the *proximal* causes of playing the game, and also more *distal* or *deep* causes. *Proximal causes* are most important in social psychological theories, and *distal causes* have been the concern of psychoanalysis.

The phenomenon of *misattribution of arousal* can help us to understand the proximal causes of Mr. K's behaviour at the squash club. *Misattribution of arousal* describes a mistaken assumption that one's feeling of arousal is due to x, when it is actually due to y. The Schachter and Singer (1962) study discussed in Chapter Three, was the early prototype for research into this phenomenon. Another classic study (Dutton & Aron, 1974), involved men meeting a woman after the men had been standing on a high, fear-arousing suspension bridge. Compared to conditions in which fear had not been aroused, men who had been afraid before meeting the woman were more attracted to the woman; had more sexual thoughts about her; and made more attempts to affiliate with her. In other words, sensations of physiological arousal, stimulated by events occurring a few moments prior to meeting the woman, were interpreted implicitly by the men as caused by the woman's attractiveness. There is now no doubt that arousal caused by one event can be *transferred* and *misattributed* to a subsequent cause (e.g., Zillmann, 1983).

> Residual excitation from essentially any excited emotional reaction is capable of intensifying any other excited emotional reaction. The degree of intensification depends, of course, on the magnitude of residues prevailing at the time.
>
> (Zillmann, 2006, p. 223)

The idea of "residues prevailing at the time" starts to get at the more *distal causes* of Mr. K's behaviour. Mr. K's subjective experience was that his hateful feelings, thoughts, and behaviour were caused by the bully at the club. But the current bully's behaviour activated more or less automatically and unconsciously a whole set of memories and feelings about his brother. These feelings about the *old object* were projected onto this *new object*. In psychoanalytic terms, Mr. K's brother *transference* was activated. In our terms, concepts used to contain sensations of a person who resembled his brother were activated. Remember, Mr. K's self-concepts were organized around the narrative of *the heroic sheriff who saves a town from a criminal*. The tendency to act to achieve his *self-ideal* was increased because he *misattributed* all his feelings of arousal to the new bully.

While we had analysed his *brother transference* in treatment, he could not activate the transference concept in this situation. It was unconscious and affected his thinking at the level of a reflex, not at the level of conscious reflection (see Bar-Anan, Wilson & Hassin, 2010). This led him to overestimate the awfulness of the current bully. In attribution theory terms, he was unable to *discount* the causal effect of his old feelings for his brother as a contributor of his current state of mind (Kelly, 1967). Cognitive mistakes like *misattribution of arousal* operate to produce distorted concepts of reality and, hence, work to deregulate thoughts, feelings, and behaviour.

Mr. K experienced both the pleasurable anticipatory excitement about defeating the man and, subsequently, Talion Dread of punishment for being successful at the task. Mr. K's negative feelings about his brother are not unconscious. He just could not connect those feelings to his current reaction to a new bully. This caused an "over-reaction" in which he forgot about his shoulder injury.

As a small child, Mr. K couldn't fight his much bigger, older brother. The frustration he experienced at the hands of his brother instinctively stimulated aggression which, in turn, he had to suppress. The suppression of aggression caused anxiety. As he grew, he learned he could not depend entirely on his father or his histrionic mother. He developed *good enough self-concepts* to work and love. But the concepts depended on a type of juvenile fantasy, albeit a type of fantasy shared by many or most adults in our culture. Since becoming an adult, his wishes to fight have been *displaced* in a socially acceptable way onto unruly students, club bullies, and others. He is especially fond of sports in which aggression and skill are regulated in time and space by the physical boundary lines of the sports field and by the "rules of the game".

Mr. K's dominant mental habit when in an aroused, anxious state was a form of *counter-phobia*. That is, his habit was to "test his worst fears". This habit was a *proximal cause* of his obsessions and compulsions. For example, Mr. K reported to me two years after this injury that he had hurt himself again playing squash. This time it was his leg. His doctor again warned him about playing squash too much or too hard. Mr. K, of course, had to get back on the court.

After playing two games and experiencing an increase in leg pain, he decided to play a third game to "make sure he was okay'" (?!). The energy available to enact a counter-phobic response to anxiety was greatly increased when combined with the stimulation of his "brother transference". In the *High Noon* situation, he could both "test to see if his shoulder was fine" and act overtly on his most cherished wish "to vanquish a bully singlehandedly". Moreover, he had an audience of appreciative townsfolk around to reflect his glory.

The mind and Mr. K's Freudian slip

Remember Mr. K's dream of a savage forcing his way into a boxing ring in which Mr. K was enjoying the sport of fighting (see Chapter Six). He woke from that dream terrified. The dream represents both his ability to enjoy using aggression "under the law", and his fear that socially regulated activity will get out of hand. He is more or less constantly processing out of awareness approach–avoidance conflicts involving aggression. Consciously, he worries obsessively about his physical health. This is in large part a derivative of the unconscious worry that his mind will disintegrate if his impulses to fight activate his concept of Talion Law. That is, he must administer to himself a punishment that fits his crime.

A fear of applying Talion Law to one's self can be trumped by a belief that one is on the moral high ground (Milton, 2000). Even murder is allowed when "morally justified", for example, in war, legal execution, and police action during riots. Feeling moral in such situations is, of course, a direct compensation for the unconscious sense that one is behaving in a most immoral manner.

Mr. K saw the film *High Noon* in 1952 when he was eleven years old. At some level he recognized not only its special meaning for him, but its universal significance. The film's director, Fred Zinnemann, said, "It is about a man in desperate need of help that no one helps. This happens every day and it makes *High Noon* a timeless movie". Mr. K as a child was in desperate need of help from his mother, father, and brothers. But their reactions to him were like those of the townspeople to the sheriff in the film. No one came to help the sheriff, except in the end, his wife. Mr. K's wife too has become a real help to him in life.

The main character Will Kane, played by Gary Cooper, gets married at 10:30 on the morning of the day depicted in the film. He has decided to quit his job upon his marriage and live a more carefree life with his new wife (played by the then unknown Grace Kelly). He had restored law and civility to the small Western frontier town after five years on the job. In the process, he made friends with the more law-abiding citizens in the town. And, he made enemies including bar and hotel owners whose businesses were somewhat reduced by the more orderly society enforced by the sheriff. His most dangerous enemy is Frank Miller, a murderer who he had sent to jail. Miller was let out of prison and was returning this day on the noon train in order to kill Cooper with the aid of three henchmen.

The murderer had also been Cooper's rival for the affections of a Mexican woman in the town. The situation is essentially an Oedipal drama. He wants to fight his murderous sexual rival, and also experience security and pleasure with a new wife. His character represents an ideal, heroic resolution of pre-Oedipal and Oedipal conflicts. He had been involved with the Mexican woman before marrying. She was a strong woman of high integrity, but the town's people considered her a whore. Cooper knew different. He saw her virtue. The reasons for their break-up are never made entirely clear. In any case, he winds up marrying the very Madonna-like Grace Kelly, a Quaker opposed to violence of any kind.

Cooper has just taken off his badge when news arrives from the train depot that the murderer is on his way and will arrive at high noon. The criminal plans to unite with his old gang of three desperados. They intend to murder the sheriff and return the town to its former lawless condition, that is, an "unregulated society" with completely "free markets".[2]

Cooper is encouraged by the wedding party to leave town at once with his new wife and avoid the coming threat. They head out of town at a gallop but after a few minutes he decides he must return. His wife says that she will leave him if he stays. The theme song, sung by Tex Ritter, continues throughout the film. The song directs the viewer's attention to the inner conflicting feelings, thoughts, and expectations of the hero. The song pleads with the wife "to not forsake" him.

The power of the film to shape Mr. K's self-concepts was enormous. The murderer, Frank Miller, is an excellent conceptual match for Mr. K's brother. The former sheriff of the town, a man who liked and had helped Cooper, refuses to join him in fending off the murderers. He is a very good match to Mr. K's father, a devotee of Judaism, the Religion of Laws. But like his father, the old sheriff in *High Noon* had no consistent, real faith in life. (Remember the father was described by Mr. K as both "a gentleman" and "a bad sport".) Near the film's climax, Cooper comes to the old sheriff to ask for help when the villains arrive on the noon train. The sheriff's refusal to help enacts what Mr. K must have experienced with his own father.

> **Cooper:** You've been my friend all my life. You got me this job.
> Ever since I was a kid I wanted to be like you, Mark.
> You've been a law man all your life .... Will you come
> down to that depot with me?
> **Old Sheriff:** No. You know how I feel about you but I ain't going
> with you .... No, I couldn't do nothing for you. You'll
> be worrying about me. You'll get yourself killed wor-
> rying about me ....

Mr. K, in my view, made a sort of heroic compromise formation by modelling himself after the hero in his favourite film *High Noon*. It enabled him to act with integrity at his job and enabled him to form a good relationship with his wife. But his compromises with reality led to habitually interpreting his aggressive impulses with guilt, leading to signal anxiety and, in turn, hypochondrical symp-toms. Aggressive impulses, concepts, expectations, feelings, and overt behaviour can be disinhibited by moral right. But what hap-pened to Mr. K's concepts and expectations about avoiding pain and injury? What about his doctor's advice? Why can't Mr. K apply jus-tice to himself?

Remember that Mr. K had been worrying about his shoulder condition for three months before this episode. And, he had been forgetting to take his SSRI. Taken together, worry about health and avoiding treatments produce a Freudian slip or *fehlleistung* (faulty action) based on an unconscious intention. In the past he had wor-ried "what if the drugs stop working". A "slip" such as forgetting to take a drug to reduce depression and anxiety is a way to enact his dominant, counter-phobic, defensive habit. It is a form of denial. We assume his mind–brain processes involved:

1. Unconscious sensations of *signal anxiety*; and conscious experience of anxiety contained by *derivative* concepts about ill health and depression.
2. Conscious activation of *ideal self-concepts*, for example, "I would like to feel better; be a hero".
3. Conscious and unconscious activation of defensive operations involving *self-concepts and self-expectations*. I have verified with Mr. K that the following are the kind of thoughts he experiences more or less implicitly:

   If I don't take the medicine it would mean I am not depressed. [Remember his habit to "act happy" to deny depression.] I need to test to see if I can feel well without pills. Maybe I feel this way because I am "bad" (e.g., have fratricidal, patricidal, matricidal, incestuous, or other taboo wishes). My punishment for having taboo ideas will be terrible pain, torture, execution. I better do the test right away and stop taking the anti-depressant. Then, if I'm not depressed when off the drug, maybe it means I'm not guilty of anti-social desires. I can't stand the suspense. *The worst thing that can happen to me is going to happen to me if I stop thinking about it happening.* When I take the drugs my worry is reduced. This puts me in danger!
4. Decides to not take the SSRI. This is in part a conscious decision based on some hazy awareness of the sorts of rationalizations shown above. The "logic" behind the decision is so distorted by defensive operations that it is like a decision made in a dream; it is an unconscious decision, a *Freudian slip*.

Neurochemistry and Mr. K's Freudian slip

If the reader can keep in mind our assumptions about Mr. K's *transference* and *misattribution of arousal* effects, we now need to add the relevant neurobiological features to this story of *acting out*. As in PTSD, where fear signals reach the amygdyla before they register in the conceptual processing areas in the neo-cortex, the biology of Mr. K's situation is working against him. Once he stopped taking his Escitalopram, he potentiated sensations, instincts, concepts, expectations, and behaviours regulated largely by dopamine. Under such neurochemical conditions, there is practically no way that Mr. K, with self-concepts constellated around the image of Gary Cooper in *High Noon*, could resist taking on the bully at the squash club.

Increases in serotonin work to suppress dopamine production. This is what causes the so-called *Prozac Poop-Out* seen with SSRIs. Some patients like Mr. K, whose depression has lessened due to an SSRI, start to feel emotionally "flat". This is due to a decrease in dopamine levels. Dopamine is the prototypical "approach pleasure" neurotransmitter. Increases in dopamine are involved in subjective experiences of seeking what the person finds exciting and fun. Its presence in synaptic clefts mediates expectations or anticipatory thoughts of pleasure such as those experienced when imagining sex, hunting, fighting, gambling, use of recreational drugs, and just about everything a particular person may like to do. Mr. K aspires to be like Gary Cooper in his role in *High Noon*. That is, a man who uses aggression in the service of morality and law.

Dopaminergic neurons in the *substantia nigra* and serotonergic neurons in the *raphe nuclei* lie close to each other in the brain stem. Their projections run alongside each other, from the brain stem to the *basal ganglia* (see Stahl, 2008). Neurons of all types (e.g., adrenergic, cholinergic, and serotonergic) have receptors for other types of neurotransmitters. Dopamine neurons have serotonin receptors. When these so-called *hetero-receptors* are occupied by a serotonin molecule, the release of dopamine by the neuron is inhibited.[3] In other words, increasing the amount of serotonin floating around because of the action of a serotonin re-uptake inhibitor drug will result in a drop in dopamine secretion. This makes it harder for the person to enjoy the usual anticipatory pleasures of life that are underwritten by dopamine. Hence, *Prozac Poop-Out*.

At least unconsciously, people who take SSRIs associate taking the drug with a flattening of anticipatory pleasures. Sometimes, of course, the person is also consciously aware of this effect. I am sure that Mr. K was not aware consciously that Escitalopram and other drugs in its class can cause emotional *Poop-Out*. He made a unconscious decision to stop taking the drug because he a felt reduction in his usual anticipatory pleasures of using aggression in sports and other ways. The increase in his ability to enjoy aggression was not a consciously intended aim of avoiding the anti-depressant. But it likely played a large role in his behaviour with the bully at the squash club.

A dopamine-mediated increase in the ability to experience anticipatory pleasures of aggression would work to increase the magnitude of his approach–aggression tendency relative to his avoid-pain tendency. Once his brother transference was activated, he "acted-out". Because he had no functionally active concept of the transference, he likely attributed all of his arousal to the bully with no accounting for the role of his own mental habits. And, indeed, he resolved his approach–avoidance conflict by approaching. The next day after his victory the memory of his joy was absent mostly from awareness. In its place was unmitigated obsession about pain, self-castigation, and remorse. Figure 7 diagrams this series of events.

Mr. K and his symptoms come and go

One month after this drama, Mr. K reports that his symptoms have mostly gone away. He then leaves therapy for five months. During this period he is advised by his internist to reduce his Escitalopram dose to 5 milligrams a day. He then became anxious, depressed, and anorgasmic and calls me. We return his SSRI dose to 10 milligrams and his symptoms abate once more. He asks now to meet once every two weeks. I agree and he comes in bi-weekly for two months.

He reports at the first bi-weekly meeting that he had thought of something I had said to him during the first year of our meetings: "You feel somehow guilty about dying. When you feel pain and imagine you are gravely ill, you always think that you are responsible. You imagine you are murdering yourself and then feel guilty". He claimed that this thought made him feel better for weeks. Then, he failed to show up for his next appointment.

At the next meeting he claimed to have "forgotten" our appointment. His relationship with me involved apparently the usual combination of transference (i.e., he interpreted my behaviour in part with old concepts); and, he had constructed some new, more valid concepts to think about me and himself. His ambivalence about the goals of treatment was communicated in the slip about the missed appointment. We were able for the first time to focus directly on his

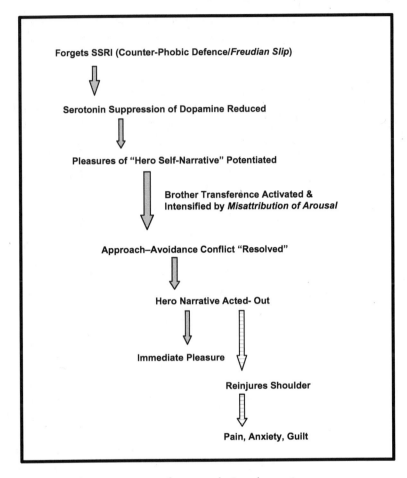

Figure 7.   Consequences of up-regulating dopamine.

transference habits of mind as applied to me, and his ambivalence about the whole project of remaking his self-concepts. In this context he reports: "I had sex with my wife after our last session [the one before the forgotten session]. I felt relaxed and then I became worried that I wasn't anxious." Shortly after this meeting he stopped coming to therapy.

Nine months later Mr. K has a scare regarding an increased Prostate Specific Antigen (PSA) level. In the meantime, his morning dysphoria, obsessions about health, and insomnia return. I discontinued the Escitalopram and switched him to Mirtazapine, with good results. He disappears again. Five months later, anticipating the results of a prostate biopsy, he becomes anxious and returns to me essentially for reassurance and security. The biopsy results are not too alarming. His urologist assumes that the increased PSA is due to an infection, starts Mr. K on an antibiotic, and the symptoms abate. He reports that he had discontinued the Mirtazapine three months ago; "I was feeling good so I went off it." Now, with his health concerns heightened and his discontinuation of Mirtazapine without my advice, his anxiety symptoms have increased.

* * *

The case of Mr. K illustrates clearly the repetitive, habitual use of invalid, incomplete self-concepts. He alternated between approach and avoidance of talk and drug therapies for two years. Criteria of success in this case would include: development of more valid self-concepts to contain sensations, concepts, expectations, feelings, and overt behaviours; and, in turn, reductions in self-injuring behaviours, anxiety, and obsessions.

The belief that one is in control of their mind is so important that if the person does not know how to feel better, they will often initiate mental operations or overt behaviours that operate to make things worse. But it is not to make things worse that these processes are initiated. Negative outcomes are "collateral damage". They occur in the course of the person demonstrating to themselves that they are in control of their thoughts and feelings. This works as a form of *self-assurance.* The negative consequences of such "control affirming behaviour" are usually unintended. This was true of Mr. K.

People do get masochistic pleasure from self-defeating behaviours, or what Reich (1933) called *moral masochism.* The self-defeating, sick person gets *secondary gains* in the form of sympathy, money, excuses from work, and so on.[4] The old psychoanalytic cliché that one "either has the *neurosis* or the *perversion*" is relevant here. Perhaps, Mr. K would be better off if he and his wife engaged in sadomasochistic sex play as a substitute for his acting out and causing real tissue injury to himself.

At this latest point in our relationship I reviewed with him his habits of denying the underlying real conditions of his body and mind: the repeated "testing" to see if he is okay by playing squash against doctor's orders, and going off his psychotropic medicines without medical advice when he feels better. I decided at this point to forego further psychopharmacological treatment beyond 0.5 mg Clonazepam per day on an "as needed" basis. I suggested to him that we begin again one-time-per-week therapy. In particular, he agrees to try Eye Movement Desensitization and Reprocessing (EMDR) treatments. The nature of EMDR and the course of Mr. K's treatment are described in the next chapter.

Notes

1. Edward Tauber (1982) believed that this sort of subjective experience of unreality results from making, unwittingly, in childhood a kind of Faustian compromise: "Some Higher Power will protect me from the worst pain, if I constantly worry about the worst pain." This sort of compromise works to constrict a feeling of aliveness seen in the *false self* syndrome (Winnicott, 1960b).

   These symptoms are somehow supported or "kept in place" in mind–brain by what I am calling *secondary defences*. These include dissonance-reducing rationalizations. In the way I am using this term, *secondary defences* also include superstitions. For example, the person holds primitive, magical beliefs in the power of touching a thing such as a rosary bead or rabbit's foot; or activating an idea such as "god loves me". A typical modern user of primitive magic is the anxious flyer who assumes more or less consciously that their worrying about a catastrophic accident works to prevent the accident. This is the "omnipotence of thought" superstition, an assumption that equates expectations or wishes with reality.

2. *High Noon* was released in the midst of the McCarthy Era when the US government made paranoid attempts to find communists and ruin their lives. Now hailed as maybe the best American Western Film ever made, *High Noon* was branded "Un-American" by John Wayne, the *Klu Klux Klan*, and other extremists.

3. The serotonin hetero-receptor on dopamine neurons cited as a cause of reduction in dopamine levels and *SSRI Poop-Out* is the inhibitory, 5HT2A receptor (Stahl, 2008).

4. In a kind of cruel consistency with economic life in our "advanced "cultures, psychopathology might be described in terms of two simple factors: 1) *Inability to make money*; and 2) A tendency for the person to "*push their luck*", that is, to have unrealistic expectations of success at overt social influence attempts. These two variables are relatively

uncorrelated. That is, any individual can be more or less competent at making money; and more or less of a "luck pusher". Competence to make money represents the person's ability to function in society to procure the essentials of life. Our "jungle" is the social world. Hunting and gathering has become "working at a job" for money. For some people their "job" is convincing other people that they are sick. It is a form of salesmanship.

Many patients have been judged by some medical diagnostic process to be incompetent to make money due to a mental or physical ailment. Others have convinced their family or friends that they are disabled and receive money that way. While many if not most people getting disability money are indeed entitled to it, being approved for government or private support rewards "appearing sick". A proportion of such patients then go on to "push their luck" in other social contexts.

By this informal, "two factor theory of mental illness", if a person can continue to get financial support from some social agent by either actually being disabled or appearing disabled, they are not mentally ill on the first criteria. They may be morally deficient, or have a "bad character" or "personality disorder", but their brains are working consciously and/or unconsciously to procure social security.

Often, at a certain point, an empirically determinable percentage of these people will start to push their luck and fail to get what they want. An example of such a case involves a patient receiving government disability payments for a mental condition. The patient owed me a significant amount of money for a portion of their treatment that was not covered by the government. The patient assured me for months that his wealthy family would pay his bill. After six months of non-payment I refused to provide further treatment. The patient then "pushed his luck" by calling and asking me to provide prescriptions for amphetamines. If this patient went on to convince some other *shmo* to write the scripts, he would, by this informal definition, not be mentally ill.

CHAPTER NINE

Eye movement therapy

E MDR was invented by Francine Shapiro (2001). It can be
effective with trauma victims or others who have repeated
unpleasant, intrusive thoughts. Mr. K qualified as a candidate
for this sort of therapy. He has repeated the same self-defeating habits
for years. He had some acute, moderate trauma (e.g., hospitalization
at five years); and, chronic moderate trauma in interaction with his
brother and mother. The interpretations we have made of his mental
processes have had descriptive validity, predictive validity, and they
make sense in light of his developmental history. Plus, we have had
the opportunity to watch his defences in action over a year and a
half. Regardless of the validity of our model of his mental processes,
knowledge of these defensive operations has not helped especially.
Mr. K's defensive, self-defeating habits of thinking and behaving
have remained largely unchanged.

Shapiro's EMDR technique involves asking the patient to think
about their past traumas and other associated ideas while they track
with their eyes the moving finger of the therapist. One holds the finger
about 18 inches from the patient's face and moves it back and forth
at various speeds and patterns for about twenty four repetitions
at a time. The patients are instructed to imagine a particular idea,

for example, the image of their car crash, and then let their thoughts go where they will. After each set of eye movements, the therapist asks the patient to report: "What did you get?" Most patients report a flowing set of associations stimulated by the target idea. Often, thoughts become stuck and repeated, and anxiety can increase. Patients are more or less able to move their eyes smoothly to follow the finger. Disruptions in tracking are diagnostic to some extent of difficulties that the patient is having with thoughts and feelings.

It is assumed that the "processing" of old memories is stimulated by experiencing them at the same time as moving the eyes. The therapist is instructed to identify "nodes" or constellations of concepts where the patient's thinking processes seem to stall. It may be around memories of trauma. The therapist can help the person "reprocess" the concepts in and around these "nodes" by various means, such as relaxation techniques. When anxiety is under some control, the therapist may suggest that the patient begin thinking, as the eye movements start, about things associated with these anxiety-provoking nodes.

The Standard Shapiro Method does not include any "interpretation" of the patient's mental processes. Merely freeing the associative processes that had been defensively blocked is assumed to promote more mental control and reduce anxiety. But as Mollon (2005) points out, EMDR has some features akin to psychoanalysis. The question asked after eye movements ("What did you get?") is essentially asking the patient to follow *the basic rule of psychoanalysis*, that is, "Report your free associations". Associations come quickly and patients often report recalling events they had previously "lost". Mollon (2005, p. 67) writes: "The mind–brain shows a natural tendency to process trauma and move towards an emotionally positive resolution when assisted by bilateral stimulation. An important part of this processing is a shift in self-related thoughts and beliefs".

If EMDR works, it must be causing a change in self-concepts and/or the manner in which they are activated. For example, positive change might involve relabeling attributes such as "victim" or "essentially defective" as *not self*; and the addition of some more valid attributes to the self-concept, such as "competent enough". Besides its therapeutic effects, EMDR is a boon to understanding a patient's defensive operations. I think of it as "psychoanalysis on the fly". Its diagnostic utility is illustrated in the cases of Mr. K and Mr. C (Chapter Ten).

Some patients learn to relax more deeply than they had ever before. Some become very anxious as a result of the technique and it has to be stopped. But there is no doubt that moving the eyes while thinking definitely makes something happen to mind–brain. Stimulating left and right ears with sounds alternately, or left and right sides of the body with touch, has similar effects. The evidence for the eye-movement effect comes from a great deal of research and clinical experience. EMDR has been used with some effectiveness in PTSD (e.g., Chemtob, Tolin, van der Kolk & Pitman, 2000); Phobias and Panic (e.g., De Jongh & Ten Broeke, 1998); dissociative disorders (Fine & Berkowitz, 2001); and other syndromes.

Activity in various brain structures has been shown to change in response to EMDR. Levin, Lazrove, and Van der Kolk (1999) report increased metabolism in the anterior cingulate gyrus and left frontal lobe after three, ninety-minute EMDR sessions with PTSD patients. Lansing et al., (2005) found drops in metabolic activity in cingulate gyrus, basal ganglia, and prefrontal cortex after EMDR in traumatized police officers. Both studies report positive changes in the subjective condition of patients. Van der Kolk (2002) says that after EMDR patients "tell more coherent narratives" about their traumas, making the memories "more coherent and manageable".

Shapiro imagines that EMDR results in the processing of old memories. What is this process? What goes on in the brain and mind of the patient helped or not helped by this method? Various mechanisms of action of EMDR have been proposed. The two most interesting hypotheses about EMDR's mechanisms of action are: (1) That eye movements stimulate REM sleep sorts of brain processes (e.g., Bergmann, 2000; Stickgold, 2002); and (2) That EMDR changes working-memory processes (e.g., Lilley, Andrade, Turpin, Sabin-Farrell & Holmes, 2009). For example, the vividness of thought and the intensity of feelings about traumatic memories are reduced by performing eye movements concurrently with attempts to recall the traumatic images.

That the therapeutic mechanism of EMDR has to involve memory mechanisms is not controversial. The person formerly plagued by memories is no longer. How is mind–brain rearranged to effect such changes? What happened when using the technique with Mr. K?

Mr. K's EMDR sessions: tolerating pleasure

Shapiro recommends introducing the technique to patients by explaining the basic logic: By thinking of troubling thoughts while moving your eyes, the areas of your mind that have been blocked from resolving what is bothering you will be freed-up. The technique can cause some increases in anxiety in the short term. So, we will start by having you imagine a pleasant idea. This can be a daydream that reliably works to calm you down. If you should become too anxious while we are using this method, tell me and we can shift attention to this comforting thought.

I asked Mr. K if he had such a calming image. He said it was, "Being at the beach". I asked him to think of being at the beach and, at the same time, to track with his eyes the back and forth movement of my finger placed about 18 inches from his face. After about twenty moderately fast back-and-forth movements (one cycle per second) I asked him, "What did you get? What thoughts and feelings did you experience?"

He said, "It was hard to keep the image of the beach in mind and track the finger at the same time. I started to feel calm and then felt tense". I then asked him to imagine the beach scene again. This time, I slowed the movement of my finger about fifty percent. His eye movements were markedly smoother this time with fewer breaks in tracking. "What did you get this time?" I asked. He reported that, "At first it was difficult but then I was able to focus on a memory of me and my wife walking on the beach and laughing. We walked to a place where we found sea shells. This is difficult but interesting". The session ended at that point.

We began the second session the next week with an attempt to imagine the pleasant beach scene. He reported that he couldn't maintain the pleasant image because he had to "multi-task" (i.e., think and move the eyes at the same time).[1] I instructed him to close his eyes and just imagine the pleasant thought without any distraction. He did this and reported a very pleasant memory of him and his wife having fun at the beach. Now I instructed him to cue this same memory but this time with eyes open and tracking slow finger movements.

He reported that he could picture the beach but that he was more able to focus on "hearing the waves" and that this sound enabled him to maintain a pleasurable feeling. In effect, Mr. K had regulated the amount and kind of sense data in focal awareness by constricting the channel of visual memory and dilating the channel of auditory memory. He had closed his mind's eye and opened his mind's ear. This self-regulation enabled him to maintain a pleasurable feeling.

I reported this hypothesis to him. He responded that he had worried after saying he had focused on the auditory rather than the visual aspects of the scene. He feared that he had "made a mistake" and "done wrong" by using this method of control. Drops in anxiety tend to cause an increase in anxiety in him. This is the vicious cycle at the centre of his malady. The range of intensity of sensation and, in turn, feeling that he can tolerate comfortably is small.

The exception to this general condition is when the *High Noon System* is operating. That is, when he feels threatened and alone and no one will come to his aid. Then, he has "no choice" but to fight and win. The *High Noon System* is arguably his greatest achievement. The alternatives to *High Noon* functioning are invalid, distorted interpretations of painful sensations in the body. The catastrophizing set of concepts he uses to contain pain are in part motivated by a wish to activate his heroic personality. If he were only in enough danger, he could triumph. Then, the mind–brain emergency mechanisms described in Chapter Four might become activated. But most of the time Mr. K is rational enough to know, or to at least behave "as if", the painful sensations coming from his foot, ankle, shoulder, stomach, and so on are not real emergencies.

The next week he reports that he has seen his orthopaedist about his ankle. The doctor told Mr. K directly that the major source of his trouble was in his mind. Mr. K told me that he started to cry upon hearing this from his surgeon. "I was so grateful that he understood. I get that feeling with you".

Mr. K has never trusted his own self-care function. A doctor must tell him his condition. In this case, an expert on ankles was able to make Mr. K feel understood. The orthopaedist recommended that he get psychological treatment. Mr. K had not told the bone doctor that he had been getting treatment from me for two years at this point. I asked why. This led to a string of associations:

> In my family one could not admit to a psychological problem even though my mother had been in psychiatric hospitals at various times over the years. I went to see her psychiatrist at the hospital once and he understood the way my mother

manipulated people. I remember after my mother's second suicide attempt my father said, "Oh my god, she did it ... it's all my fault". I was so angry with mum for doing this. She always made everyone feel responsible and "wrong" about everything. I knew how it fed into my Dad's worrying. I felt like the James Dean character in *Rebel Without a Cause*. I wanted to shove my father and say, "This is not your fault!" ... My wife showed me a picture the other day of me at the beach at three years of age. I remember being on the beach and how much I liked it. It was a sunny, warm feeling. I welled up with tears.

I asked him to think of this picture of himself at the beach and began to lead him in eye movements. He tracked smoothly my finger moving at a rate of one complete left to right shift in under one second. He reported that he had recalled a memory from his eighth year:

I heard my mother say, "Let's go to the concert at the bandstand next to the beach. You love the concerts". I felt real good. I was with her walking to the concert and eating ice cream while my older brother was goofing off. It was a nice feeling. I could visualize some, but the good feeling was stimulated by sound. Hearing her say, "Let's go to the concert", and then I could see the band and focus on the sound of the French Horn.

It had taken two months of once-a-week treatments including EMDR about every other session for Mr. K to achieve a durable, pleasant feeling while moving his eyes relatively quickly. He had learned regulatory methods involving the titration of sensation from visual and auditory channels that kept him in a pleasurable state. It became apparent to me that his mother, while undoubtedly a histrionic character, was competent enough to relate to a young, pre-pubescent child. There was love in this family but only under the sort of low-stress conditions characterizing interactions between adults and young children, or humans and domestic animals. This assumption is consistent with the report of Mr. K that his older, bullying brother had a great affection for animals.

The concepts used by members of Mr. K's family to interpret sensations derived from interacting with young children, cats, and dogs contained positive attributes. Pleasure was expected when one interacted with children and animals. The brother and the mother were competent in relation to naïve living things. Mr. K's memories of childhood and his subsequent development were built on a foundation that included durable, valid, positive, and relatively non-conflicting concepts and feelings for simple creatures. But his self-concepts were not fully competent to regulate the more complex forms of subjective experience and overt behaviour involved in adult aggression and sexuality.

Mr. K's EMDR sessions: anxiety

Since the patient had developed some competence at regulating his mind during the eye movements, I suggested that he frankly consider anxiety-causing ideas while tracking my finger with his eyes. He reports today that he has told his orthopaedist that he has been in psychotherapy, but that he did not tell him my name. "I didn't know if I should do that. But I felt better telling him I was in psychotherapy. I had sex with my wife later in the day and had a normal, nice feeling but then started to feel panicky". This, of course, reaffirms the hypothesis that pleasure and a lowering of anxiety automatically cause an increase in his anxiety levels. He says he is noticing more about himself and obsessing less. He then reports this dream:

> I am in a classroom in a consulting role to do something. The administrator says, "No, that's not it, we need you to do something else". It was something less important than I had imagined. My brother the bully was there and said, "See, you are doing an unimportant thing. You are a liar and a phony".

I instructed him to think about this dream and track my finger with his eyes. Then I asked him to report what occurred to him during the tracking.

> I had a memory of after my father died. My older brother had come to my house and made insulting comments about my dog. I had both auditory and visual images of the scene.

I asked him to rate his current level of anxiety on a scale running from zero (indicating no anxiety at all) to ten (the highest anxiety). He rated his anxiety an eight. Then, I asked him to pick up the memory where it left off and track my finger. Afterwards, he reported:

> This was different. I remembered reading a letter my brother had sent to me stating that I was incapable of handling the family finances after my father's death. I wasn't really depressed. I was angry reading the letter. I said to my wife, "Look at this shit! I'm going to read this to my mother to show her what chaos she's caused by pitting everyone against each other".

He then rated his anxiety a six, but his anger with his brother a nine, and for his mother, a seven. He said, "I was looking forward to showing her this letter". He then added, gratuitously, "It's easier for me to imagine negative things than positive things". The session ended at this point.

Over the next two weeks we used eye movements while he thought about various somatic symptoms and situations that stimulated feelings of anxiety, loneliness, and anger. Many times he reported being conflicted about whether or not to take his Clonazepam when he started to feel anxiety. Interestingly, he has never been able to pronounce correctly the word "Clonazepam" or the word for any other drug I have given him. I assume that this is a defensive operation not unlike the superstition Jews have about saying the word "god". It is as if the drug or god will stop working on his behalf if he clearly annunciates the word for the powerful agent. It is similar to his reluctance to tell his orthopaedist my name. These symptoms are manifestations of the more general difficulties he has using valid semantic concepts to describe reality and, thereby, regulate his mind. A valid concept, that is, the truth, is powerful and it will be somehow damaged or rendered ineffective if it is unambiguously recognized or used.

His back was bothering him and he went to a back specialist where his blood pressure was measured at 130/90. This worried him. Today his pressure is 110/66 with a pulse of 66. He reports this dream from two nights ago:

> I was swimming in a pool with a friend, who is a surgeon, and the actor Pierce Brosnan. We had to do sprints. I was getting tired and looked at my friend and we laughed. I woke up

and it wasn't the usual feeling on waking. It was not an unhappy feeling. It was a good feeling I hadn't had for a long time.

I reflect back to him that he is waking up feeling better and ask what happened the next day. "I woke the next two days not feeling good. I had an empty feeling". I ask him to think about the empty feeling and start eye movements. He reports remembering that his wife said, "What's wrong now?"

> I told her, "I don't feel like getting out of bed. I have stomach pain and anxiety". She said, "Why don't you take a Clonazepam?" I wanted to get up but was reluctant to take the pill. I have that empty feeling right now. I got up and washed my face and told myself "you are going to be alright". I saw something on TV that I liked. The emotion I got was that "tearing-up feeling". I shed tears during wonderful times.

I ask, "What is the relationship between feeling anxiety and tearing-up?"

> First, the tearing-up feels like a relief … but then it's not. For example, I will know something about a film and can answer some trivia question asked about an actor and then I get a teary, nostalgic feeling. Others ask, "How do you know this?" Then I feel ashamed, embarrassed, and nostalgic about knowing this stuff. The same thing happens with my knowledge of sports, religion, and things in general.

I repeated the question, "What is a possible connection between this and your anxiety?" He says, "Someone is acknowledging me and I'm so happy, I'm crying. Similarly, I saw an artist on TV that my wife likes and I got teary because I know she likes him …"

These remarks indicate that positive feelings about himself and empathic feelings about others both stimulate his dominant habit to activate negative self-concepts and, in turn, anxiety, guilt, and sadness. This is the mental analogue of having difficulty in simultaneously patting the head and rubbing the stomach; or moving the eyes and thinking. He can make both movements independently under low arousal, but the processes become under-differentiated when he experiences relatively strong sensations of either pleasure (e.g., pride) or pain (e.g., a twinge in his ankle). His self-concepts are not fully differentiated from concepts of people in parental, caring relations with him. *Self-concepts* and *caregiver concepts* are activated automatically and simultaneously when arousal is high. At such moments he feels "he can't live without these other people". The DSM-IV would call his a *dependent personality*. Object Relations Theorists might say that Mr. K's self-concepts are not differentiated well from the parental objects.

While sitting with Mr. K at this moment, I think of my cats, of helpless infants, of retarded people, of creatures who have limited conceptual competence to care for themselves. It is a sad, nostalgic feeling. At once, Mr. K says, *"This is the first time that I am feeling in your office the sorts of feelings I tell you about that occur outside your office"*.[!] It seems quite plausible that my subjective experience was transmitted to Mr. K, and his experience transmitted to me, in part via non-verbal channels. I was having tender feelings for Mr. K and cats, who have limited competence to know reality by means of words. He sensed this somehow and was, therefore, able to experience dependent, longing feelings in the office with me present. Unlike the cats whose brains are less sophisticated, we assume that Mr. K's limitation is a functional one and can be altered.

The transference

The late Anne Alonso of Massachusetts General Hospital thought that the hours in the analyst's office should be "the worst part of the patient's week". The rest of the patient's life should get better as analysis gets more difficult. Mr. K, who always used meetings with doctors for reassurance and comfort, was now speaking openly about his positive feelings for me which involved, in part, a *transference* to me. He told me immediately at the start of our next meeting that, "I don't feel good outside of here". He reports that his wife has started to complain that he spends all his time at doctors' offices. Relations with her have become strained. They have stopped talking altogether, something very unusual in their long relationship.

Perhaps I was making some mistake in Mr. K's treatment. By Alonso's theory shouldn't he be feeling worse in therapy than outside of it? I would argue that "feeling good depending on some-one" was indeed the worst part of his week, worse than having trouble with his wife. But he didn't quite know it yet. The situation reminds me of Dr. Otto Speilvogel, the psychoanalyst in Philip Roth's *Portnoy's Complaint* (1969). After Portnoy complains uninterruptedly from the couch for over two hundred pages, Dr. Speilvogel makes his only remark in the entire book: "So. Now vee may perhaps to begin. Yes?"

Mr. K's positive attitudes about me would become more negative when I, inevitably, disappointed his wishes for perfect empathic understanding (e.g., Wolf, 1995). But as often happens in treatment, his negative attitudes were largely unconscious and/or unexpressed. A barrier or *resistance* to improvement was his strong habit to suppress aggression towards his caretakers for fear of reducing their motivation to care for him. Somewhat more suppressed were the unconscious wishes and fears that he might harm his minders.

The mental sequence for Mr. K and other patients is: empathic failure by the caregiver → frustration and aggression in the dependent person → guilt and anxiety. Mr. K's invalid self-concepts worked to habitually interpret his aggressive sensations and instincts about caregivers as indicating physical disease and impending doom. He was anxious much of the time. The compromise formation of "aggression interpreted as illness" is perfect in a way. It brought him constantly into attachments to caregivers, that is, doctors. And, he never gets well. Getting well would put him in danger of being alone and without help. He can't win and he can't lose. He can only repeat this way of coping until he gets a new valid idea that integrates his conflict between aggressive and attachment needs.

His work with me to date, and the diagnosis he received from an orthopaedist of uncommon psychological sophistication, has resulted in him being conscious of my descriptions of his self-concepts and the processes by which they became activated. As we know, mere knowledge of valid concepts is not enough to effect real change in people. Somehow, new, more valid ideas need to become "realized" or "operational" in brain–mind. New mental habits must supplant the dominant, defensive ways of interpreting sensations and *signal anxiety*. EMDR seems to help rewire the conceptual system. It causes associations to flow. It seems to potentiate the brain's natural tendency to come up with a new concept to resolve endlessly repeated conflict.

After saying, "I don't feel good outside your office", he reports a dream: "I'm in an academic situation and I don't know what I'm doing there, what my role is … I'm just walking around". Then we had an exchange that might have come from Absurdist Theatre or a Marx Brothers movie:

WMB: I think the dream refers to this treatment.

MK: No. As much as I'd like others to help me, I have to live my life.

WMB: What does that mean as a response to what I said?

MK: Usually, when I leave here I feel okay.

WMB: Your relationship to me is like your relationship to your tranquilizer.

MK: I can't remember feeling good.

WB: Really?

MK: I was at a party. I felt anxious at first and then I felt good.

WMB: When was that?

MK: Three days ago. But now I have ankle pain and tension with my wife. I always want to take a Clonazepam, every-day. I told my wife she had to save money for a trip she wants to take. She told me I was spending all the money on doctors. She doesn't understand. It frustrates me.

WMB: Your dream suggests that you don't know what role you should play with your wife, me, and other helpers. The "academic situation" in the dream is like the therapy situation in which conflicting intentions and expectations confuse you. When we have found medicines that make you feel better, you have stopped taking them. When your orthopaedist advised you to not play squash, you played. I think you have two conflicting intentions in coming to see me: to feel better and to not feel better. And, you have trouble being aware of both intentions at once.

MK: I have a dependent personality.

This interchange had some diagnostic utility but little therapeutic utility. He was in the grips of the repetitive habits. His mentation was dreamy and almost devoid of logic. So, I asked him to think about whatever came to mind while tracking my finger with his eyes. He reported after the eye movements: "I thought of breaking the ice with my wife by asking her how her day went". I told him to imagine asking her that question as he tracked with his eyes. He reports that he imagined, "She asked me if we are we going to go running tomorrow. Then I wondered if my ankle would hurt tomorrow? And then that I could deal with it".

I congratulated him on using sensible thinking and anticipating that he could likely cope with whatever pain might come up. EMDR moved what seemed to be a non-productive psychoanalytic discussion about *transference* and a dream, albeit an important dream, into a somewhat more useful process in which he practiced coping with pain.

The next meeting

The next week he reports more frequent panicky feelings. This is not uncommon when EMDR methods are used. Presumably, the activation of formerly "frozen" episodic and semantic concepts in memory is partly responsible for patients' increases in anxiety. But Mr. K had a different explanation. "Maybe I'm not taking the Clonazepam right". He is forever tinkering with this medication. It is a way of externalizing the source of his anxiety. Moreover, his new internist warned him that, "Clonazepam can be dangerous. If you take it every day it may cause memory problems".

It is worth noting emphatically at this point that many well meaning clinicians do and say things that negatively affect patients with somatoform disorders. This is especially true in cases like Mr. K's. Most somatoform patients who present as cordial and friendly are projecting intense, unconscious aggression onto caregivers. The physician who is unaware of this phenomenon is especially vulnerable to *identifying with the projections* and, in turn, traumatizing the patients in the manner of the early caregivers. Mr. K has consulted with six other health care providers from various specialties in the two and a half years I have seen him. At least two of them have unwittingly *acted out*, essentially scaring the hell out of him with remarks that reinforced his anxieties and did nothing to promote his overall health. His orthopaedist was unusual in that he recognized the psychogenic nature of Mr. K's symptoms and, as importantly, he communicated his impressions openly to Mr. K. When multiple people are treating the same somatoform patient, the person charged with treating the mental condition itself should ideally take an active role as leader and educator of the treating team.

Given the internist's remarks about the "dangers of Clonazepam", it was not surprising that Mr. K reported having an intense anxiety attack anticipating a lunch meeting with a friend who happened to be a retired physician. "I worried he would think I was a noth- ing. But he talked with me as if he respected me. He asked me for advice on a matter that he was dealing with. I wondered why this guy thought I was any good. I must be a great actor".

He then reports that he debated about coming to our appointment because he was worried about having enough money to pay me. That night he had this dream: I was with five or six students, each a member of some minority group. We were having a hard time lifting a large, bright orange, rubber tub. I start to lift and thought, "This is impossible". Then, the tub is on top of me, crushing me. I had trouble breathing.

So, *the day residue* involved conflict about getting help from me because of what it will cost him. The feared cost is that his relationship with me or, more exactly, with the part of himself that identifies with me, will crush him, destroy him. I say, "The way you think about what we are doing here is central to this dream". His response is typical of how he manages often to cleverly miss the point. "Yes, I think about the things you say to me".

* * *

Somatoform cases in general are among the psychopathologies most resistant to treatment. Mr. K has various factors working against him. One is his age. He is in his mid-60s. His defensive habits of mind are very entrenched, and the brain loses plasticity with advancing age. Working in his favour are overall good health, high intelligence, and a desire to learn.

He has made modest but important advances with treatment. He now thinks somewhat logically before using his body in sports and other activities in ways that might harm him. EMDR helped him to reflect upon his self-concepts. He began to think systematically about how sense data emanating from the external social environ- ment and from his own mind and body work to activate strategies for controlling feelings and overt behaviour. Perhaps Mr. K's greatest achievement was to take seriously the idea that the main cause of his anxiety has been psychogenic.

Mr. K was a sort of *Oedipal Victor*. When asked to identify who in his life was most like the Gary Cooper character in *High Noon*, Mr. K pointed wrongly to his father. His father was the old sheriff not Gary Cooper. Mr. K himself most personified the man who does his duty under the law, alone, without help. While Mr. K had done difficult jobs where he had to rely on his own resources and courage, he was plagued by a belief that success is sure to be punished. He was in the grips of a superstition involving Talion Dread. He could defeat bullies and exceed the courage of his father. But he couldn't quite enjoy it.

I will make a case in Chapter Ten that the best chance to alter habits of using flawed self-concepts may involve the use of both hallucinogenic drugs and valid descriptions of regulatory habits. These assumptions are based, in part, on my experience with another patient, Mr. C.

Mr. C is younger than Mr. K and his anxiety disorder is without somatoform features. Various diagnostics and treatment modalities led to important, circumscribed improvements in Mr. C's functioning. They included: psychopharmacology, neuropsychological testing of executive functions, EMDR and psychodynamic interpretations. Comparisons between the cases of Mr. K and Mr. C will help illustrate various assumptions we have been making about the workings of mind–brain, psychotropic medicines, and EMDR.

Note

1. The task of thinking and moving the eyes at the same time is something like the child's game of attempting to pat the head while rubbing the belly. The ability to perform the patting–rubbing tasks simultaneously depends on differentiating two separate sets of signals sent from the brain about how to move the two arms. Similarly, thinking while moving the eyes calls for differentiation of two separate tasks that are carried out at the same moment.

    Mr. K's difficulty with doing two things at once is related to the general difficulty in making competent decisions regarding objects that stimulate both pleasure-approach and pain-avoidance motives. He has complex mental habits to approach pleasure that involve the stimulation of anxiety when pleasure is achieved. He solved the problem of thinking a positive thought while tracking the moving finger by diminishing access to conscious awareness of too much visual sensation. The benefit of this "compromise solution" or "compromise formation" was that it prevented conscious awareness from being overwhelmed by "too much pleasure", that is, multi-sensory pleasure. This functioned, in turn, to diminish the likelihood of the stimulation of *signal anxiety*, which he experiences whenever he feels "too good". The down side of the compromise, of course, is the limit it places on the amount of pleasure he can experience.

CHAPTER TEN

Memory processes and mind–brain change

M r. C is a fourty five year-old man with a PhD in a scientific discipline. He is working productively in his chosen sub-specialty. He loves his work. He has been married to his current wife for ten years and they have three children aged from five to nine. He comes in with a DSM-IV diagnosis of Obsessive Compulsive Disorder. He counts silently to himself, dwells on fears, and often feels very anxious. He has no other medical diagnoses. He had one short course of Cognitive Therapy eight years ago. He sought treatment at the time for anxiety about finding a suitable job. He reports that the therapy was somewhat helpful. He is a nor-mal appearing, slender man. He talks rather easily and has a good sense of humour.

He reports that his obsessional symptoms appeared first when he was in graduate school. He is already receiving medications for his obsessional habit from a local psychiatrist. He was started six years ago on 200 mg of Fluvoxamine two times a day. This is an SSRI often used for OCD. The Fluvoxamine alone reduced his symptoms by fifty percent. Two years ago he had convinced his psychiatrist to add Dronabinol to his psychopharmacological regime. Dronabinol is Tetrahyrdocannabinol (THC), the active psychotropic agent in marijuana. Compared to using the SSRI alone, the patient had found that smoking marijuana along with using the SSRI reduced his obsessional thinking markedly. He uses 10 mg taken three times a day and it is as effective as the smoked *Cannabis Sativa* plant. He has also been using 1.0 mg of Clonazepam most nights to aid sleeping.

Mr. C was referred to me for psychotherapy by his psychiatrist. Mr. C says, "This was because I tend to provoke people verbally. I am bothered by authority figures". A year ago he had gotten in trouble at a shopping centre for arguing with a security guard who had forbidden his children to play on a fountain. The guard called the police. Complaints were filed by both parties and nothing of significance came of the incident. It seems plausible that the anxiety-reducing effect of the THC, begun about the time that these sorts of provocative behaviours increased, worked to disinhibit his aggressive impulses.

He also reports that, "My marriage has been a bit rocky because of my mental and behavioural problems". This turns out later to be an understatement. While he and his wife are able to enjoy themselves together to a reasonable extent, he started having sexual performance difficulties immediately after they were married. He had been sexually competent reliably during their one-year courtship. This pattern, of course, strongly indicates incomplete resolution of Oedipal conflicts.

Object relations

Mr. C grew up as an only child. His parents are Fundamentalist Christians. He reports no separation anxiety upon entry to school. He had a cat that functioned as a transitional object. He experienced no acute traumas due to illness or assault. He describes his mother as "clueless", "nice", and "Asperger's". He says the mother understood him to a degree. His father is described as "smart", "strict", and "depressed". He also felt somewhat understood by the father. He and his father built model aeroplanes, devised various science experiments, and generally had a good time playing together with such things. He had a repeated dream as a child until age ten: "I ran down a corridor in school, fell into a hole in the floor and at the bottom of the hole a man would drop kids down a pipe".

First two meetings

Mr. C was encouraged into psychotherapy by his wife who had made an amateur diagnosis of his condition as a form of *Asperger's Disorder*. Asperger's is an autism-like disorder characterized by repetitive motor behaviours (e.g., hand twisting). Mr. C has none of this. Rather, he does have some of the more psychological and social symptoms of Asperger's listed in DSM-IV such as an "encompassing preoccupation with one or more restricted patterns of interest that is abnormal either in intensity or focus"; and impairment in social performance (e.g., his "provocative" behaviours).

Mr. C was trained to think in a formal scientific manner. He knew the sorts of things that support the validity of concepts and those that do not. When his wife showed him some of the Asperger's symptoms listed in the DSM, he recognized them as descriptive of his mother and, to a limited extent, himself. That there might be a genetic, biological aspect to his problems encouraged him to seek treatment. He had imagined psychology to be a "junk science" and this was one reason he had avoided therapy. To him biology and chemistry were "real sciences". His mental condition had been helped by drugs, biochemical things. And, Mr. C could recognize that his love of science was an "encompassing preoccupation" that was, at least statistically, "abnormal in intensity and focus". Of course his interest in science was not merely an "autism spectrum psychopathology". It was his passion. I have seen many patients like Mr. C who are excellent scientists. And, like Mr. C, their social competence is often relatively primitive compared to their competence at work.

Mr. C was a naïve scientist when it came to explaining his own behaviour and the behaviour of others. But he was also a formal scientist. Accordingly, I decided to use Mr. C's strengths in the service of his treatment. I gave him on our first meeting the chapter on treating obsessions from Hawton, Salkovskis, Kirk, and Clark (1989). This is an excellent guide to Cognitive Behavioural Treatments of various disorders. Hawton et al. describe a treatment for obsessions and compulsions. The goal of the method is to *extinguish* symptomatic habits. The patient is instructed to carry a rating sheet for assessing their anxiety (i.e., a scale running from 0 = not anxious to 10 = very anxious). When they have an impulse to think an obsessional thought or act on a compulsion, they are to attempt to suppress it and instead record the time on the form and rate their anxiety using the ten-point scale.

The rating exercise itself works, in part, as a distraction, an alternative habit. It shifts the patient's focus of attention towards a valid, *proximal cause* of the obsession (i.e., anxiety), and away from the concrete effect of the anxiety (i.e., the obsession itself). One finds that when refraining from the obsession or compulsion, anxiety normally goes down after a minute or so. The technique is easier to use with overt compulsions but can also be used in the context of refraining from mental activity. Obsessions and compulsions are, in effect, the "treatments" that the patient uses to reduce their anxiety. This technique demonstrates to the patient that their anxiety will fall without performing the compulsive behaviour or thinking the obsessional thought.

Mr. C. came in the next week and said that he found the chapter very helpful. He had tried the method and noticed the predicted effect of reduced anxiety. He then went on to talk of other things. At one point he noted, "It would make me so anxious to tell a police officer he is right about something". So, we can infer that his provocative behaviour has a *counter-phobic* quality. Mr. C has an impulse to be in a good relation with the police and, instead, he fights with them. In Mr. K's case, he had a wish to be healthy but found that this would make him think obsessively that he was not healthy, which led to performing "tests" to see if he was ill. These tests sometimes made him ill.

So, some central self-concepts regarding aggression and pain are imagined implicitly to be in a zero-sum relationship in both cases. The feared idea activates anxiety and sometimes overt behaviour that is the opposite of some unconscious intention. *Counter-phobia* is a simple suppression of one part of one's motivation (e.g., to engage a police officer in a positive fashion), by activation of the opposite motivation (e.g., to fight with a police officer). All the various symptoms of defence involve invalid concepts or ill-timed activation of valid concepts. They involve more or less a denial of reality (A. Freud, 1936).

By definition, all defences are motivated attempts to counter a fear. A defence must become activated when the fear itself is subjectively experienced at some level of awareness. Freud's concept of signal anxiety describes how defences are activated in general. When the fear is experienced, a defensive operation to counter the fear is activated. All pathological defences are literally *counter-phobias*.

Mr. C's scientific way of thinking led him to define two goals for his treatment: (1) To better control his social behaviour and obsessional thoughts; and (2) To understand the underlying causes of his symptoms. He was in effect asking for both symptom relief and a deeper understanding of himself. One wishes, of course, that more patients came to treatment with this level of sophistication. We decided to meet for one hour each week.

The next two months of treatment

I asked him to describe more exactly what happens when he "confronts authority figures". He went on to describe three scenarios:

> I feel anger and rage when confronted by a policeman for any reason. I question their authority, for example, once I said to a traffic policeman, "Why should I show you my driver's licence?" This got me in a bit of trouble. But I enjoy this sort of defiance.
>
> Sometimes if I'm corrected by someone like my boss or my wife, I feel I have been abused, unjustly violated.
>
> Sometimes I get annoyed by a slow driver in front of me. I feel I have been wronged, or at least inconvenienced by the other driver. Then I give them "the finger" and think, "I've failed". Then I feel kind of guilty.

Mr. C and I reviewed the three situations. We attempted to devise a system of conceptual categories for some of the different feelings and thoughts he experiences when frustrated by authority or merely a slow driver. He nominated first, "anxious" and "impatient". He said, "I get *impatient* waiting for the traffic light to change. It's not a very intense feeling but I have it often. I use the word *anxious* when there is no obvious reason for being afraid or nervous".

So, Mr. C had differentiated two different causes of unpleasurable feelings. *Impatience* is an everyday sort of annoyance that occurs when he is frustrated by someone. We all feel this more or less. He reserves the concept *anxiety* for objectless situations. That is, there is no obvious external, physical, or social cause of his feeling uneasy. This is what psychoanalysts call *floating anxiety*. This is why Mr. C has a "DSM anxiety disorder" and not an "impatience disorder". But the continuum implied should be obvious. The difference between the concepts involves, primarily, intensity of displeasure or tension. *Anxious* is more intense than *impatient* for Mr. C, and most users of English. Not surprisingly, Mr. C, versed in mathematics, created categories representing quantities rather than qualities of tension.

I suggested to him that a more complete control of his feelings and behaviour might be achieved if he created at least one additional concept that is suggested by his three scenarios. One might call the concept "being mad and enjoying it". This concept would include attributes such as "enjoying anger does not mean that one is mentally ill", or "behaving provocatively is not always a moral or legal crime", or "a person who enjoys aggression is not necessarily a bad person". I also suggested a concept we named "indifference" since he sometimes was not bothered by authority figures. Naming concepts to contain and explain sensations has a great utility. It enables the person to think explicitly about conceptual inconsistency (e.g., aggressive and positive feelings about others). In somatoform cases like Mr. K, troublesome sensations "stay in the body". The patient can't think effectively about the underlying causes of their subjective experiences. In contrast, Mr. C was consciously troubled by moral questions about science and religion. And, he made a conscious decision to pursue a career in science.

Mr. C was plagued by a form of "perfectionism" in which he would feel guilty and anxious about having a "non-Christian thought" or "a thought that Jesus never had". Especially as a child, Mr. C was plagued by not being a perfect Christian. The cliché that "the perfect is the enemy of the good" applies here and in virtually all of these anxiety cases. Mr. K too suffered from this type of perfectionism. But he wanted to be perfectly healthy (cf. Tauber, 1982).

Mr. C's parents were "Fundamentalists", or, in other words, "perfectionists" of some kind. In their church people talked explicitly about the advisability of attempting to suppress "bad" or "immoral" thoughts, feelings, and behaviours. At bottom, Fundamentalist religious thinking is always based on an assumption something like that articulated by The Christian Scientists: "There is no death without sin". If one could just figure out how not to sin, well, they would live forever.

One might consider a Fundamentalist background as merely a hindrance to a child's development. But the belief system of Mr. C's parents was at least explicit and social. They talked about what they believed. Open discussion helps give children some freedom to examine a subject from various angles. Mr. C's family belonged in the "Eccentrics' Wing" of The Fundamentalist Nut House, rather than being dangerous and fanatical like Al Qaeda or Nazis. And, his parents did support his efforts in school.

Mr. C became committed to science early on. Being a thoughtful lad, he wrestled with the role religion should play in his life. He felt that there were flaws in his parents' system of beliefs. He did serious reading of theological literature. Like Mr. K's parents, Mr. C's parents did seem to be able to relate to him as a small child. They appreciated animals and nature. But they were not sophisticated enough to be of much help to an older child attempting to regulate his feelings and thoughts. One way he comforted himself in college was by becoming attached to Kurt Gödel's (1931) theorem concerning the impossibility of disproving some hypotheses. Gödel's mathematics was a relief to Mr. C because it had shown that some things are not knowable perfectly.

Third month

Mr. C's impulsive, aggressive provocations stopped for the most part after two months of treatment. The use of more valid concepts to contain his impulses seemed to be the reason for his improvement. Then, as often happens in psychodynamic therapy, the patient carries out an unconscious intention to avoid treatment. He "overslept" for our regular meeting time. I interpreted it as a resistance to the treatment. He accepted my premise and added, "I have become afraid of my rage at your failure to understand me any more deeply than you do".

He then states that the first goal of treatment, getting his anger under control, has been achieved. He now wants to work on what is currently his most salient problem, his relationship with his wife. The request indicates a shift has occurred in his mental operations from problems with aggression to problems with intimacy.

Next four months

Mr. C reports that his wife feels his behaviour has improved since he began treatment. But that she complains that he is too dependent on her and is ineffectual as a parent. It becomes clear that Mr. C regresses in relations with his wife. He plays the role of a child who is not fully understood by her. Understandably, she is turned-off by the idea of sex with someone behaving like a needy child. Together they engage in a constant sort of bickering in which he attempts to use formal logical proofs to counter her criticisms of him.

Currently, they are sleeping in separate rooms. I suggest to Mr. C that he try to discern his wife's perspectives on him: "How do you think she sees you?" "What is her subjective experience of you?" I encourage him to make her psychology his subject. I tell him I will act as his consultant in this. Our goal will be to try to get him back in the bedroom with her.

A key instruction for patients who endlessly repeat ineffective behaviours is to have them refrain from enacting such behaviours. This logic is similar to that underlying the cognitive treatment for obsessions and compulsions. In Mr. C's case, for example, I point out that we know the behaviours that do not work to improve relations with his wife. These include endless arguments that serve only to make her infuriated with him. The first step in such cases is to instruct the patient "to not do what doesn't work" to promote achievement of your goals. Mr. C's goals involved both more social intimacy with his wife as well as physical intimacy. While the patient may not know what does work, we know certainly what does not work. For Mr. C the advice was simply to "shut up" when he perceived that his wife was entirely fed up with his arguments. He was able to do this to some degree.

Often, of course, both people in a marriage are colluding at some level to make sure that the level of intimacy does not change. Mrs. C was surely getting something out of Mr. C's ineffective behaviour. A wife or therapist may fear being overwhelmed by a person's neediness for perfect empathic understanding. So, one also must warn the patient that when he stops doing what doesn't work, he may be subjected to increased provocations on the part of the other person to indeed keep up the old repetitive behaviours.

For the most part, it seemed Mrs. C did not attempt to goad Mr. C. Instead, he reported that she was pleased that he had become a less irritating partner. After four weeks of Mr. C suppressing attempts to be "more exactly understood", Mrs. C asked him to return to their bedroom. They began talking more effectively about the children, and were enjoying watching movies and taking vacations together. But they did not resume sexual relations.

Next seven months

We spent the next five months exploring the nature of his anxiety about not being accurately understood by his parents. I gave him Winnicott's work (1960a) on the holding function of the mother. He understood these papers. We also explored why he became less sexually competent immediately after the marriage. He clearly had felt guilty about feeling sexual pleasure. The Fundamentalist teachings of his parents did help in this regard. Marriage usually involves a decision to have the partner perform both security operations somewhat similar to those performed by a parent in addition to adult sexual functions.

When Oedipal conflicts are inadequately resolved, the patient's self-concepts do not allow him to conceive of the wife as both a comforter and an arousing sexual partner. Mr. C was handicapped in this regard. He had a variant of a Madonna–Whore Syndrome: a zero-sum conceptual scheme in which the wife was conceived to be either a caretaker or a sex partner, but not both at the same time. He behaved most of the time as if his wife was a surrogate mother. This reduced her sexual attraction to him. But we can also assume that their constant bickering was an alternative to sex that involved some form of gratification for both of them. This is in contrast to some couples who are somehow able to use their less than completely positive feelings for each other in some mutually satisfying sex play.

The couple had been sharing a bed for months but was still not having sex—apart from some heated bickering. At this point Mrs. C asked him for a divorce. Mr. C was "shocked". "I'm miserable. I never fall out of love with anyone". Of course, this inability to free the system of self-concepts from a fragment of a parental other was at the centre of Mr. C's difficulties. His self-concepts had never become differentiated sufficiently from his concepts of his parents. Being separated from a caretaker like his wife was tantamount to dying. He reacted to his wife's statement, in part, as if he were a child, too young to care for himself.

The next week he reports this dream: "I'm driving to work, fast, around curves. I notice I'm in the wrong lane with a car headed straight at me. I felt numb but was thinking, 'At least it's over'". The dream seems consistent with the idea that he is relieved at some level to be out of a social arrangement in which he had compromised parts of his mental competence in exchange for some imagined security. This, of course, is what Mr. K had done.

Separation and EMDR

Mr. C feels very sad as he moves out of his house and into a house with four men about his age. It is like a college dormitory environment. For his dysthymic mood his psychiatrist has added 2.0 mg of Aripiprazole per day. This is in addition to his regular drug regime of 200 mg of Fluvoxamine two times a day; 10 mg of Dronabinol three times a day; 20 mg of Methylphenidate twice a day; and some Clonazepam as needed for sleep. He has instant companions and a host of visitors coming through his new home including attractive, available woman. And, of course, he is less in contact with his wife. He keeps up visits with the children. The Aripiprazole and his interesting social environment work to lessen his depression considerably over a three-week period. We decide at that point to begin EMDR treatments.

I ask him to recall a positive memory and track my finger. Before starting he rates his anxiety level at "seven" on the ten point scale. After thinking and tracking for about 30 seconds he reports: "I was driving at night to a bar. Then it was daytime and I was in a beautiful field with wild flowers. I was with R [a woman he had a tortured, non-sexual relationship with for seven years]. We were having a fun time at the beach climbing over rocks. The thought of R was very pleasant in this instance". He rated his anxiety at "five" after the eye movements.

The next week he reports being at a party and worrying if he would ever be able to meet a woman. I ask him to think about that as he tracks my finger with his eyes. He reports that he imagined talking with a woman at a party, then about arguing with his wife, then being at the party again. Then he makes a very telling comment: "The [eye movement] wasn't as good this time because I wasn't as depressed and anxious as I was last week". I asked him to elaborate on this idea. He said, "Because I was feeling worse last week I really wanted this method to work so I was able to concentrate more intensely on the memory of being with R on the beach".

In effect, Mr. C was saying that he used anxiety to regulate the intensity of his attentional focus. He becomes worried when he is not worried. This is a process similar to that found with Mr. K. Mr. K worried when he was not worrying about his health. But Mr. C had found a use for the anxiety. He could concentrate more intently if he berated himself with guilt-inducing ideas which produced anxiety. This worked to enhance concentration even when background arousal levels were high. Plausibly, the habit to activate self-hating cognitions is reinforcing because it causes release of adrenergic neurotransmitters such as epinephrine and dopamine. These neurotransmitters are normally elevated in response to threat. In anxiety disorders, the person "threatens himself". The result is increased sympathetic arousal and, in the short term, increased attentional focus. Adrenergic stimulant drugs are used to treat attention deficit disorders. In effect, self-hate co-opts the normal flight or flight mechanisms in the service of attentional regulation. Such a mechanism might explain the almost universal presence of self-hate or *harsh superego* in mental disorders.

In this case, with the EMDR technique, he noticed that with relatively low background anxiety, he could not sustain as vivid a flow of associations as he had last week. One can see too how this method of regulating thinking is not dissimilar to how masochistic sexual behaviours can increase the intensity of sexual pleasure. That is, being injured more or less materially, or in an "as if" imaginary game, enlists the sympathetic nervous system's arousal that is channelled hallucinogens cause alterations in subjective experience and overt behaviour is still unclear. Perhaps the most that can be said with some certainty is that: "The physiological manipulation that most closely simulates the behavioral actions of LSD is stimulation of the raphe [nucleus], leading to decreased habituation to repetitive sensory stimuli" (Cooper, Bloom & Roth, 2003; page 301).

To decrease habituation to sensation is more or less to make it harder to stop paying attention to sensations. So, when under the influence of hallucinogens, the old concepts one uses habitually to interpret, contain and shut off sensation are insufficient. More extensive or deeper interpretive processing of sense data is called for than in more usual states of mind. In short, hallucinogens may work by motivating the creation of new concepts. The incentive to think creatively should increase when habituation to sensation is reduced. Creating new, or using old concepts in new ways, is instrumental for regulating sensation; and interpretation of sense data is more pleasurable than sensation itself (e.g., Biederman & Vessel, 2006).

In addition to the two hallucinogens, Mr. C already had onboard: THC (a cannabinoid receptor agonist); Aripiprazole (a partial dopamine agonist); Fluvoxamine (an SSRI); and Methylphenidate (a norepinephrine and dopamine reuptake inhibitor). The combined effect of this unusual combination of drugs is very hard to know.

Mr. C also had on board the interpretation I had made the week before about how he had used anxiety- and guilt-causing concepts as aids to his ability to concentrate on his work. They were "deserved" punishments for the pleasure he derived from thinking. The pain rectified the sin of his pleasures and provided energy and sensations that potentiated to some degree his conceptual work.

Somehow, the amalgam of this interpretation, his separation from his wife, and this unusual combination of psychoactive chemicals provided the necessary and sufficient conditions for a real change to occur in Mr. C's mind and brain. Mr. C came to his session with me the morning after this party having had just two hours of sleep. Sleep deprivation itself can be thought of as a type of drug. He recounted to me the events of the evening and the drugs he had taken. We decided then to leave my office and take a walk around the streets as we talked.

As we walked, Mr. C reported calmly, "It just hit me like a ton of bricks. I know what you mean about how I use anxiety to control my thinking. There is really no need for me to feel guilty and anxious all the time". At once, this realization had worked to make his anxiety and guilt feelings stop. This was the moment we wait for in psychoanalysis: when a valid interpretation of an unwanted mental process works to stop the process. But in practice it doesn't usually work that way. Now here we had an accurate interpretation, delivered a week ago and repeated by myself to Mr. C as we walked. The brain state of this man at that moment is impossible to describe completely. But we do know he had used two hallucinogens, TCH, and a third generation anti-psychotic just hours before. And, he had recently separated from his wife whom he had used as some sort of surrogate parent.

When asked to describe how the way he was now was different from the way he had felt for years up until now, he said: "Freedom, more degrees of freedom. I have more options in what I think and what I choose to do. I am not *required* to become as grief stricken as I thought I was. I enjoyed in a twisted way the grief. It was required of me to feel grief about the loss of my wife. Previously, I knew these things intellectually, but now the ideas are engaged".

The next week he went on to describe the change: "Now when I am trying to develop a mathematical proof I don't have to constantly be checking back to the equations leading up to the equation I am working on in the moment. In that sense my memory is better since [the realization that I needn't use worry and self-criticism as a way to operate and focus more intensely]". In effect, Mr. C was now using some means other than anxiety to regulate his thinking. He was not constantly interrupting himself unnecessarily to check to see if he was feeling guilty or anxious enough to satisfy some invisible judge of morality. He was enjoying his work more and being more productive. Apparently, there is a way to think effectively without being hard on the self. And, the efficiency of thinking regulated by something other than pain is much increased.

The next week the change was still in place but "not perfectly" he said. He still had some anxiety but essentially he had felt free and good all week. Moreover, his work was progressing well. He had delivered a talk that was very well received and he felt optimistic about his career. I saw him three more times over a six-week period. The change still held and we terminated treatment at that point. His psychiatrist continued management of his ongoing psychopharmacological regime.

What were the key factors promoting this mind–brain change? And, what exactly changed? I am assuming some attributes in Mr. C's self-concept system changed. Why has Mr. K been unable to change in this way? What are the neurochemical conditions for change? What are the processes in the brain that underlie changes in one's subjective experience of the self and the external world? We have a variety of clues to start answering these sorts of questions.

Memory processes and psychopathology

Mid-way through the eighteen months of Mr. C's treatment he had told me that despite the fact that his work involves complex mathematics, he had difficulty doing simple arithmetic and remembering what people had just told him. Also, if he was attempting to work out a series of mathematical equations he had to constantly look back at the prior equations in order to continue with his proof. This is consistent with an "absent-minded professor" aspect to his demeanour. I tested Mr. C's executive functions at three points during his Eighteen-month treatment. The results suggest that if an important change occurs in a regulatory self-concept and/or the process by which the new self-concept is used, measurable changes will occur in memory processes.

The relations between symptoms, personality (habits of mind), and memory are of course central in psychoanalytic theory. Freud and Breuer (1895, p. 7) wrote that their early hysteria patients were suffering "mainly from reminiscences". The assumption was that patients' memories of trauma and/or imagined bad behaviour were inaccessible to awareness and caused disorders of feeling, thought, and behaviour.

If relatively accurate representations of episodes from one's life and relatively valid semantic concepts are stored in memory, they can be used to cope with a current situation. For example, "The last time I said 'Hello' to Irving, he ignored me (*an episodic memory*). Perhaps this means he doesn't like me (*the semantic concept 'Irving' might contain the attribute 'doesn't like me')*". This might lead to an experiment: "This time I'll ask him if something is wrong. Then I can refine or alter my concept of Irving". In short, the person can test the validity of the attributes contained in concepts. A more neurotic individual would conclude at once that he is disliked, that the concept "Irving" certainly contains the attribute "dislikes me", and then suffer anxiety whenever Irving came around.

The ability to think in social and vocational context depends, in part, on the speed and accuracy of recall of episodes and semantic concepts stored in memory (e.g., Tulving & Szpunar, 2009). A Theory of Neuropsychoanalysis should ultimately be able to spell out how executive functioning is compromised by defensive operations based on invalid self-concepts learned during development.

Neuropsychological testing

A computer-based test battery, CNS Vital Signs (Gualtieri & Johnson, 2006), was used to test Mr. C's and Mr. K's neurocognitive functioning. The exam is comprised of seven tests: Verbal and Visual Memory; Finger Tapping; Symbol Digit Coding; the Stroop Test; Shifting Attention Test; and Continuous Performance Test.[1] An individual's performance on the tests is compared to a population similar in age, gender, and education. Results from the seven tests are combined to generate one overall functioning score and five scores indicative of specific executive and other neuropsychological competencies: Memory; Reaction Time; Psychomotor Speed; Complex Attention; and Cognitive Flexibility. This battery is used in clinical practice to screen patients for cognitive disorders such as attention deficits and dementias. If dysfunctions are discovered, *Dose Response Studies* may be called for. This involves testing patients before and after administration of medications aimed at treating symptoms. The method facilitates assessment of the effectiveness of medications. Results for the two patients Mr. C and Mr. K are shown in Figure 8.

Mr. C was given the exam three times while in treatment with me over Eighteen months. The Baseline, or *Time One Exam*, came about one year into the treatment after he complained about his memory. Then, a week later, we redid the test 35 minutes after administering a 10 mg dose of Methylphenidate (*Time Two*). The third exam (*Time Three*) was six weeks after his "realization" about not needing to be anxious while attending to his work. The figure also includes results from Mr. K taken after over two years in treatment.

	MR. C			MR. K
	T1	**T2**	**T3**	**Tx**
Overall Function	3	8	27	25
Memory	*34*	*7*	*95*	*8*
Psychomotor Speed	8	30	47	45
Reaction Time	45	13	45	14
Complex Attention	1	1	1	53
Cognitive Flexibility	1	3	4	21

Mr. C: **T1** = Baseline; **T2** = 35 min. Post 10 mg Methylphenidate; **T3** = Six weeks Post Self-Concept Change.
Mr. K: **Tx** = Post Two Years Treatment.

Pharmacological regimes at each testing period

Mr. C:

Baseline: Fluvoxamine 200 mg BID; Dronabinol 10 mg TID; Clonazepam 2.0 mg qhs
Post-Methylphenidate: Baseline + Methylphenidate 10 mg
Post Self-Concept Change: Baseline + Methylphenidate 20 mg BID; Aripiprazole 2.0 mg qd;
[Six weeks earlier: MDMA; Psilocybin]

Mr. K:

Clonazepam 1.0 mg PRN

Figure 8.   Executive functioning of Mr. C and Mr. K.
The results are shown in *percentile* form. For example, Mr. C's 3rd percentile rating for his Overall Cognitive Function at Baseline means that his performance was better than only two percent of those in his reference group (i.e., fourty five year-old men with more than twenty years of education). Mr. K.s reference group is sixty five year-old men, with eighteen years of education.

There are several remarkable features of these results. *The result most central for our discussion is Mr. C's very large improvement in memory function at the third exam. He scored at the 95th percentile for memory function six weeks after the moment when it hit him "like a ton of bricks" that he was compelling himself to be anxious all the time.* This score compares to his *Baseline* performance of thirty four, and seven on the second exam. I am assuming that the change in memory functions took place on the day of the *realization* of my description of his defensive habit of using anxiety to focus attention. In comparison,

Mr. K who never achieved a realization that worked to halt his defensive processes, scored at the 8th percentile on memory function after two years of therapy.

These findings are consistent with many others that have found episodic memory function and attentional deficits in anxiety disorders (e.g., Airaksinen, Larsson & Forsell, 2005). These executive function deficits are especially pronounced in Obsessional Disorders, that is, the syndromes that best describe the repetitive, anxious thoughts of Mr. C and Mr. K.

Two tests contribute to the Memory Score on the CNSVS battery. The Verbal Memory Test involves displaying fifteen words for two seconds each on the computer screen. The subject is instructed to attempt to remember these words. Immediately after the display of the fifteen target words, a longer list of thirty words is presented. Half the words will have appeared on the first list that was to be remembered. The task is to press a key if the subject remembers having seen the word on the first list. The test is then repeated at the end of the whole battery to get a measure of delayed recall. The delay is about 25 to 30 minutes. The other memory measure is The Visual Memory Test. The same protocol is followed as with the words but simple geometric shapes are used as the target items.

These are tests of episodic memory for words and shapes. That is, does one remember the episode of seeing the word or shape or not? But remembering words must involve semantic memory too. Figure 9 shows Mr. C's raw memory scores.

	T1	T2	T3
	Verbal/Visual	Verbal/Visual	Verbal/Visual
Correct Hits (Immediate)	9/15	11/13	15/15
Correct Hits (Delay)	7/11	13/11	14/15

T1 = Baseline; T2 = 35 min. Post 10 mg Methylphenidate; T3 = Six weeks Post Self-Concept Change

Figure 9.   Mr. C's raw memory scores.
(Note that the Percentile scores for Overall Memory shown in Figure 8 are based on 'correct hits' plus 'correct passes' which are not shown here. Mr. C had more 'correct passes' at Time 1 than at Time 2. This accounts for his Memory Percentile being higher at Time 1 than Time 2.)

Note that his Visual Memory was relatively better than his Verbal Memory. This result is consistent with our idea that Semantic Concepts and defences involving their activation are central to defensive processes. Verbal Processes are usually located in the left hemisphere and Visual Processes in the right. This gives a clue of sorts as to the brain areas involved in defensive operations.

Memory function as a marker for change

Mr. C, an accomplished scientist, came into treatment with very poor executive functioning. This is indicated by his *Baseline* results. In simple cases of Attention Deficit, memory scores are typically normal but the measures of attentional performance are low. The Cognitive Flexibility, Complex Attention, and Continuous Performance scores are indicative of competence in deploying attention consciously. Mr. C's Baseline results included both poor memory and attention scores. His *Baseline* Overall Functioning score was at the 3rd Percentile. His attentional control was poor at all three time periods. His control of attention did improve somewhat with the addition of 10 mg of Methylphenidate. But the change was small in comparison to the change in memory function that accompanied his subjective transformation.

The improvement in Cognitive Flexibility from 1st percentile at *Baseline* to 3rd percentile *Post 10 mg Methylphenidate* may appear small. But scores at the far end of a distribution like this can represent a meaningful shift. For example, The Shifting Attention Test, a component of The Complex Attention Score, has a mean error rate of five. Mr. C made twenty four errors at *Baseline*; fourteen errors *Post Methylphenidate 10 mg*; and sixteen errors after *Self-Concept Change*. Clinically, it made sense to start Mr. C on a stimulant. After some experimentation, he felt best on a Methylphenidate dose of 20 mg in the morning and 20 mg at noon. But even when on the larger dose of the stimulant, that is, at *Time Three*, his attentional control was still relatively poor.

The large change in his episodic memory function had to require other factors in addition to insight. He had been aware of my description of his anxiety operations for one week. The morning after his wild party, we took a walk; he "gets it" and starts to feel less anxious. Over the next few weeks he notices that he is more effective and efficient doing his mental work. He no longer needs to keep checking his previous work before moving ahead in his writing. Why did the anxiety-generating process stop when it did?

It is most probable that his change was due to a combination of factors: (1) Awareness or ability to reflect upon and, hence, stop the use of the process which depended upon the concept "I must use guilt and anxiety to focus attention"; (2) Real time sensory data of a present, comforting other (that is, his therapist); and (3) Some continuing activity of two hallucinogens he had taken the night before. We can likely rule out the role of the Methylphenidate in producing his important mind–brain change inasmuch as he was using Methylphenidate at *Time Two*, albeit at a lower dose than at *Time Three*. The most important psychopharmacological difference between *Time Two* and *Time Three* was the presence of the hallucinogens.

Hallucinocis, sleep, and memory

It is interesting to speculate how hallucinogens, or a combination of hallucinogens such as MDMA (methylene-dioxy-methamphetamine) and psilocybin (4-Phosphoral-Dimethyltryptamine) might potentiate change in chronic cognitive habits. MDMA has a well known affect of increasing users' subjective sense of empathy, well-being, and energy. It also affects both verbal and visual memory, decision making, and self-control (Kalant, 2001). Psilocybin has long been used by native cultures and is known to produce life-changing experiences (e.g., Grob, 2002; Leary, Litwin & Metzner, 1963; Wasson, 1980; Weil, 1980). Hallucination of course is the subjective experience occurring during dreaming. The brain makes its own hallucinogens. Dimethyltryptamine (DMT) for one has been hypothesized to play a role in dreaming sleep, especially lucid dreaming (e.g., Callaway, 1988; LeBerge, 1990; Wallach, 2009).

We now know that various sleep stages are involved in the storage of different sorts of memories (e.g., Hobson, 1999; Mishkin, 1982; Stickgold, 2005; Winson, 1992; Zhang, 2004). Different sets of brain regions, electrical patterns, and neurotransmitters are involved in processes for storing so-called *Declarative Memory* for episodes and semantic concepts; and, for storage of *Non-Declarative Memories* such as procedural motor skills, unconsciously primed ideas, and associations made by means of classical and instrumental conditioning.

Sleep involves cycling about four times per night between Slow Wave Sleep (SWS) and Rapid Eye Movement (REM) sleep. At the beginning of the night we enter Stage one Sleep characterized by regular *alpha waves*. Then, Stage two Sleep occurs with the appearance of *sleep spindle waves* having both regular, synchronous and irregular, non-synchronous qualities. SWS encompassing stages three and four is characterized by synchronous, predictable, *slow wave* electrical activity. REM sleep has the least synchronous Electroencephalograph (EEG) activity. And, hallucinogens seem to induce EEG activity that is similar to REM activity, that is, low synchrony, fast, noisy wave patterns (e.g. Fairchild, Jenden, Mickey & Yale, 1980).

During REM, the eyes move rapidly back and forth, voluntary muscles are paralysed and the person is in a generally aroused state. People awakened during REM sleep almost always report dreaming. Dreaming occurs in SWS too. But SWS is the most quiescent sleep physiologically and is associated with restoration of somatic functioning (e.g., Hoshikawa et al., 2007; Shapiro, Bortz, Mitchell, Bartel & Jooste, 1981). The recognized sleep states are not entirely distinct from each other or from waking consciousness. This is consistent with the somewhat common experience of finding oneself awake and paralysed momentarily because REM-state muscle immobility has intruded upon wakefulness.

Consolidation of memories for *Non-Declarative*, procedural motor skills such as tapping a learned sequence of numbers on a keyboard are enhanced by time spent in Stage two Sleep (Stickgold, 2005). Remembering associations between behaviours and spaces (e.g., how to run through a maze), is consolidated by firing patterns in the hippocampus during sleep which repeat the neuronal activity occurring during the waking acquisition of maze-learning in lab animals. This repetitive firing occurs during Slow Wave Sleep and during REM sleep (Louie & Wilson, 2001).

Consolidation of *Declarative Memories* for word pairs in the human seems to involve hippocampal processes similar to those identified in encoding spatial memories (Gais & Born, 2004). That is, after learning associations between words, memories become more durable with time spent in SWS. In that period, hippocampal neurons that fired during the acquisition of learning, fire again. The enhancement of Declarative memory depends on very low levels of acetylcholine in the hippocampus during SWS. This contrasts with the necessity for high levels of acetylcholine for consolidation of Non-Declarative Memories during REM sleep and the recall of memories during wakefulness. (Drugs that work to increase acetylcholine levels are used in Alzheimer's disease.)

Also, the ability to recognize patterns in complex stimuli seen during wakefulness is mediated by hippocampal activity (Wagner, Gais, Haider, Verleger, & Born, 2004). That is, patterns recognized only implicitly during wakefulness become explicit when the complex stimuli "replay" in the hippocampus the night following initial exposure. These reactivated representations of stimuli are transferred to neocortical regions for storage (e.g., Buzsaki, 1989; Hasselmo, 1999).

It seems likely that our knowledge about the relationships between memory processes involving implicit procedures and explicit semantic concepts will evolve rather quickly. In the meantime, it is safe to say that memory benefits from processes characterized by synchronous EEG wave forms (e.g., Stage three and four Sleep); partially synchronous waves (Stage two Sleep); and non-synchronous waves (REM sleep). Very likely new relations will be found between sleep states, neurotransmitter systems, and brain regions that underlie changes in concepts and in concept-activation habits. Meanwhile, Wagner et al. described how implicit and explicit processes might operate together:

> Our results show that sleep acts on newly acquired mental representations of a task such that insight into hidden task structures is facilitated ... Specifically, subjects [who solved a problem by recognizing algorithms hidden in an array of numbers] appear to have incipient representations of the [to be discovered, explicit] rule overlapping with that required for implicit task performance. By amplifications during sleep, this novel representation could eventually start to dominate the implicit memory representation, a process expressing itself in insightful behavior as a consequence of an overall restructured representation ... Thus, our data support the concept that sleep, by hippocampal-neurocortical replay, not only strengthens memory traces quantitatively, but can also "catalyse" mental restructuring, thereby setting the stage for the emergence of insight.

(Wagner et al., 2002, p. 354)

In the Wagner et al. (2004) and Gais and Born (2004) experiments, we see the central role played by *repetition of neuronal firing* in facilitating the solution of a problem. The subjective experience of dreaming *and the waking process of reflecting upon dreams* have meaning for mind–brain development. During dreaming, repetition is automatic but not entirely unconscious. We can remember dreams which occur presumably contemporaneously with automatic memory consolidation process and think about them while awake.

Reflecting on dreams while awake

Some claim the waking, re-experience of a dream is not especially central to mind–brain development. For example, Hobson (2002) points out that many people who don't remember dreams seem to function well. But my clinical experience indicates that a complete inability to remember dreams is a marker of psychopathology. Most patients who claim to not remember dreams will start to remember them if instructed to put a pad and pencil next to their bed. But there is a segment of the population who cannot recall dreams at all. These people almost always have anxiety disorders of one kind or another.

Most importantly for our current theory, dreaming sleep is a subjective experience of hallucination that occurs contemporaneously with objectively understandable brain processes involved in the storage and management of concepts in memory. The development of the person may proceed without use of hallucinogenic drugs because Nature has provided an endogenous system for *hallucinocis*. But in cases of chronic psychopathology, Nature can use some help. Dreaming sleep alone does not work especially to help the patient change. In Post Traumatic Conditions dreams repeat unchanged night after night.

For Mr. C, an insight about the way that he habitually regulated his attention became *activated* while he was awake and under the influence of hallucinogens. This is a sort of "double processing". It is analogous to *Lucid Dreaming* in which the person is aware that they are dreaming and involves both dream-like and wakeful, conscious mentation. This Lucid State preceded a change in the way that Mr. C controlled his mind–brain and, in turn, improvements in his memory function. The psychoanalytic practice of analysing dreams while patients are not taking hallucinogens is good for increasing insight, but relatively poor at *activating insights* to cause important psychological change.

Wishful thinking

We have assumed throughout that all thinking is more or less "deciding". More exactly, thinking always involves an attempt to decide whether to approach or avoid objects in the world and in the mind. Freud (1900) thought that dreams represented wishes or wish fulfilment. Inasmuch as we try to make the best decisions, and since dreaming is a type of thinking, then all dreams represent a process connected with a wished for or ideal solution to some problem.

The "problems" come from the *day residue*. These are dream experiences from events in the preceding day that activated instinctual tendencies to respond to biological releasers. Most likely there was some suppression or less than ideal regulation of the instinctual tendencies. How might we have reacted differently to the events of the day? The person made probably "good enough", "compromise decisions" in response to his instincts. Of course, in wakefulness we were limited by the need to compromise, to act in socially acceptable ways and to control anxiety. But maybe after we have repeated thinking about the day's problem in a dream, and perhaps created new anxiety-containing concepts and/or concept-activation habits, we will have a better response to such a situation tomorrow.

Implicit activation of explicit semantic concepts

Our central thesis has been that mental competence depends on two general factors: (1) The validity of concepts; and (2) Habits or procedures for activating concepts so that they appear in conscious awareness. The sleep research indicates that there are two different processes involved in memory storage: one for Declarative Semantic Concepts; and another for Non-Declarative Procedures. Although the distinction is not entirely clean, the evidence to support its validity includes:

1. Non-Declarative Procedural Memory consolidation depends in large part on non-synchronous REM Sleep (Juliana et al., 2006;

Maquet, 2001); and high levels of Glutamate (Steffen, Bjorn, Ullrich & Born, 2008).

2. Declarative Semantic Memory Consolidation seems to involve especially synchronous, Slow Wave Stage three and four Sleep, and partially synchronous Sleep Spindles in Stage two Sleep (Born & Wagner, 2004); and, low levels of hippocampal acetylcholine (Gais & Born, 2004).

Declarative concepts and *non-declarative* procedures for becoming aware of concepts are seemingly stored by means of separate processes occurring in different parts of the brain. But the subjective experience of thought and feeling depends on some dynamic linkage in time and space between concepts and concept-activation procedures.

The difference between the way concepts and activation procedures are processed in sleep may be what makes dreaming mentation possible. During wakefulness the person, especially an anxious person, is using concepts habitually, implicitly, constantly, and quickly. During sleep, the procedural habits of concept activation and the concepts themselves are more distinctly separated than in wakefulness. The suspension of habitual, fast activation of concepts may allow for the odd images in dreams. Ideas are activated in novel, unusual ways, different from the way that concepts are combined in normal waking awareness. Normally, novel sequences of *concept-activation complexes* make up a dream. And, perhaps the new complexes can confer some insight into the way that the self operates. On the other hand, in PTSD and other severe pathologies old sequences of concept-active complexes based on the traumatic event itself repeat unchanged, over and over. Dreaming in PTSD is essentially non-productive.

Infants, REM sleep, and self-development

The neonate's brain exists almost entirely in REM State (Dement, 1994). Early in life, without many concepts on board, the brain seems to be searching for rhythm, regularity, or perhaps—*meaning*. Time spent in the relatively non-synchronous, high energy REM Sleep State decreases over the mammalian life span. This is consistent with the idea that a reduction in the degrees of freedom of mind–brain occurs in old age. This is due, in part, to the aging of the underlying brain that supports mental functions. It is also likely a result of the degree to which the self-system of semantic concepts becomes organized or, in pathology, "over-organized", and "locked up" by conflicting, zero-sum assumptions.

Self-development has to involve the development of new concepts (structures) and changes in the way that concepts are used (procedures). Specifically, the habits to activate newer, more valid concepts have to become stronger than habits to activate older, less valid concepts. The tendency to activate the foundational representations of the self, modelled on early caregivers, may need to weaken relative to the tendency to activate new concepts if the person is to grow "beyond the level" of their early teachers. Moments of *insight*, experienced while asleep or awake, may be defined as those in which new self-concepts (i.e., mind–brain structures) and new ways of processing sensation, come into awareness.

It is conceivable that the more valid are one's self-concepts, the easier it is to access them in the service of regulating instinctual behaviours potentiated by the sensation of evolutionarily meaningful stimulus arrays. This ease of access might be due to the greater simplicity of a system composed of valid concepts in logical relationship, compared to a system composed of invalid concepts in illogical relationships that developed initially in the service of the denial of reality and logic.

Mr. C was not changed at a deep, foundational level. Rather, his insight involved a suspension of his dominant habit to activate *derivative self-concepts*, not the underlying, conflicting concepts the derivatives contained. His deepest, *foundational self-concepts* were formed early on in his interaction with his parents who endorsed zero-sum, Fundamentalist Religious concepts, such as "there is no death without sin". These set up the conditions for pleasure to chronically activate *signal anxiety*. Somehow, hallucinogenic drugs promoted awareness of how he processed this signal anxiety with derivatives of the foundational conflict.

Hallucinogens in psychotherapy

These speculations are consistent with the enthusiasm of Naranjo, Shulgin, and Sargent (1967) regarding the utility of using MDA; and, more recently, MDMA (e.g., Bouso, 2010), as aids to psychotherapy.

Philip Wolfson made the case for allowing research into MDMA's use in testimony before a committee of the Food and Drug Administration:

> MDMA is a potentially valuable therapeutic agent that should not be lost to the psychiatric profession or to human beings. Its uses and value as a psychotherapeutic agent demand exploration in the interests of all of those people who are doomed to a life of chronicity. In sophisticated psychotherapeutic hands, within an overall program of psychotherapy, I believe MDMA will prove to be a boon to those of us interested in helping individuals going through terrible states of mind ... I would urge its exploration. A Schedule III or lower designation would enable this to occur.
>
> (Wolfson, 1985, p. 13)

In the next chapter, cognitive and motivational variables that operate in both the maintenance and the change of defensive habits of mind will be described. The chapter explains recent research results on *thought suppression* that has employed *semantic priming techniques*. The research provides a model for processes occurring in anxiety disorders.

Note

1. The three attentional measures are The Stroop Test, Shifting Attentional Test, and Continuous Performance Test.

   The Stroop Test involves displaying on a computer screen words for colours (e.g., blue, red, green). Subjects are instructed to press a key as soon as the word appears. Reaction Time is measured. Then, the colour words are presented in the colour they represent (e.g., blue is painted blue) or they are not (e.g., blue is painted red). The subject's task now is to press the key only if the word is painted in a consistent colour, for example, blue is painted blue. If blue is coloured green the subject must refrain from pressing the key. Then the rule is reversed and the subject must press the key only if the word is painted in an inconsistent colour (e.g., blue is painted red).

   The Shifting Attention Test requires subjects to adjust their responses to randomly changing rules. A figure (circle or rectangle) is presented at the top of the computer screen in blue or orange.

At the bottom of the screen are two other shapes, one a circle and one a rectangle. These are either blue or orange. Underneath the shape at the top, a rule is printed: "match shape" or "match colour". The rule and the colours of all three figures change randomly every two seconds. The task is to accurately execute the matching rule by pressing a key as quickly as possible. Low scores on the test are especially diagnostic of attentional problems. Mr. C made fifty percent fewer errors on this test after taking Methylphenidate.

The Continuous Performance Test taps the ability to sustain attentional focus. Single letters (e.g., B, R, H) are flashed in the centre of the computer screen every few seconds for five minutes. The subject is instructed to press a key only if the letter is a "B".

CHAPTER ELEVEN

Cognitive load and defence

An experiment described in Chapter Five concerned the attempt to approach a beautiful woman (Bernstein et al., 1983). It demonstrated something about how the person regulates thought, feeling, and behaviour in a conflict situation. We found that the subjects were able to exploit the conceptual ambiguity inherent in a social condition, camouflage their true intentions, and thereby reduce the likelihood of a painful rejection. There are of course countless ways to reduce mental anguish in the service of one's motives. Perhaps the simplest method for reducing the pain of a negative thought is to not think it. "Thought suppression" is more or less equivalent to changing one's focus of attention.

Much research has shown reliably that attempts to "not think about x" work briefly to suppress awareness of "x". But, in various ways, the intention to suppress a thought often results in increased conscious awareness of it (e.g., Wegner & Erber, 1992). The maddening repetition of obsessive thoughts is an example of a "suppression boomerang effect". I assume the failure of thought suppression attempts is due in large part to the general tendency of mind–brain to attempt constantly to make connections. Ultimately, every thought in mind and every nerve in brain is connected to all the other thoughts and nerves.

The connectionist tendency of mind–brain can be understood, in part, as *Spreading Activation* (Collins & Loftus, 1975). When a node in a semantic-neural network is activated, nodes near to it go into a "readiness state". An important method for studying spreading activation is called *Semantic Priming* (see Chapter Four: Note 3). When a concept in a person's semantic memory is activated, neural structures representing proximal concepts are *primed*. That is, the threshold for the activation of related concepts is lowered after priming.

For example, if the word "dog" is stimulated, the mind–brain representation of "pet" becomes "primed". Primed words are recognized more quickly than "non-primed" words. Something like this explains the well-known phenomenon in which one hears a word and then often "hears it again". It is not that the word in question has suddenly become extremely popular. Rather, after it is heard once (primed), the likelihood of noticing it and its semantic associates increases because their activation thresholds for awareness have been lowered.

Semantic priming can occur in or out of conscious awareness. Words presented visually for no more than 200 milliseconds and appropriately "masked" do not appear in consciousness (see Chapter Three: Note 4). But consciousness is not needed to produce spreading activation and priming. Spreading activation is a basic, automatic brain process. Its constant operation makes clear that any attempt to suppress associations is going to encounter resistance. Thought suppression efforts are always more or less swimming against a current.

For our purposes, *it makes sense to see the connection-making tendency as more or less in the service of the motive to know reality. Spreading neuronal activation is the automatic tendency to approach proximal and usually meaningful associates of the contents of current consciousness. A process something like spreading activation is likely involved in how the body communicates its needs to the brain–mind.*

McClelland and his colleagues demonstrated that food deprivation causes people to think about food and related concepts such as fork and plate (McClelland & Atkinson, 1948). Similarly, sexual abstinence increases thoughts of sex (Clark, 1956). McClelland, like Miller and Lewin, never restricted his analysis of motivated behaviour to what were called *tissue needs*. His group determined that thinking about *social motives* such as affiliation and achievement, increase with deprivation in the manner of thoughts of hunger and sex (McClelland, Atkinson, Clark & Lowell, 1953; Shipley & Veroff, 1952). It should be obvious today that *all cognitive and social motives are tissue needs*. The needs of the mind were separated from the needs of the body only because until recently what went on in the gelatinous mass of brain tissue had been entirely arcane. Mental needs were seen as something other than biological. The behaviourists chose, somewhat wisely at the time, to "look under the light for the key".

Freud's method of free association essentially tried to watch the person's mind move from one concept to another. He assumed and verified that if the person was relatively *compes mentis*, they could move around in their own mind without too much fear and avoidance of ideas. But what we find always in psychoanalysis are *resistances* to *free association*. The patient becomes anxious, or has "no thoughts". Or, they attempt to steer away from a concept in mind and move to a safer area, for example, "Did you see that game on TV last night, Doc?" Resistances to free association are mental avoidances. One may be able to "change the subject" for brief periods. But all nodes of semantic and episodic memory are connected more or less distantly. In the long run, if one does not learn new concepts about him or herself, it becomes impossible to change the subject.

What is the nature of the processes that regulate resistance to apprehending thoughts consciously? The individual's self- and non-self-concepts are stored in memory and new concepts may be developed "on the fly" in the present. We know that attempting to suppress a conscious thought often backfires, resulting in repeated awareness of the thought. This happens especially in Obsessive Compulsive and Post Traumatic Stress Disorders.

Asymmetries in activation of concepts and attributes

Najmi and Wegner (2008) found an *asymmetrical priming effect* when people attempted to either suppress or focus on words. They asked subjects to "think about" (*Concentrate Condition*) or "not think about" (*Suppress Condition*) words such as "house" and "mountain". Half of the subjects in the *Concentrate* and *Suppress Conditions* were under *High Cognitive Load*. The other half experienced Low *Cognitive Load*.

Cognitive Load or *Stress* was operationalized by having subjects rehearse either a two digit number (Low Load), or a nine digit number (High Load). These numbers appeared at the bottom of the computer screen upon which the semantic priming task took place. While continuing to suppress or think about, for example, "house", all subjects were run through the Semantic Priming Procedure. They were primed on different trials of the experiment for 200 ms with the focus word itself ("house"), its associates (e.g., "roof", "door"), or unrelated words (e.g., "moon"). The key measures were the amount of time it took subjects to recognize after priming the prime itself (which sometimes was the overarching concept "house"), its associates ("door", "roof"), and unrelated words.

The results were essentially the same in three of the four experimental conditions: *Concentrate/Low Load: Concentrate/High Load;* and *Suppress/Low Load.* Compared to subjects primed with unrelated words, subjects asked to "Think About House" or to "Not Think About House" recognized associates (e.g., "door") faster than unrelated words if they had been primed with "house". They recognized "house" faster if they had been primed with "door" or "roof". And, they recognized "house" faster if they were primed with "house" itself. That is, recognition of both the containing concept "house" and its attributes was facilitated by priming regardless of whether subjects were intending *"to think"* or *"not think"* about the containing concept.

The central finding had to do with results in the *Suppress/High Load Condition.* In this condition priming with an associate of a suppressed word speeded reaction time to the suppressed word itself (i.e., "door" facilitates recognition of "house"). But priming with the higher-order containing concept did not speed reaction time to its associated attributes (i.e., "house" did not facilitate recognition of "door"). That is, under high cognitive stress, there was an asymmetry between the effects of priming on speed of recognition of the suppressed word and its semantic associates. Conscious suppression attempts worked better under High than Low Load but in one direction only. Spreading activation from concept to attributes was suppressed under High Load. The prime failed to cause activation from concept to attributes.

Most simply, we can describe Najmi and Wegner's results like this: When a person is performing many cognitive tasks and is then stimulated unconsciously by a concept they are attempting to not think about, stimulation by priming of the concept does not work to facilitate recognition of the attributes contained in the concept, but stimulation of an attribute of the concept will activate the concept. The conscious effort to suppress is focused on the containing concept (house). For some reason the suppression is more effective when the person is experiencing high stress (Figure 10). Why?

The processes of thought suppression

The ability to execute *simple suppression operations* of the form "Don't think of an elephant" must be learned by everyone. Simple control attempts amount to changing one's focus of attention. They work in the present as long as one is spending energy focusing on "distracters", for example, those things that are "not an elephant". But they do not affect more general dynamics regulating thought, that is, spreading activation. One cannot rid the mind of the neural structures encoding "elephant". One can only "push it out of awareness" by focusing attention on another node in memory or on incoming sense data. Simple suppression is a displacement of attention onto a distraction. It requires a lot of glucose (Gailliot et al., 2007).

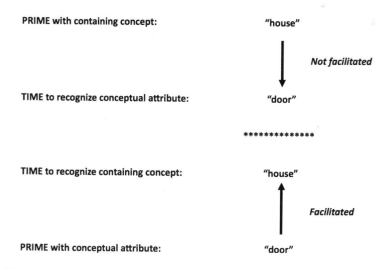

PRIME with containing concept: "house"

Not facilitated

TIME to recognize conceptual attribute: "door"

****

TIME to recognize containing concept: "house"

Facilitated

PRIME with conceptual attribute: "door"

Figure 10. Asymmetric semantic priming effects involving intentionally suppressed concept under high cognitive stress.

Because displacement uses a lot of fuel, it makes sense bioenergetically to exert effortful control on as few semantic nodes as possible to perform the suppression task. Logically, any attempt to exclude an item from conscious awareness has to include the ability to recognize the item. How else would one know what not to think about? Suppression, like negation, is an extra-cognitive operation. It does not "get rid" of the idea one wants not to think about. Something extra and energy-consuming must be employed. The process must logically involve:

1. Holding the suppressed word in an area of mind (out of focal awareness) in which it can be used as a standard to test items emerging in awareness.
2. Comparing incoming items to the standard.
3. Changing the focus of attention to non-standard items if the incoming item matches the standard.

It should be apparent that these steps constitute a Test-Operate-Test-Exit process. At least part of the process is consciously intentional in the Najmi and Wegner experiments. That is, the subject must attempt to comply with the experimenters' instructions to "think about" or "not think about" a word. I assume the intentional aspect of the process takes the form of inserting the word to be suppressed in some liminal area of awareness.

One gets "the biggest bang for the energy buck" from using as few standards of comparison as possible. That is, one does less work when suppressing the higher-order concept than when attempting to suppress awareness of all its attributes. When instructed to "not think house" the subject does not make a list of the attributes of a house and then use TOTE functions with all of them. Instead, they activate a process that uses the summary containing concept itself as a single standard for comparison.

This hypothesized process can explain the *asymmetry in priming* found by Najmi and Wegner (2008). This process must be continuous in order to ban the suppressed word from awareness. Since the *Test Operation* uses the summary concept "house" as a condition for initiating distraction operations, and since the concept "contains" all the attributes, suppressing "house" works to restrict from awareness a house's attributes. But if defences are not placed on the attributes, that is, if they are not used in TOTE operations, attributes used as primes *will* activate the concept. In other words, the defence is subverted via a "back door". This creates a constant stress to suppress awareness of the concept itself. In anxiety disorders, stimulus arrays or releasers that potentiate forbidden thoughts and actions are everywhere in the social environment. They prime the "defended against concept" all the time.

This line of reasoning suggests that we may differentiate neurotic repetition processes such as OCD from other more normal TOTE processes by assuming that there is "No Exit" when one is chronically on guard against a particular idea. Maybe this was what Sartre was talking about in the Play *Huis-Clos or No Exit* (1946) in which a character says, "Hell is other people". For our purposes we might say, "Hell is ideas one can't avoid".

Besides being expensive, attempting to defend against many ideas sooner or later will induce feelings of confusion and anxiety. It is more efficient in the short term to defend one fort than the entire countryside. Attempts to defend against every thought emerging from the external world or the unconscious can lead to depression and in some cases psychosis. The "ideal" secondary defence against the numerous attributes of feared concepts that cannot be managed by simple suppression is *paranoia*.

If one can attribute all mental disturbances to a single malevolent force in the external environment then defensive efforts are simplified. The paranoid already knows the reason for everything: "They are out to get me". Paranoia is the ultimate, simple method for "explaining" the world. It is the grandfather of all forms of simple-minded theories of the form, "It's all about X". The person's quest to understand reality is co-opted more or less entirely by the defensive need to protect against *disintegration anxiety*. We should note too that there are optimistic forms of paranoia in which the person imagines a single benevolent force to be causing everything. Mystical states are of this sort. But the underlying mental mechanism, that is, a process by which all events are attributed to a single cause, is the same.

But why did Najmi and Wegner find no asymmetry in the Low Load/Suppress Condition? That is, under *Low Cognitive Load* using the *concept as a prime* facilitates recognition of *attributes*, and using the *attributes as primes* facilitates recognition of the *concept*. Why do attempts to suppress a concept from causing spreading activation to the concept's associates only work under High Load?

If inhibitory processes are weak or not operating, spreading activation across a semantic network will occur spontaneously in the brain. High Cognitive Load may be considered an operationalization of the mental conditions underlying the well known *Zeigarnik Effect*. Kurt Lewin's student Bluma Zeigarnik (1927) proved convincingly that the person with many incomplete tasks has a better memory for the tasks than the person with only a few such tasks. The classic example is that compared to a waiter serving one table, the waiter with multiple tables is much more likely to remember the customers' orders. The validity of the *Zeigarnik Effect* has been supported by many other researchers (e.g., Greist-Bousquet & Schiffman, 1992; Wicklund & Gollwitzer, 1982). The effect has been described as: "the tendency to experience intrusive thoughts about an objective that was once pursued but left incomplete. The automatic system signals the conscious mind, which may be focused on new goals, that a previous activity was left incomplete" (Baumeister & Bushman, 2008, p. 122).

Najmi and Wegner's *High Load* subjects were rehearsing nine-digit numbers during the priming task. Their *Low Load* subjects were rehearsing two-digit numbers. Therefore, *High Load* subjects are much more likely to be in an "incomplete" state regarding their rehearsal task than *Low Load* subjects. The two-digit rehearsers are achieving almost 500% more completions per unit of time than the nine-digit rehearsers as they perform the semantic priming tasks. In effect, compared to the *Low Load* rehearsal tasks, the *High Load* tasks are creating more tension due to more *incompletion*.

According to the Zeigarnik phenomenon, the attempt to suppress awareness of the concept "house" from awareness should be more energized under *High* than *Low Cognitive Load*. In general, Lewin (1936) assumed that energy from incomplete tasks can be "borrowed" in the pursuit of other goals. So, the suppression operations are more competently performed under *High* than *Low Load*. This is a good model for what happens in OCD and other anxiety disorders. The anxious person always has "something else" they ought to be doing. Their ability to defend against thoughts is thereby enhanced. But it is easy to imagine how constant vigilance and TOTE defensive operations might interfere with all *executive functions*, especially memory. There is just not enough time and energy left over to attend to, encode, store, and retrieve items in memory when defence is the first priority of mind–brain.

I assume that resisting or denying valid ideas is more costly in terms of energy and time than resisting invalid thoughts. For example, denying a painful memory takes more energy in the long run than allowing the memory to have access to conscious awareness. It can result in mental and physical illness. This is really most remarkable. The mind and brain become ill if the tendency to approach valid ideas is resisted. This was essentially what Freud was saying about the problems caused by what he called *repression*.

These semantic priming experiments are very relevant to both normal and abnormal mental control processes. Mental illnesses all represent some failure to control the mind–brain. These failures to control the contents of consciousness result from a few basic factors:

1. There is a constant tendency for stimulation of any particular node in a semantic conceptual network to "spread" to proximal nodes.
2. If one cannot put in place valid self-concepts and processes to automatically perform inhibitory functions, excluding thoughts and feelings from consciousness becomes more or less a constant, effortful, energy-intensive TOTE process with "No Exit".
3. As the person ages, complicated mental control systems that might have worked in the past when more energy was available, will start to fail. Personalities that were functional in youth can no longer be afforded. Logically, the motivation to learn and to use more valid concepts should increase as time and energy decrease.

Semantic concepts and memories of episodes

Najmi and Wegner's results provide a model to understand defensive operations. And, they are consistent with Snyder's assumption that concepts contain attributes. (See also Mishkin, Suzuki, Gadian & Vargha Khadem, 1997). Compared to low stress situations, people under high stress are better at blocking the entry of the particular associates of concepts they are intending to block from focal awareness. The results are also consistent with the idea that dominant habits of thought are potentiated and enacted more forcefully when arousal or anxiety or cognitive stress is higher than usual.

Metaconcepts can suppress subordinate concepts (Snyder, Bossomaier & Mitchell, 2004). For example, the concept "psychoanalysis" contains the attributes "transference", "resistance", "ego", "id", and so forth. Thinking of the word "psychoanalysis" will momentarily suppress awareness of its attributes. So it is a matter of the generality or specificity of our focus of attention that determines, by definition, what is "concept" and what is "attribute".

Brain–mind is very flexible in this regard. And, this flexibility gives us great potential to "think big" and to "think small". We can think about the containing concepts or about the details making up the concept. It is most helpful when thinking about an "asymmetry in activation" to remember that the relation between concept and attributes or associates is already asymmetric. These relationships are *matters of truth*, at least as given by language. "House" is a higher-order concept than "door".

By definition, more valid conceptual systems are organized with more *true* relationships between concepts and attributes than less valid systems. Semantic memory probably provides structure for episodic memory. Semantic self and non-self concepts are our theories for explaining data. The data are the events in our lives, the episodes. Dreaming sleep is a process for lodging events in the meaning system.

Dreaming and all forms of thinking are more pleasurable if logic, rather than flawed assumptions, is used to determine the relationships between items in mind. It is a tremendous handicap to have self-concepts that interpret pleasurable sensations or memories as certain to result in pain. The extreme case is when all pleasure is imagined a "sin" and arouses Talion Dread. There is great variation in the ability of people to process the data of their lives. The more valid in a scientific sense are the self- and non-self concepts, the less difficulty there will be in development. One can operationalize the flexibility of the mind by assessing the *validity* of *metaconcepts* for understanding the theoretically possible relationships between things and events.

A *metaconcept* can concern "relationships between events". Logically possible relations between things, plus illogical ones, may be attributes of such a metaconcept. On the logical side, events can be related in a unidirectional causal manner (a causes *b, or b* causes *a*); in a bidirectional causal manner (*a* and *b* effect each other);

in multivariate, partial causal relations (*a* causes 70% of *b* which in turn causes 50% of *c*); in a coincidental relationship (*a* and *b* happened at the same time but do not cause each other); and so on. Events can also be in zero-sum relations. In truth, of course, some things are mutually exclusive (e.g., "life and anoxia"). But illogical zero-sum assumptions are made by many people. For example, "If I love her, I can't have sex with her"; "If he is of religion *X*; I can't like him"; "If one is good at maths, they can't be good at languages". As we have maintained throughout, holding too many invalid zero-sum assumptions leads to problems with work, social life, feelings, thoughts, and behaviour.

Theoretically, if one had perfectly valid concepts for understanding the world, they would never need to engage in ad hoc attempts to regulate the mind. The valid concepts in memory would process events effortlessly. One would then be in more or less of an optimal *Flow State* instead of a stopped, anxious state (see Csíkszentmihályi, 1990; Wicklund & Vida-Grim, 2004).

Such a conceptual system might be thought of as similar to *The Logos* or "The perfect wisdom of the word of God". More prosaically, the hypothetical individual with perfectly valid concepts for interpreting the causes of the events in their life, especially painful, traumatic events, would have the competence to be "philosophical" about such memories. They could "get over it". Painful episodes in memory could be transformed from constant dangers that stimulate suppression, projection, obsession, "acting out", and so on, into mere "data" that validated some law of nature. Instead, *nostalgia and romance operate as almost universal compromise formations when people consider their past, present, and future.*

But Nature has made ignorance and denial of ideas more costly in the long run than open consideration. Denied thoughts will repeat sooner or later. They can be controlled best if considered consciously with the aid of logic. The truth can hurt until it is accepted. It may still hurt after it is realized, but never as bad as when it is denied.

* * *

In the next and final chapter the theory developed so far is used to spell out a way to categorize mental illness in general, and systematize the relationships of mental illnesses to one another and to common etiological factors.

CHAPTER TWELVE

Diagnosing mental illness

Scientific understanding progresses through three basic stages: description, prediction, and control. Careful observation and description of salient, palpable aspects of natural phenomena is where understanding begins. It is the "fire and water" stage: an Aristotelian differentiation of one thing from another. Once objects are defined, the questions become: "How are these things related in time and space?" "Are they in causal relationships?" This is where experimental science comes in. Galileo's experimental studies of gravity stand in contrast to Aristotelian methods based on the hope that describing every last detail on an object's surface will reveal some "essence" or truth lying underneath.

The Diagnostic and Statistical Manual of Mental Disorders (DSM) contains descriptions of mental conditions. The first DSM was issued in 1952. It has been revised four times to date and a fifth revision is expected in 2013. The impetus for creating such a manual was the wide disagreement about what constituted "mental illness". The old story was that if you had ten psychoanalysts examine the same patient you would get back ten different diagnoses. It made sense to try to develop reliable categories for psychiatric disorders.

Psychometric Reliability has two aspects that are of interest here: *Inter-Rater Reliability* and *Inter-Item Reliability*. Both are easily quantified statistically (e.g., *alpha coefficient* for items; *kappa coefficient* for raters). *Inter-Rater Reliability* involves agreement between observers. For example, if all clinicians decide that a patient belongs in diagnostic category x and not y or z, inter-rater reliability is perfect. In practice, if about 85% of observers agree, inter-rater reliability is more or less acceptable.

The basis on which different observers make their decisions about the type of illness the patient has is the similarity of the assumptions they make about what is pathognomonic for a particular disorder. The DSM-IV uses sets of symptom descriptions that define each of over 400 presumably distinct disorders. The items making up the sets of symptoms are presumed to occur together more or less for each disorder. This is called *Inter-Item Reliability*. For example, the symptom list for Major Depressive Disorder includes: "depressed mood most of the day as indicated by subjective report or observation made by others"; "markedly diminished interest or pleasure in all or almost all activities of the day nearly every day"; "significant weight loss"; "insomnia"; "feelings of worthlessness".

Since most but not all patients with major depression have insomnia, for example, the alpha coefficient will be something less than perfect (i.e., 1.0). In practice, alphas over .80 are pretty good. The idea behind the DSM is that if you give all the clinicians lists of symptoms with high inter-item reliability, you should get good inter-rater reliability about the diagnoses.

All the versions of the DSM have had had moderate to poor inter-rater and inter-item reliability (e.g., Kirk & Kutchins, 1994). But one should not be too surprised or disturbed by that. The DSM-V will also have poor reliability if the strategy for producing it is similar to the previous versions.

The DSM was a good idea. One must attempt to first describe explicitly the phenomena one wants to ultimately predict and control. And, symptom descriptions are helpful in choosing and modifying psychopharmacological regimes which, of course, are used primarily to treat symptoms. But producing a DSM-V is "gilding the lily". Making finer and finer descriptions of the same old data is not the way to go forward. Continuing to cluster symptoms in slightly different combinations to define what are imagined to be unique syndromes is now largely a waste of time.

An appeal of the DSM is that it makes psychiatry like other branches of medicine. It too now has diagnostic codes for each disorder. (And, the medical insurance industry in the US uses these codes for a variety of their less than admirable purposes.) Such pseudo-precision makes it seem that psychiatrists and other doctors know more than they really do. Daniel Amen (2003) noted that until recently psychiatry was the only branch of medicine that knew practically nothing about its special organ of interest. This is changing and so too should our diagnostic scheme.

The major barrier to increasing the reliability of DSM diagnoses is that there are not over 400 totally unique, underlying mind–brain processes working to produce all of these symptom presentations. Similar symptoms appear in many patients; hence the diagnostic categories cannot be differentiated neatly and reliably from each other by means of symptom presentations alone. The brain, like all other organs, goes wrong 80% of the time in a relatively small number of predictable ways. The mind, conditioned by culture, is more creative with its manifestations of illness. But one of Freud's great insights was to see common mental processes underneath the apparent variety of psychopathological presentations.

The five dimensions of a DSM diagnosis

A complete DSM diagnosis includes ratings made on five different dimensions or "axes". Axis III includes the patient's medical, nonpsychiatric conditions, and Axis IV attempts to identify social stressors in the patient's environment. Axis V is a summary rating of the person's functionality. These are important things to account for. The most important and problematic ratings involve Axes I and II.

Axis I is used to rate mood, anxiety, cognitive psychotic, and somatoform disorders. These include Unipolar Depression, Bipolar Depression, Generalized Anxiety, Dementia, Schizoaffective Disorder, and Hypochondria. Most Axis I disorders can be treated today more or less effectively with drugs. The major exceptions to this rule are somatoform conditions and dementias. Axis II is the remnant of psychoanalytic diagnostic ideas. It contains Ten Personality Disorders, including Dependent, Histrionic, Avoidant, and Antisocial. It also includes Mental Retardation. Why is that?

Probably the best way to differentiate Axis I from Axis II is that Axis I disorders can be treated more effectively, usually with drugs, than personality disorders and mental retardation. Politics and economic issues affect, in part, DSM decisions. Patients and doctors would rather deal with a treatable Axis I disorder than a harder to treat Axis II disorder.

Fourteen different committees each comprised of people from different schools such as psychiatry, clinical psychology, and psychoanalysis produce the DSM. The manner in which obsessive-compulsive anxiety problems have been classified may indicate how such committees operate to some degree. They use *compromise formations*. For example, OCD can be treated more or less effectively with drugs and with cognitive therapies. It is classified as both an Axis I Disorder *and* an Axis II Personality Disorder, thereby satisfying both the pharmacologists and the clinical psychologists.

Everyone knows that the DSM is inadequate. There is no reason to make another edition. We should be making attempts to base our diagnostic taxonomy on *valid theories* of the etiology, the mind–brain processes, and the courses of mental illnesses. The reliability of measuring instruments are essential for assessing the validly of concepts. But we are not interested primarily in the reliability of the thermometer. Rather, reliability is in the service of finding true causes and effective treatments for the fever.

Personality

The psychoanalytic school now has published their own diagnostic scheme, the Psychodynamic Diagnostic Manual or PDM (2006). As we might have imagined, their Axis I includes Personality Disorders and their Axis II describes symptoms. They have used most of the Personality Disorders from the DSM but made a good change by relegating the term "borderline" to its original usage as a severity variable, rather than having it as a discrete type of personality. The PDM is more thoughtful than the DSM but it too is largely an Aristotelian definitional approach to mental illness. It is concerned primarily with mental structure but not mind–brain processes.

As stated before, personality is the sum total of all the person's mental habits. The entire set of habits is systematically influenced by the first foundational self-concepts. In mental illness these foundational concepts are in a more or less chronic state of unresolved conflict. Sensory stimulus arrays or *releasers* of conflicting instincts, and learned habits to both approach and avoid objects in the external world and the mind itself, stimulate signal anxiety.

In response to signal anxiety, individuals develop compromises in the form of mental habits that work more or less well to regulate thought, feeling, expectations, and overt behaviour. These compromise habits usually work to suppress awareness of the self-concept conflicts that cause signal anxiety. The foundational conflicts are frightening. They imply severe punishment for imagining taboo pleasures. The concepts were formed early on when young children behaved like primitive people who are governed by the *Rule of Talion* or an "eye for an eye". Incestuous and aggressive impulses are imagined to result certainly in severe, painful punishments.

At the foundational level, mind–brain conflicts are set in zero-sum relationships of the form: "Pleasure is a sin and must be followed by pain"; "If I live or am happy, mummy must die or be unhappy"; and so on. Of course, such concepts develop in the first years of life when the child is without the benefit of formal logic. Later in life, when adults come to treatment, I tell them that "reality is your friend; logic can help you create more room for thinking and allow you to consider many potential options for coping with conflicting wishes".

The compromise formations resulting from unresolved conflict are *derivative* or *secondary defences* such as rationalization and pseudological thinking. "Personality Traits" such as dependence, avoidance, histrionics, and so on, are also types of *derivatives*. Both Mr. K and Mr. C were dependent types. Their personality traits worked to get them into treatment, into their marriages, and to be able to be comforted by me, their wives, and others. But most of these habits did not operate as *proximal causes* of their prominent symptoms. Rather, they are deeper, *distal causes* working to both stimulate and support the *proximal* defensive habits that caused symptoms. This relationship between distal and proximal causes is revealed when using EMDR and analysing dreams. Attending in dreams or during EMDR to recent troubling events, leads to activation of concepts and memories associated with the events such as childhood traumas.

Perhaps we could neutralize the anxiety-producing effect of foundational conflicts by stunning the brain structures supporting them with *Deep Transcranial Magnetic Stimulation* (e.g., Levkovitz et al., 2009). Remember, Snyder was able to turn-off concepts by applying magnetic pulses to the surface of the brain at the left, occipital cortex (see Chapter Three). In any case, therapeutically important change is most likely to occur when treatment focuses on the *proximal causes* of disordered executive functioning. More or less of the personality supports these proximal causes. The case of Mr. C illustrates this point. He did not "resolve his Oedipus Complex" in treatment. Rather, he gained some flexibility in regulating his attentional focus without anxiety. In turn, his memory function increased dramatically. Ideally, these sorts of changes will, in turn, promote further development of more valid self-concepts to regulate the hard to change foundational structure of the self.

Figure 11 illustrates some of these ideas in the context of our overall model. It should be apparent that DSM diagnoses focus on the box at the top: "Overt behaviour including self-reports of symptoms". The PDM focuses on Foundational Conflicts and the entire personality and not especially on the proximal causes of executive dysfunction. Cognitive Therapy and my brand of treatment both concentrate

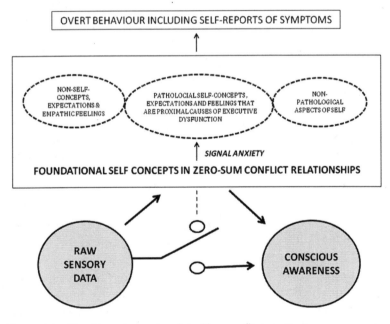

Figure 11. Signal anxiety, stimulated by conflict, activates compromise concepts and processing habits that may cause symptoms.

on the self-regulatory processes and self-concepts that are *proximal causes* of executive dysfunction. But the Cognitive School does not recognize the psychodynamics that are important parts of these pathological processes. Drugs work primarily by moderating something about the way that sensory data is processed and reduce anxiety, depression, and thought disorders. These sorts of changes, like the changes we saw in Mr. C's case, can have subsequent positive effects on the entire personality. This was described well in the popular book *Listening to Prozac* (Kramer, 1993).

Model for a diagnostic system

The underlying assumption of this whole book is the now commonly accepted idea that the mind is the functioning of the brain. It makes sense therefore to search for valid mind–brain relationships when devising a diagnostic scheme for mental illness. There has been an explosion of studies using scanning technologies including functional MRI to correlate subjective phenomena with brain activity (e.g., Sörös et al., 2007). This sort of work will produce valuable knowledge and controversy for years.

In the meantime, few workers have done as much as Daniel Amen to correlate brain activity with psychopathological presentations of symptoms (e.g., Amen, 2001; Amen, Hanks & Prunellla, 2008). Amen (2003) presents a set of Single Photon Emission Computed Tomography (SPECT) scan images that he correlates with different forms of psychopathology. I have adopted parts of his results and those of others to differentiate a basic set of mental disorders with different underlying brain activity.

I am proposing six basic forms of functional mind–brain pathology as the foundation of a neuropsychoanalytic diagnostic system. The six basic syndromes are: Anxiety, Cognitive Dysfunction, Depression, Bipolar Disease, Psychosis, and Somatoform Disorders. They are functional psychopathologies as distinct from psychological problems caused by relatively unchangeable underlying neurological conditions such as Mental Retardation, severe forms of Autism, Tourette's Syndrome, and Dementias caused by Alzheimer's Disease or extensive brain damage. The six syndromes satisfy important criteria for scientific validity:

- **Face Validity:** One can recognize each syndrome from words used in natural speech.
- **Predictive Validity:** We can specify predisposing factors and the course for each.
- **Discriminant Validity:** Different brain regions are affected in each condition. And, particular drugs work for some conditions but for not others.

The syndromes represent not only valid constructs supported by brain research, but also about the right amount of specificity for what we know today about mental illness. The over-precision of the DSM doesn't help. The inclusion of the entire personality and symptoms common to the six major categories such as insomnia, sexual problems, addictions, social avoidance, and so on, gives rise to all sorts of confusion. Treatment methods based on all of patients' symptoms are likely to miss the key mental habits that are the proximal causes of dysregulation of feeling and thought. Amen's SPECT scan results, plus results from others, are shown in summary form in Figure 12.

I have developed a set of symptom measures for each disorder. The items come from a variety of sources and include classical and some less widely recognized indicators of anxiety, depression, and so on. The clinician rates the extent of each symptom at initial evaluation of each patient on a 5-point Likert Scale (0 = none; 1 = slight; 2 = moderate; 3 = great; 4 = very great). Sometimes we make the rating ourselves and sometimes we ask patients to make ratings while we are talking. We don't give them a rating sheet to fill out. See Appendix I for the form used on the initial diagnostic meeting including the symptom

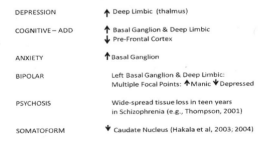

DEPRESSION	↑ Deep Limbic (thalmus)
COGNITIVE – ADD	↑ Basal Ganglion & Deep Limbic ↓ Pre-Frontal Cortex
ANXIETY	↑ Basal Ganglion
BIPOLAR	Left Basal Ganglion & Deep Limbic: Multiple Focal Points: ↑ Manic ↓ Depressed
PSYCHOSIS	Wide-spread tissue loss in teen years in Schizophrenia (e.g., Thompson, 2001)
SOMATOFORM	↓ Caudate Nucleus (Hakala et al, 2003; 2004)

Figure 12. Anatomical/functional correlates of symptom types based on scanned variations in blood flow/metabolism (cf. Amen, 2003).

lists. Appendix II lists psychopharmacological treatments for each syndrome and their variations. Symptoms displayed in Appendix II in bold type are particularly pathognomonic, for example, "diurnal variation in mood" for depression, and "reduced need for sleep presently or in youth" for bipolar.

Causal system of pathologies and etiological factors

If we have identified reliable disease constructs, we can start to study the causal relationships between the disorders themselves and common etiological factors. Multivariate statistical methods are particularly suited for such purposes (e.g., Heise, 1975; Kerlinger & Pedhazur, 1973). Figure 13 depicts hypothesized positive and negative linear, as well as curvilinear causal relationships between etiological factors and disease syndromes.

The model specifies that *Biological and Social Factors* work directly to increase or decrease *Internal* and *External Stress, Self-Concept Validity, Competence at Regulating Sense Data, Success at Love and Work,* and *Psychiatric Disorders.* Biological factors include genetics and metabolic processes. For example, it is beyond doubt that *temperament* is largely determined by genes (e.g., Buss & Plomin, 1984). Temperament varies on perhaps five dimensions: emotionality, soothability, activity, attention span, and sociability (Rowe & Plomin, 1977). If one is genetically predisposed to be very emotional and non-soothable, *Internal Stress* might be magnified. *Internal Stress* and *External Stress* affect each other (the bi-directional arrow between *Internal* and *External Stress*). For example, a stressed baby can irritate a parent who then acts out and increases the baby's internal stress.

Genetics also have some role in producing diagnosable psychiatric disorders (e.g., Burmeister, 2006). This is indicated by the arrow from *Biological and Social Factors* to *The Five Psychiatric Conditions* in the box on the right-hand part of Figure 13. *Biological and Social Factors* certainly affect *Anxiety* too, but the model assumes that these effects are indirect and mediated by *Self-Concept Validity, Competence at Regulating Sense Data,* and *Success at Love and Work.* While many variables mediate the effect of *Biological and Social Factors* on *The Five Other Conditions,* these are not specified in the model. Non-specified causes will cause prediction errors when these sorts of models are tested statistically. But an advantage of statistical modelling is that the amount of error can be quantified and, hence, can guide further specification of variables.

Social Factors such as family income and education surely influence the amount of physical, social, and mental stress a person is exposed to, as well as their ability to develop coping mechanisms (e.g., Marmot, 2004). For example, living in an abusive social environment causes stress and impedes psychological development.

An enormous number of *Biological and Social Factors* influence *Stress Levels, Self-concept Validity, Competence at Regulating Sense Data,* and *Success at Love and Work.* And, each variable has its own more or less unique sort of causal effect on variables downstream in the sequence of events leading to mental competence or mental illness. For example, social status might simply lower *External Stress* (an inverse, linear relationship). Or, moderate levels of social status might lower stress, but very high or very low status might increase stress (a curvilinear relationship). Similarly, the stress of intense physical pain is likely to decrease the development of *Competence at Regulating Sense Data* (an inverse linear effect). But there is reason to believe that moderate levels of stress experienced at the hands of the mother best promote regulatory competence. This is the sort of curvilinear relationship between stress levels and development described by Kohut's (1977) concept of *optimal empathic failure* (see Chapter Six). The figure uses arrows without explicit (+) or (−) signs to indicate that causal effects may include positive and inverse linear effects as well as curvilinear relations.

The model is more definitive regarding the hypothesized causal relationships between *Self-Concept Validity, Competence at Regulating Sense Date, Success at Love and Work, Anxiety,* and *The Five Other Conditions.* The relations between these variables have been at the centre of the book. We have assumed that *Self-Concept Validity, Competence at Regulating Sense Data,* and *Success at Love and Work* (i.e., one's overt behavioural competence) are in bidirectional, positive, linear causal relationships. That is, *Self-Concept Validity* promotes *Regulatory Competence* and *Success* in life. And, *Regulatory Competence* and *Success* in life tend to promote the development of *Self-Concept Validity.* These relationships are indicated in the figure by the bidirectional arrows tagged with (+) signs.

We have also discussed at length that high *Competence* at *Regulating Sense Data* and the *Success* in life it fosters, operate to reduce

Anxiety. And, that *Anxiety* affects *Regulatory Competence* and worldly *Success*. These are assumed to be bidirectional, inverse (–), linear relationships. *Competence at Regulating Sense Data* and *Sucess at Love and Work* are also assumed to be in inverse, linear, bidirectional causal realtionships with *The Other Five Psychopathologies*. For example, low *Competence at Regulating Sense Data* can cause *Cognitive* disorders; and *Cognitive* disorders can lower *Competence at Regulating Sense Data*.

Anxiety, especially chronic anxiety, is arguably the first and most important cause in a chain of events leading to more serious mental disorders. Control of *Anxiety* after all, if based on real threats to life and limb, confers an evolutionary advantage to the individual by stimulating fight or flight behaviours. This implies that there should be strong evolutionary pressures promoting competent anxiety regulation. The other disorders do not seem to promote survival. But some have argued that being depressed might improve decision making (Andrews & Thomson, 2009). Defensive operations are focused on controlling anxiety. There are really no comparable "defences" against *Depression, Somatoform, Cognitive, Bipolar* or *Psychotic* Disorders. The model assumes that these syndromes are caused, in large part, by failures in anxiety regulation.

Freud felt that mental development depended on coping competently with loss and grief. He claimed famously that "the superego is the residue of lost object cathexses" (Freud, 1923). That is, grief is processed by incorporating some of the valued attributes of those we have loved and lost in our own self-concepts. Does this process require a major depression to operate? Maybe, but clearly the issue determining the utility of any mental condition is *chronicity*. A little psychotic perspective now and then might give one insight. I am even recommending the use of hallucinogens in psychotherapy. But it seems implausible on the face of it that being chronically anxious, depressed, or psychotic can be especially useful. Chronic depression, for example, has been strongly associated with cardiovascular disease and diabetes (e.g., Everson-Rose et al., 2009).

In any case, that mind–brain states resembling mental illness might have some beneficial effects is not central to this diagnostic scheme. What is more central is the assumption that the *Five Other Disorders* in our system are related to each other and that each is downstream from *Anxiety*. The model in Figure 13 specifies that the

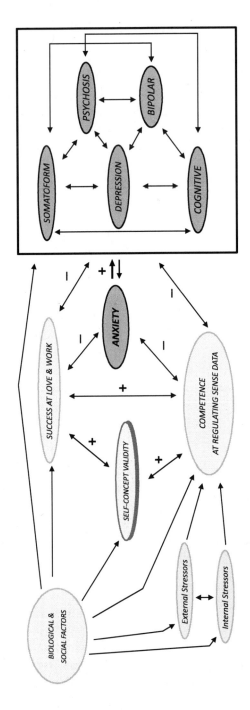

Figure 13. Causal system of six pathologies and etiological factors.
Note: Arrows indicate directions of hypothesized causal effects. (+) marks indicate linear positive effects; (–) marks indicate linear inverse effects. Arrows without (+) or (–) marks indicate positive **and** inverse linear effects, **and** curvilinear effects.

Other Five Psychopathologies increase as a direct linear function of *Anxiety*. Classic vegetative depressions serve as a prime example of this causal sequence.

Many or perhaps the majority of cases of *Depression* result from chronic *Anxiety*. At a certain point after suffering from uncontrolled anxiety for an extended period, catecholamine and other neurotransmitter systems become deranged and high levels of cortisol are produced. Then, post-synaptic catecholamine receptor systems become altered, usually by an increase in the number of post-synaptic sites. This can cause *disuse-hypersensitivity* (Freidman, 1977; Ghose, 1975). Once the number of receptor sites increases abnormally, small amounts of catecholamine in the synapses result in large sympathetic responses, especially on cardiac output (Meck, Martin, D'Anno & Waters, 2003) and subsequently, hypertension. An array of such complex processes in response to chronic stress and anxiety leads to vegetative depressions. If not treated, depressions may escalate via regressive defensive operations into *Cognitive, Bipolar, Psychotic, or Somatoform* syndromes.

The model also specifies that *Depression, Cognitive, Somatoform, Bipolar, and Psychotic* conditions affect *Anxiety* levels. How these syndromes affect *Anxiety* is complicated. For example, in the *Somatoform* condition of *Conversion*, otherwise free-floating anxiety is contained or explained by physical symptoms such as paralysis or pseudo-seizures. This sort of defensive operation can reduce felt anxiety (e.g., *la belle indifférence*). Accordingly, the model depicts the effects of the *Other Disorders* on *Anxiety* with an arrow indicating that these effects may be positive, inverse, and/or curvilinear. In any case, *Anxiety* is almost always a feature of the *Other* types of mental illness depicted in Figure 13. This is consistent with the idea that it is a temporal precedent of the other conditions, and that it usually persists as symptoms ramify (see Paterniti et al., 1999).

What about the relationships between *Depression, Cognitive, Somatoform, Bipolar, and Psychotic* forms of illness? Certainly, the symptom presentations for these syndromes are much correlated. The model assumes some of the correlations indicate causal relations. Certainly, the etiology of each syndrome involves some unique factors and some factors common to them all. The common sorts of factors include: distal genetic, metabolic and social causes; derangements in neurotransmitter levels and transmitter receptor systems;

changes in intracellular *second messenger systems* affecting protein synthesis; changes in functioning in various brain regions; and psychological causes, such as information-processing habits.

The nature and magnitude of the relationships between the disorders (correlation and causal) can only be specified with more validity by empirical research. The first step in such research is to unambiguously describe hypotheses about the relationships. Then, the research must be done to disconfirm and refine the hypotheses. And, the amount of error in any presumed relationship can be specified quantitatively by structural equations. The model depicted in Figure 13 is composed of reliable concepts of disease entities and plausible relations between them. It is underspecified in many ways. It is a model for making better models.

* * *

Appendix III outlines statistical methods for testing the model in Figure 13; and, proposes laboratory experiments to test some of the other central theoretical assumptions in the book.

EPILOGUE

The high level of competence to remember, process, and reflect upon semantic concepts makes the human brain–mind unique. Compared to how evolution operates via genetic changes and selection pressures among other creatures, human viability is more dependent on the validity of concepts learned over the history of the species—that is, culture—and during the life of each individual.

In non-humans, genes and the instinctual *fixed action patterns* that they promote, determine mostly the survivability of species and individuals. Individuals carrying genes conferring high selective advantages will be eliminated at a slower rate than others and produce more offspring. With raw evolutionary forces operating as "executive" the entire organism is killed for being less than optimally competent instinctively.

Changing mind–brain by learning and activating valid concepts about nature and the self can substitute for complete organismic death. A key executive function is to *deactivate invalid concepts and activate better ideas.* In other words, the executive must use a sort of *Kill Switch* to turn off repetitive, non-helpful ideas. Mental illness involves deficits in executive functioning. Those suffering from psychopathology habitually repeat thoughts, expectations, feelings, and

213

behaviours that are based on invalid self-concepts. These processes have been the central focus of this book. It is of course difficult to kill something, especially perhaps an idea that one is familiar with and has, in a fashion, come to love. But nostalgia for old crap is perhaps the greatest barrier to human growth.

Science and educational institutions have important roles in finding more and more valid concepts to explain biological, psychological, and social aspects of nature. Governments, businesses, legal authorities, and religions are responsible for using these ideas. In particular, there is an urgent need for increased cooperation between science and government regarding health care.

The strain on health care resources throughout the world is based to a large extent on ignorance about the relationships between mental and physical illness. Estimates of the proportion of patients presenting to primary care physicians for symptoms due to psychosocial stress range from 30 per cent to 72 per cent (Rosendale et al., 2005; Shaibani & Sabbagh, 1998). In one large hospital's Emergency Department, 76 per cent of patients presenting with "chest pain" had no discernable cardiac abnormalities (Abbass et al., 2010). "Patients with somatization have overall health care expenditures nine times that of unaffected persons, and over 82 per cent of patients with somatization stop working because of their health problems" (Shaibani & Sabbagh, 1998, p. 2486).

It is difficult to differentiate and integrate diagnoses of mental and physical illnesses. But not attempting to do so routinely causes patients and world economies to suffer. Every illness affects the mind and body. For example, heart disease causes anxiety and depression and anxiety and depression cause heart disease. Somatoform illnesses such as fibromyalgia, hypochondria, conversion disorders, and chronic pain syndromes are widespread. This does not mean that there are no tissue changes outside the brain in such cases, but that the primary cause of the illness is psychological. Somatoform patients usually present first to Emergency Departments, internists, rheumatologists, and neurologists. So, they are rarely given treatments for their psychological problems (for an exception, see Abbass et al., 2010). Instead they often receive expensive diagnostic workups, useless surgeries, and inappropriate medication regimes.

Post-Traumatic and Somatoform Disorders are among the most difficult syndromes to treat effectively. My experience interviewing fibromyalgia patients, who are mostly female, is that virtually all of them have a history of early sexual trauma. I think the sorts of tissue injury associated with normal aging cause pain and fatigue in these patients because they are under a constant cognitive overload similar to that created experimentally by Najmi and Wegner (2008). This idea is consistent with the impression of John Sarno (1991) that physical treatments for somatoform illnesses are usually useless. A brain-mind that is not attempting constantly to suppress concepts and memories can learn to "turn-off" signals from pain neurons.

There has been a well documented historical change in presentations of functional somatoform illnesses (Shorter, 1992). With new imaging technologies such as MRI, doctors can see, for example, that "there is nothing visibly wrong with your back". Patients have learned, in turn, to locate their pain in more arcane conceptual containers. In Freud's day, sexual abuse and other trauma victims might complain of not being able to move a limb, or feel anything in it. Doctors learned over time that many of these sorts of symptom made no sense physiologically. Today, the victims of psychological trauma present often with fibromyalgia and chronic fatigue. So far, no one (except perhaps Hakala et al., 2002; 2004) can find "fatigue" on an MRI.

The medical community needs to provide a valid diagnostic container for these patients. The case of Mr. K illustrates how a valid somatoform diagnosis works as a form of empathy and can help effect moderate improvements in such a patient's condition. The hypochondriac with chronic pain is more likely helped by a valid somatoform diagnosis than by, for example, back surgery.

Today, we can often help patients to alter habits that are the proximal causes of the dysregulation of thought, feeling, expectations, and behaviour. Awareness of these habits, which are derivatives of underlying conflict, is near the "top of mind". That is, these are not "deeply repressed" but rather "nearly conscious thoughts". Deep, foundational self-concepts are hard or maybe impossible to change. But basic self-concept change is not necessary to relieve most mental suffering. Conflict at depth will continue to generate signal anxiety more or less regardless of alterations of habits relatively accessible to conscious awareness. But remodelling the *derivative habits and concepts* can help regulate the anxiety. Drugs which act on the entire brain offer relief to patients, but there is often little we can do to change deep structures by talking to patients. Treatments such as EMDR and hallucinogens have good promise as effective therapies.

The classical method of psychoanalysis usually is not fully effective at achieving its stated aim of altering psychological depth. Freud was essentially a research scientist and theorist. The psychoanalytic method of free association is an excellent way to learn about the mind. It never was a very effective therapy except for some patients. Many of the patients it worked for best may have became psychoanalysts.

But deep structures and processes do evolve more or less over time. Developments at depth are very likely affected by changes in the dynamics of thought processes just outside of awareness. Everything in mind–brain is connected. The task of psychotherapy is to start where important change is possible. Over time, change processes gain momentum. Mind–brain grows in some deep way as do all living things. I don't know how my plants grow, for instance. But given sun, water, air and earth—they grow.

Initial diagnostic exam

NAME: _____ DOB: _____

GENDER: _____ EDUCATION: _____

TYPE OF WORK: _____

MARITAL STATUS:_____ CHILDREN:_____

SIBLINGS: _____

BP: _____ PULSE: ____ HT: ____ WT: ____ PAIN (1–10 max): ____

CURRENT COMPLAINT

PSYCH HISTORY

(INCLUDE TRAUMAS AND PREVIOUS TREATMENTS)

CURRENT SYMPTOMS

(0 = NONE; 1 = SLIGHT; 2 = MODERATE; 3 = GREAT; 4 = VERY GREAT)

DEPRESSION

Rating   *[Take notes here as well as ratings]*

_____ Sad

_____ Anhedonia

_____ Guilty

_____ Self-Esteem Problem

_____ Suicidal

_____ **Diurnal Variation** *(bolded items are especially pathognomonic)*

_____ Psychomotor Retardation

_____ Sleep Disturbance

_____ Eating

_____ Sexual (orgasm, interest)

_____ Low Energy

COGNITION

_____ Attention
_____ Memory
_____ [Neuropsych Testing Results]
_____ Reading and Language Difficulties
_____ Mathematics Difficulties

ANXIETY

_____ Generalized
_____ Bored
_____ Panic
_____ Agoraphobia
_____ Obsessive
_____ Compulsive
_____ Histrionic
_____ Afraid to be Alone
_____ Social Avoidance
_____ Post-Traumatic
_____ Startle Response
_____ Phobias
_____ Counter-phobias

BIPOLAR

_____ Racing Thoughts
_____ Pressured Speech
_____ Agitated
_____ Angry/Irritable
_____ Aggressive/Violent
_____ Impulsive ($, sex, drugs)
_____ *Decreased Need for Sleep, Now or in Youth*
_____ Elevated Mood
_____ Mood Changes (note periodicity)

PSYCHOSIS

_____ Reality Testing
_____ Disassociation/Depersonalization
_____ Loose/Tangential
_____ Delusions
_____ Hallucinations
_____ Paranoia
_____ Odd Behaviour/Appearance
_____ Negative Symptoms (flat, alogia, avolition)

SOMATOFORM

_____ Conversion
_____ Hypochondriasis
_____ Pain Disorder (note type, location)
_____ Fibromyalgia
_____ Body Dysmorphic Disorder
_____ Eating Disorders

Three additional important diagnostic questions

_____ Relationship Problems _____ Substance Abuse _____ Unable to Remember Dreams

Neuropsych testing results

(In percentiles _vs._ patient's reference group)

_____ Summary Index
_____ Memory
_____ Psychomotor Speed
_____ Reaction Time
_____ Complex Attention
_____ Cognitive Flexibility

MEDICATIONS

Allergies to Medications?   Yes/No _____

History of Seizures?   Yes/No _____

History of Head Injury?   Yes/No _____

Pregnancy Risk?   Yes/No _____

Smoke?   Yes/No _____

Drink?   Yes/No _____

ALL CURRENT MEDICATIONS

Meds	Dose	Why/For How Long
1.		
2.		
3.		
4.		
5.		
6.		
7.		
8.		
9.		

Previous Psych Meds	Dose	Why/For How Long
1.		
2.		
3.		
4.		

Favourite Recreational Drugs (ask about hallucinogens)
1.

2.

3.

SYSTEMS

Current/History/Genetics

Neurological

Cardiovascular

Pulmonary

Gastro-Intestinal/Hepatic

Kidney/Bladder

Endocrine/Metabolic

Dermatology

Muscular/Skeletal

Reproductive/Sexual

Eye, Ear, Nose, Throat

Immune

Cancers

Surgeries

Last Check-Up

Relevant Labs

Brief object relations interview

[Depression] Did you have a happy childhood?

[Separation Anxiety] Do you remember being anxious when you were first separated from your parents (e.g., first day at school, hospitalization)?

[Transitional Objects] Did you have a blanket or teddy bear, or a real pet like a cat or dog that you liked? Did you take it to sleep? Until what age?

[Estimate Transference] What three words would you use to describe your mother? Your father? Did they understand you? Three words for any other important adults or siblings?

> **Note:** Healthier patients will usually nominate two positive words and one less than positive word when describing one or both parents. Sicker patients will use either all positive or all negative words. Some patients will block on the third word.

[Trauma] Any illnesses or surgeries when you were a child or later on? Were you ever attacked verbally or physically by a parent or other caretaker? Were you ever sexually molested?

[Unconscious] Do you remember your dreams? Tell me your most recent dream. Did you as a child, or do you now, have any recurring dreams?

Initial diagnostic formulation

One should make an overall diagnosis using one or more of the six categories after the first interview. Also, develop some plausible, working hypothesis about the proximal causes of executive dysfunction or mood dysregulation and central self-concept compromise formations. Data from the Object Relations History and the Symptom Lists are useful for imagining how foundational self-conflicts may work to produce anxiety. Usually it takes about three meetings to generate a valid model of the person's defensive operations.

Consideration of psychopharmacological interventions should be made. Treating sleep difficulties and anxiety should be a priority at the start of treatment. Take account of what has worked or not worked for the patient in the past and their preferences in recreational drugs. Some people prefer being stimulated; others tranquilized. Anxiety can be reduced with tranquilizers and, for some patients—especially those with attention deficient and dementias—stimulants.

Treatment plan

Psychotherapy

EMDR

Psychopharmacology

Combinations of Treatments

Frequency of Visits

Referrals

Patient Informed of Possible Treatment Effects and Side Effects: Yes/No

Pharmacological treatments for six valid categories of functional psychopathology

Anxiety

_____ Generalized Anxiety
_____ Bored
_____ Panic
_____ Agoraphobia
_____ Afraid to be Alone
_____ Obsessive Thoughts
_____ Compulsions
_____ Phobias
_____ Social Avoidance
_____ Post-Traumatic
_____ Startle Response
_____ Counter Phobia

Antidepressants
Preferable to benzodiazepines

Benzodiazepines
Avoid Alprazolam if possible
Use longer ½ life agents (Clonazepam)
Impaired liver function: Lorazepam, Oxazepam

Buspirone
Rarely effective

Panic
Diagnosis most responsive to psychotherapy

Obsessions/Compulsions
High dose SSRIs and Dronabinol

Note: SSRI = Selective Serotonin Reuptake Inhibitor

225

Depression (Rule Out Bipolar, or Treat it First)

_____ Sad
_____ Hopeless
_____ Low Energy
_____ Anhedonia
_____ Guilty
_____ Self Esteem Problem
_____ Suicidal
_____ **Diurnal Variation**
_____ Psychomotor Retardation
_____ Sleep Disturbance
_____ Eating
_____ Sexual (interest, orgasm)
_____ Chronic Pain
_____ Attention/Concentration
_____ Memory

Sad, Guilty, Low Self-Esteem, Anxious
5HT: SSRIs

Low Energy, Anhedonia, Cognitive Sx
DA + NE: Buproprion, Stimulants
5HT: SSRIs
NE: Atomoxetine

Insomnia, Anxiety
5HT + NE: Mirtazapine, Tricyclics
(e.g., Amitriptyline)

Treatment Resistant, Atypical, Anxiety
5HT + NE: Duloxetine, Venlafaxine,
Tricyclics, Stimulants
5HT + NE + DA: MAOIs

Chronic Pain
Duloxetine, Tricyclics

Suicidal
Li+

Note: 5HT = Serotonin; DA = Dopamine;
NE = Norepinephrine; MAOI = Monoamine
Oxidase inhibitors; Li+ = Lithium

Bipolar

_____ Pressured Speech
_____ Agitated
_____ Angry/Irritable
_____ Impulsive-$, sex, drugs
_____ Aggressive
_____ Grandiose
_____ **Decreased need
for sleep**
_____ Increase in energy
_____ Elevated Mood
_____ Mood Changes
(note periodicity)

> **Bipolar I & II**
> *DA-2 antagonist; 5HT-2A antagonist*
> Risperidone, Quetiapine, Ziprazadone
> Avoid Olanzapine due to metabolic side effects
>
> *DA-2 partial against; 5HT-2A antagonist*
> Aripirazole
>
> *No⁺ channel block, glutamate release inhibitors*
> Lamotrigine, Oxcarbazepine
>
> *No⁺ channel block, GABA Increase*
> Valproate
>
> *GABA potentiation, Cl⁻ channel opened*
> Benzodiazepines (Clonazepam, Lorazepam)
>
> *Mechanism unknown*: Li⁺
>
> **Bipolar Depressed:** Quetiapine, Lamotirgine, Li⁺
>
> **Aggressive:** Risperidone
>
> **Weight Gain:** Ziprazadone, Aripiprazole,
> Lamotrigine

Note: DA2 = Dopamine Receptor Type; 5HT-2A =
Serotonin Receptor Type; GABA = Gamma-Amino
Butyric Acid; Li⁺ = Lithium

Psychosis

2nd Generation Anti-Psychotics
DA-2 antagonist; 5HT-2A antagonist
Rieperidone, Quetiapine, Ziprazadone

3rd Generation Anti-Psychotics
DA- 2 partial against; 5HT-2A
antagonist Aripiprazole

_____ Dissociation/Depersonalization
_____ Loose Associations/Tangential
_____ Delusions
_____ Hallucinations
_____ Paranoia
_____ Odd Behaviour/Appearance
_____ Negative Symptoms

1st Generation Anti-Psychotics
DA-2 antagonists worsen negative
symptoms & movement disorders
e.g., Thorazine, Haloperidol

Anxiety, & Depression
Benzodiazapines, SSRI's

Obesity, Weight Gain
Ziprazadone, Aripiprazole

Note: DA2 = Dopamine receptor Type;
5HT-2A = Serotonin Receptor Type.

Cognitive—Attention Deficit
Methylphenidate Dose Response Study, 49 y.o. man

Computer-Based, Real Performance and Reaction Time Test with Normative Comparisons (%tiles)

DOMAIN	BASELINE	POST 10 mg METHYLPHENIDATE
Neurocognition Index	10	32
Memory (verbal and visual)	18	18
Psychomotor Speed (finger tap, SDC)	7	30
Reaction Time (aggregate)	21	68
Complex Attention (Stroop Test, CPT)	6	16
Cognitive Flexibility (Shifting Attention)	6	34

Somatoform

_____ Hypochondriasis
_____ Conversion
_____ Pain (note type, location)
_____ Fibromyalgia/Chronic fatigue
_____ Body image
_____ Eating disorders
_____ Obesity

Sometimes Effective
Duloxetine, SSRIs, Pregabalin, Benzodiazepines, Tricyclics, Amphetamines, Modafinil, NSAIDS, Opiates, 2nd and 3rd Generation Anti-Psychotics.

Four types of testable hypotheses from the theory

This book spells out various neurobiological and cognitive operations that affect the competence of human thought, feeling, and behaviour. The validity of these presumed processes are testable empirically. The ideas come from neurobiology, cognitive-social psychology, psychoanalysis, medical psychology, and psychiatry. As these putative mechanisms involve variables at multiple levels of analysis, research must involve methods from the various schools used more or less together. Four types of assumptions might be tested initially to assess aspects of the theory's validity: .

1. Foundational self-concept conflicts, signal anxiety, and defence.
2. Psychopharmacological effects on mental habits that are proximal causes of executive dysfunction.
3. Multivariate statistical modelling of common etiological and functional relations between the six psychopathologies proposed by the theory.
4. Brain imaging studies to locate underlying brain areas and mechanisms for the Six Syndromes.

Foundational self-concept conflicts, signal anxiety, and defence

Incest is a primary taboo and its overt enactment occurs rarely. But the motive to commit the act is chronically stimulated, as is all sexual behaviour, by the presence of biological *releasers* (e.g., sensory stimuli such as prominent secondary sexual characteristics) that operate automatically in mind–brain regardless of social conditions.

I did a laboratory experiment to see if and when subjects acted defensively when a taboo idea was made salient to them (Bernstein, 1981, 1984). Male college students were asked to rate the physical attractiveness of their mothers; the intensity of their own sex drive; and their social closeness to their mother. These ratings were taken during a pre-term, psychological testing session including measures from other researchers. Three months later I brought 124 of these pre-tested subjects into the laboratory to take part in what was presented as a "cognitive psychology experiment". They were unaware of the connection of this experiment to the initial testing. There were two experimental conditions: In the *Incest Salient Condition* subjects had to arrange a set of nine tiles, each containing one word, into a grammatical sentence. Taken together, the set of tiles could only make the sentence, "I would like to have sex with my mother". In the *Control Condition*, the sentence was, "I would like to have tea with my friend."

Defensive behaviour was operationalized by asking subjects questions after the *Incest Salient* or *Control Manipulation*. They were asked to rate "the number of times they had seen their mothers naked" and "the number of times they might have imagined their mother naked", and so on. The assumption was that a way to deny incestuous wishes was to claim to have never seen or even thought about the naked mother.

As predicted, male subjects whose pre-test results indicated *High Drive* (sexual deprivation, no girlfriend); *High Sexual Incentive* (attractive mothers under 45 years of age); and who were Socially *Close to Mother* (e.g., "We hold hands while sitting together"); behaved more defensively in the *Incest Salient Condition* than the *Control Condition*. Subjects in the *Incest Salient Condition*, who had *High Sex Drive* and, who were *Socially Close to Mother*, claimed to have "never" or "maybe once" seen or thought about their mother naked. Subjects in the *Control Condition* with the same levels of *Drive* and *Closeness* claimed to have seen and thought about mother more than all other subjects. In other words, there was a three-way inter-action between: (1) High Drive to Commit Incest (attractiveness of the goal object plus sexual deprivation); (2) Close Social Distance; and (3) Semantic Salience (i.e., Activation of the Incest Concept), on the tendency to deny ideas associated with incest.

Psychoanalytic theory has never made explicit how unconscious conflicts worked to produce psychological symptoms. How might unconscious stimulation of taboo concepts affect the subjects with low and high motivation to perform forbidden acts? The idea is to use the lexical priming procedures developed by Meyer and Schvaneveldt (1971), Posner and Snyder (1975), and Marcel (1980), but to use more provocative social stimuli. The basic design of Najmi and Wegner (2008) used with normal subjects can be used to test some assumptions regarding thought suppression in pathological anxiety.

Basic study design

The relationships between anxiety and cognitive processes of spreading activation will be studied using lexical priming meth-ods in a "Between–Within" Experimental Design. The "between variables" will include individual differences between subjects' lev-els of chronic anxiety, anxiety symptoms, and neuropsychological function, especially memory. Executive function will be measured by the CNSVS computer-based method (Gualtieri & Johnson, 2006). Compared to others, subjects with chronic anxiety should have poor memory function (e.g., Airaksinen, Larsson, & Forsell, 2005). The "within variables" are the repeated trials of various sorts of seman-tic priming for each subject. The key dependent variable is "time to recognize words" displayed after subjects are shown various prim-ing words for about 200 ms and appropriately masked.

The aim is to discern more exactly how cognitive defensive proc-esses work outside of conscious awareness in normal and pathologi-cal conditions. Najmi and Wegner (2008) have learned something basic about how spreading activation can and cannot be inhibited by intentional attempts to suppress awareness of relatively neu-tral, non-emotional words. The question here is, "How is this basic process employed and perhaps altered in cases of chronic pathology where defensive processes, stimulated by signal anxiety, work more or less well to inhibit conscious awareness of particular semantic self-concepts and anxiety"?

The information needed for each subject is the type described in the case of Mr. K. He had a chronic anxiety disorder. It was due in large part to intense, largely unconscious conflict about his feelings of aggression. People who evoked ideas of his older bullying brother (i.e., transference objects) stimulated conflicting tendencies to aggress and suppress aggression. The relevant aspect of Mr. K's dynamic system is shown below:

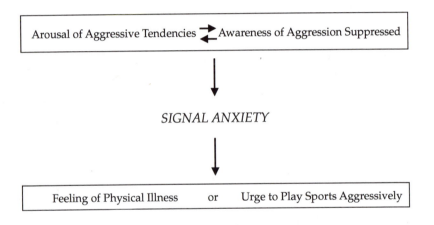

He developed various means to cope with this largely unconscious conflict: (1) Automatically converting aroused aggression into anxiety in the form of hypochondrical symptoms; (2) Holding a belief that it was permissible to express aggression in sports or other "legal", organized activities, especially when the provocative other person was clearly "in the wrong" or "immoral"; and then, (3) Playing sports which reduced his anxiety.

Experimental protocol for individual subjects. The pre-experimental task is to discern the specific, foundational self-conflicts and the central, habitual compromise defences of each subject. A model after the fashion of the one made for Mr. K (shown above) will be developed for each subject. These can be made by a clinician familiar with the current theory in about two or three hours of interviews for each subject. Note that the "between–within design" is very powerful statistically and, hence, only about 20 subjects will be needed for this first experiment.

Each subject's model includes specification of: (1) Central self-conflict (e.g., "I want to be aggressive but it is wrong"); and (2) Dominant habit of conceptual defence (e.g., "I can use my aggression in controlled conditions like sports"). For example, if Mr. K was a subject in the experiment. we would use a masked prime stimulating aggression such as "bully", "older brother", "humiliated", "frustrated", or some such word that triggers his aggression. Then we would measure the time it took him recognize words such as "hurt", "revenge", and "aggress".

We expect already anxious subjects to be able to better suppress recognition of associates of their particular anxiety-causing primes compared to less anxious subjects. That is, a Mr. K-like subject's reaction time to post-prime words such as "hurt", "revenge", and "aggress", will be slower than on trials where they are given neutral primes, for example, "moon" and "mountain". And, the subject will recognize such words slower than less chronically anxious subjects.

A Cognitive Load variable can be used to assess how increased contemporary cognitive load, over and above their normal chronic defensive readiness, might affect thought suppression. The assumption from Najmi and Wegner (2008) is that suppressive attempts are especially potentiated by being in a state of High Cognitive Stress. Subjects with chronic conflict and anxieties are already in a High Cognitive Load Condition. That is, they have a ready, strong repetitive habit to suppress awareness of aggression when it is stimulated by *releasers* in the social environment.

Najmi and Wegner (2008) found that High Cognitive Load enhanced subjects' ability to suppress higher-order containing concepts. For example, under high load subjects instructed to suppress the word "house" from mind reacted more slowly to attributes of house such as "door" or "roof". But these same subjects' recognition of "house" itself was potentiated when they were primed with the attributes of house. That is, the activation of the relevant nodes spread to consciousness through a "back door" to undefended associates of the intentionally suppressed concept. I would expect this "back door" route to be especially active in those with chronic suppressive habits. In short, we should expect a larger "asymmetry" between the effects of priming in anxious subjects than others. Recognition of the containing feared concept (e.g., "aggression") will be faster the more defensive and anxious the subject is about their aggression. To test this sort of idea subjects will be asked "to not think about" words we have identified as triggers for defence; and in other conditions we could ask subjects to concentrate on their trigger words. *Concentrate* and *Suppress* instructions might be operationalized as either within- or between-subjects variables.

Psychopharmacological effects on proximal causes of executive dysfunction

This general sort of design is amenable to many variations including using drugs such as benzodiazepines, stimulants, and anti-depressants to see how they might modulate reaction times and anxiety. Also, functional Magnetic Resonance Imaging (fMRI) might be used during the priming tasks to locate particular brain regions involved in the recognition and suppression operations. Additionally, the effects of therapy using hallucinogens such as MDMA to alter the dominant mental habits in anxious patients might be tested by lexical priming procedures such as these.

Multivariate statistical modelling to discern causal relations between etiological factors and six functional psychopathologies

Variables: There are 12 classes of variables in the model (Figure 13). Measures for the six types of pathologies are those listed in Appendix II (e.g., Anxiety is rated by self-reports of some versions of the 12 items including "general anxiety", "bored", "panic", "obsessions", and "startle response"). Responses will be made on five-point Likert scales. Measures of the etiological factors can be easily developed and will be collected in a similar fashion. Factor analysis will be used to reduce the complexity and increase the reliability of the classes of variables. Age and gender should also be added as demographics.

Subjects: Experimentation with the prediction equations will involve multiple predictors per each dependent variable. One would like to have 100 subjects per variable. This suggests a sample size of at least 1200 survey respondents. Controlling for effects such as age and gender will be done statistically so there is no need for making extensive, pre-study sampling decisions. But data should be collected within a time period of about one month or less.

Analysis: Path Analysis or another multivariate method can be used to determine the effect sizes of the variables in the model and the error terms for each predicted item. The design will be a "snap shot". We can do longitudinal studies later if needed. But a one-time measurement approach is simple and gives a good "bang for the buck" in regard to learning about the relations between these types of variables.

Brain imaging studies to locate underlying brain areas and mechanisms for the six syndromes

The fourth type of study suggested by the theory involves extensions of the work already started by others to find brain correlates of subjective mental experience in mental illnesses. The results from the study of etiology and relations between the hypothesized six syndromes should be valuable in helping to plan imagining research.

REFERENCES

Abbass, A., Campbell, S., Hann, S. G., Lenzer, I., Tarzwell, R. & Maxwell, D. (2010). Cost savings of treatment of medically unexplained symptoms using intensive short-term dynamic psychotherapy (ISTDP) by a hospital emergency department. *Archives of Medical Psychology*, 1(2): 34–43.

Airaksinen, E., Larsson, M. & Forsell, Y. (2005). Neuropsychological function in anxiety disorders in population-based samples: Evidence of episodic memory dysfunction. *Journal of Psychiatric Research*, 39(2): 207–214.

Amen, D. G. (2001). Why don't psychiatrists look at the brain: The case for the greater use of imaging. *Neuropsychiatry Reviews*, 2(Summer): 19–21.

Amen, D. G. (2003). *Healing Anxiety and Depression*. New York: Berkley.

Amen, D. G., Hanks, C. & Prunella, J. (2008). Predicting positive and negative treatment responses to stimulants with brain SPECT imaging. *Journal of Psychoactive Drugs*. 40(2): 131–138.

Andrews, P. W. & Thomson, J. A. (2009). The bright side of being blue: Depression as an adaptation for analyzing complex problems. *Psychological Review*, 116(3): 620–654.

Archer, R. L., Hormuth, S. E. & Berg, J. H. (1979). Self-disclosure and self-awareness. Paper presented at the American Psychological Association, New York.

239

240   REFERENCES

Arlow, J. A. & Brenner, C. (1964). *Psychoanalytic Concepts and the Structural Theory*. New York: International Universities Press.

Aronson, E. (1969). The theory of cognitive dissonance: A current perspective. In: Berkowitz, L. (Ed.), *Advances in Experimental Social Psychology*: 1–34. New York: Academic Press.

Aruffo, R. N. (1995). The couch: Reflections from an interactional view of analysis. *Psychoanalytic Inquiry*, 15: 369–385.

Bagemihl, B. (1999). *Biological Exuberance, Animal Homosexuality and Natural Diversity*. London: Profile Books.

Bailey, A., Luthert, P., Dean, A., Harding, B., Janota, I., Montgomery, M., Rutter, M. & Lantos, P. (1998). A clinicopathological study of autism. *Brain*, 121: 889–905.

Bar, M. (2009). Predictions: A universal principle in the operation of the human brain. *Philosophical Transactions of the Royal Society–Biology*, 364(1521): 1181–1182.

Bar-Anan, Y. B., Wilson, T. D. & Hassin, R. R. (2010). Inaccurate self-knowledge formation as a result of automatic behavior. *Journal of Experimental Social Psychology*, 46: 884–894.

Baumeister, R. F. & Bushman, B. J. (2008). *Social Psychology and Human Nature*. Belmont, CA: Thomson Wadsworth.

Beck, A. T. (1967). *Depression: Clinical, Experimental and Theoretical Aspects*. New York: Harper & Row.

Beck, A. T. (1976). *Cognitive Therapy and Emotional Disorders*. New York: International Universities Press.

Beck, A. T., Freeman, A. & Davis, D. D. (2004). *Cognitive Therapy of Personality Disorders*. New York: Guilford.

Becker, E. (1973). *The Denial of Death*. New York: Free Press.

Bergmann, U. (2000). Further thoughts on the neurobiology of EMDR: The role of the cerebellum in accelerated information processing. *Traumatology*, 6: 175–200.

Bernstein, W. M. (1981). *Denial and Ego Defense*. Unpublished Doctoral Dissertation, University of Texas, Austin.

Bernstein, W. M. (1984). Denial and self-defense. *Psychoanalysis and Contemporary Thought*, 7: 423–457.

Bernstein, W. M. (1995). On integrating cognitive and motivational explanations in psychology. In: Oosterwegal, A. & Wicklund, R. A. (Eds.), *The Self in European and North American Culture: Development and Processes*: 159–168. The Netherlands: Kluwer Academic.

Bernstein, W. M. (2001). Alternating patient posture. *Psychoanalysis and Contemporary Thought*, 24(3): 309–334.

Bernstein, W. M. & Burke, W. W. (1989). Modeling organizational meaning systems. In: Woodman, R. W. & Passmore, W. A. (Eds.),

Research in Organization Change and Development: 117–159. Greenwich, CT: JAI Press.

Bernstein, W. M. & Davis, M. H. (1982). Perspective-taking, self-consciousness, and accuracy in person perception. *Basic and Applied Social Psychology*, 3: 1–20.

Bernstein, W. M., Stephan, W. G. & Davis, M. H. (1979). Explaining attributions for achievement: A path analytic-approach. *Journal of Personality and Social Psychology*, 37: 1810–1821.

Bernstein, W. M., Stephenson, B. O., Snyder, M. L. & Wicklund, R. A. (1983). Causal ambiguity and heterosexual affiliation. *Journal of Experimental Social Psychology*, 19: 78–92.

Biederman, I. & Vessel, E. A. (2006). Perceptual pleasure and the brain. *American Scientist*, 94: 249–255.

Bion, W. R. (1961). *Experiences in Groups*. London: Tavistock.

Bion, W. R. (1962a). *Learning from Experience*. London: Tavistock.

Bion, W. R. (1962b). A theory of thinking. *International Journal of Psycho-Analysis*, 43: 306–310.

Boring, E. G., Langfeld, H. S. & Weld, H. P. (Eds.) (1948). *A History of Experimental Psychology* (2nd Ed.). New York: Appleton.

Born, J. & Wagner, U. (2004). Awareness in memory: Being explicit about the role of sleep. *Trends in Cognitive Science*, 8: 242–244.

Bossomaier, T. & Snyder, A. W. (2004). Absolute pitch accessible to everyone by turning off part of the brain? *Organized Sound*, 9(2): 181–189.

Bouso, J. C. (2010). MDMA-assisted psychotherapy using low doses in a small sample of women with chronic post-traumatic stress disorder. *Journal of Psychoactive Drugs* 30(4): 371–379.

Bowlby, J. (1973). *Attachment and Loss*. New York: Basic Books.

Brehm, J. W., Wright, R. A., Solomon, S., Silka, L. & Greenberg, J. (1983). Perceived difficulty, energization and the magnitude of goal valence. *Journal of Experimental Social Psychology*, 19: 21–48.

Brenner, C. (2006). *Psychoanalysis or Mind and Meaning*. New York: The Psychoanalytic Quarterly.

Bruce, T. J., Spiegel, D. A. & Hegel, M. T. (1999). Cognitive-behavioral therapy helps prevent relapse and recurrence of panic disorder following alprazolam discontinuation: A long-term follow-up of the Peoria and Dartmouth studies. *Journal of Consulting and Clinical Psychology*, 67: 151–156.

Burmeister, M. (2006). Genetics of psychiatric disorders: A primer. *Focus*, 4: 317–326.

Buss, A. & Plomin, R. (1984). *Temperament: Early Personality Traits*. Hillsdale, N. J.: Erlbaum.

Buzsaki, G. (1989). Two stage model of memory trace formation: A role for "noisy" brain states. *Neuroscience*, 31(3): 551–570.

Byrne, D., Ervin, C. R. & Lamberth, J. (1970). Continuity between the experimental study of attraction and real-life computer dating. *Journal of Personality and Social Psychology*, 16: 157–165.

Callaway, J. (1988). A proposed mechanism for the visions of dream sleep. *Medical Hypotheses*, 26(2): 119–124.

Caplan, G. (1970). *The Theory and Practice of Mental Health Consultation*. New York: Basic Books.

Carhart-Harris, R. L., Mayberg, H. S., Malizia, A. L. & Nutt, D. (2008). Mourning and melancholia revisited: Correspondences between principles of Freudian metapsychology and empirical findings in neuropsychiatry. *Annals of General Psychiatry*, 7: 9.

Carver, C. S. (1975). Physical aggression as a function of objective self-awareness and attitudes toward punishment. *Journal of Experimental Social Psychology*, 11: 510–519.

Carver, C. S. (2006). Approach, avoidance, and the self-regulation of affect and action. *Motivation and Emotion*, 30: 105–110.

Carver, C. S. & Scheier, M. F. (1981). *Attention and Self-Regulation: A Control-Theory Approach to Human Behaviour*. New York: Springer-Verlag.

Chemtob, C. M., Tolin, D. F., van der Kolk, B. A. & Pitman, R. K. (2000). Eye movement desensitization and reprocessing. In: Foa, E. B., Keane, T. M. & Friedman, M. J. (Eds.), *Effective Treatments for PTSD: Practice Guidelines from the International Society for Traumatic Stress Studies:* 139–155. New York: Guilford Press.

Clark, R. A. (1956). The relationships between symbolic and manifest projects of sexuality with some incidental correlates. *Journal of Abnormal Social Psychology*, 50: 327–334.

Clifford, M. & Walster, E. (1973). The effect of physical attractiveness on teacher expectation. *Sociology of Education*, 46: 248–256.

Collins, A. M. & Loftus, E. F. (1975). A spreading activation theory of semantic processing. *Psychological Review*, 82: 407–428.

Cooper, J. R., Bloom, F. E. & Roth, R. H. (2003). *The Biochemical Basis of Neuropharmacology* (Eighth Edition). New York: Oxford University Press.

Courchesne, E. (1995). New evidence of cerebellar and brainstem hypoplasia in autistic infants, children and adolescents: The MR imaging study by Hashimoto and colleagues. *Journal of Autism and Developmental Disorders*, 25(1): 19–22.

Craig, A. D. (2009). Emotional moments across time: A possible neural basis for time perception the anterior insula. *Philosophical Transactions of the Royal Society–Biology*, 364(1525): 1933–1942.

Csíkszentmihályi, M. (1990). *Flow: The Psychology of Optimal Experience.* New York: Harper and Row.

Davis, M. H. (1983). Measuring individual differences in empathy: Evidence for a multi-dimensional approach. *Journal of Personality and Social Psychology,* 44: 113–126.

Davis, M. H. (1994). *Empathy: A Social Psychological Approach.* Madison, WI: Westview Press.

Davis, M. H. & Stephan, W. G. (1980). Attributions for exam performance. *Journal of Applied Social Psychology,* 10(3): 238–245.

Dawkins, R. (1976). *The Selfish Gene.* New York: Oxford University Press.

Decety, J. & Jackson, P. L. (2004). The functional architecture of human empathy. *Behavioral and Cognitive Neuroscience Reviews,* 3: 71–100.

Deci, E. L. (1971). Effects of externally mediated rewards on intrinsic motivation. *Journal of Personality and Social Psychology,* 36: 451–462.

De Jongh, A. & Ten Broeke, E. (1998). Treatment of choking phobia by targeting traumatic memories with EMDR: A case study. *Clinical Psychology and Psychotherapy,* 5: 1–6.

Dement, W. C. (1994). History of sleep physiology and medicine. In: Kryger, M. H., Roth, T. & Dement, W. C. (Eds.), *Principles and Practices of Sleep Medicine*: 3–16. Philadelphia: W. B. Saunders.

Deutsch, M. (1977). *The Resolution of Conflict: Constructive and Destructive Processes.* New Haven: Yale University Press.

Diagnostic and Statistical Manual of Mental Disorders, Fourth Edition (1994). Washington, DC: American Psychiatric Association.

Dias-Ferreira, P., Sousa, J. C., Melo, I., Morgado, P., Mesquita, A. R., Cerqueira, J. J., Costa, R. M. & Sousa, N. (2009). Chronic stress causes frontostriatal reorganization and affects decision-making. *Science,* 325(5940): 621–625.

Dion, K., Berschied, E. & Walster, R. (1973). What is beautiful is good. *Journal of Personality and Social Psychology,* 24: 285–290.

Dollard, J., Doob, L. W., Miller, N. E., Mower, O. H. & Sears, R. R. (1939). *Frustration and Aggression.* New Haven: Yale University Press.

Dubreuil, E., Bouterice, B., Pérusse, D. &. Pihl, R. O. (1998). Reactivity to a looming stimulus: Twin study. *Infant Behaviour and Development,* 21(1): 389.

Dutton, D. G. & Aron, A. P. (1974). Some evidence for heightened sexual attraction under conditions of high anxiety. *Journal of Personality and Social Psychology,* 30: 510–517.

Duval, T. S. & Wicklund, R. A. (1972). *A Theory of Objective Self-Awareness.* New York: Academic Press.

Einstein, A. (1936). Physics and reality. *Journal of the Franklin Institute,* 221(3).

Ellenberger, H. F. (1970). *The Discovery of the Unconscious: The History and Evolution of Dynamic Psychiatry*. New York: Basic Books.

Emde, R. N. (1980). Emotional availability: A reciprocal reward system for infants and parents with implications for prevention of psychosocial disorders. In: Taylor, P. M. (Ed.), *Parent–Infant Relationships*: 88–115. New York: Grune & Stratton.

Everson-Rose, S. A., Lewis, T. T., Karavolos, K., Dugan, S. A., Wesley, D. & Powell, L. H. (2009). Depressive symptoms and increased visceral fat in middle-aged women. *Psychosomatic Medicine*, 71: 410–416.

Eysenck, H. J. & Wilson, G. D. (1973). *The Experimental Study of Freudian Theories*. London: Methuen.

Fairchild, M. D., Jenden, D. J., Mickey, M. R. & Yale, C. (1980). EEG effects of hallucinogens and cannabinoids using sleep-waking behavior as baseline. *Pharmacology, Biochemistry and Behavior*, 12(January): 99–105.

Fechner, G. T. (1860). Elemente der psychophysik (Elements of psychophysics). In: Wozniak, R. H. (Ed.), *Classics in Psychology, 1855–1914: Historical Essays*. Bristol: Thoemmes Press, 1999.

Fenigstein, A., Scheier, M. F. & Buss, A. H. (1975). Public and private self-consciousness: Assessment and theory. *Journal of Consulting and Clinical Psychology*, 43: 522–527.

Festinger, L. A. (1957). *A Theory of Cognitive Dissonance*. Stanford, CA: Stanford University Press.

Festinger, L. A., Pepitone, A. & Newcomb, T. (1952). Some consequences of deindividuation in a group. *Journal of Abnormal and Social Psychology*, 47: 382–389.

Fiedler, F. E. (1964). A contingency model of leadership effectiveness. In: Berkowitz, L. (Ed.), *Advances in Experimental Social Psychology*: 149–190. New York: Academic Press.

Fine, C. G. & Berkowitz, S. A. (2001). The wreathing protocol: The imbrications of hypnosis and EMDR in the treatment of dissociative identity disorder and other maladaptive dissociative responses. *American Journal of Clinical Hypnosis*, 43: 275–290.

Fonagy, P., Gergely, G., Jurist, E. L. & Target, M. (2004). *Affect Regulation, Mentalization, and the Development of the Self*. New York: Other.

Frazer, J. G. (1910). *Totemism, Endogamy and Exogamy*. London: Macmillan.

French, J. R. P. & Raven, B. H. (1959). The bases of social power. In Cartwright, D. (Ed.), *Studies in Social Power*: 150–167. Ann Arbor: Institute for Social Research.

Freud, A. (1946). The *Ego and the Mechanisms of Defense*. New York: International Universities Press.

Freud, S. (1900). The Interpretation of dreams. *S.E.*, IV–V. London: Hogarth Press.

Freud, S. (1904). The psychopathology of everyday life, *S.E.*, VI: 1–279. London: Hogarth Press.

Freud, S. (1905). Three essays on the theory of sexuality. *S.E.*, VII: 135–243. London: Hogarth Press.

Freud, S. (1912a). On the universal tendency to debasement in the sphere of love. *S.E.*, XI: 179–190. London: Hogarth Press.

Freud, S. (1912b). Totem and taboo. *S.E.*, XIII: 1–161. London: Hogarth Press.

Freud, S. (1915). The unconscious. *S.E.*, XIV: 159–204. London: Hogarth Press.

Freud, S. (1920). Beyond the pleasure principle. *S.E.*, XVIII: 7–64. London: Hogarth Press.

Freud, S. (1921). Group psychology and the analysis of the ego. *S.E.*, XVIII: 67–143. London: Hogarth Press.

Freud, S. (1923). The ego and the id. *S.E.*, XIX: 3–66. London: Hogarth Press.

Freud, S. (1924). The dissolution of the Oedipus complex., *S.E.*, XIX: 173–179. London: Hogarth Press.

Freud, S. (1925). Negation. *S.E.*, XIX: 235–239. London: Hogarth Press.

Freud, S. (1926). Inhibitions, symptoms and anxiety. *S.E.*, XX: 77–174. London: Hogarth Press.

Freud, S. (1930). Civilization and its discontents. *S.E.*, XXI: 57–145. London: Hogarth Press.

Freud, S. & Breuer, J. (1895). Studies in hysteria. *S.E.*, II: 75–312. London: Hogarth Press.

Friedman, M. J. (1977). Depression and hypertension. *Psychosomatic Medicine*, 39(2): 124–142.

Gailliot, M. T., Baumeister, R. F., DeWall, C. N., Maner, J. K., Plant, E. A., Tice, D. M., Brewer, L. E. & Schmeichel, B. J. (2007). Self-control relies on glucose as a limited energy source: Willpower is more than a metaphor. *Journal of Personality and Social Psychology*, 92(2): 325–336.

Gais, S. & Born, J. (2004). Low acetylcholine during slow-wave sleep is critical for declarative memory consolidation. *Proceeding of the National Academy of Science USA*, 101: 2140– 2144.

Gallese, V. (2001). The "Shared Manifold" hypothesis: from mirror neurons to empathy. *Journal of Consciousness Studies*: 33–50.

Ghose, K. (1975). Intravenous tyramine pressor response in depression. *Lancet*, 1: 1317–1318.

Gibbons, F. X. (1978). Sexual standards and reactions to pornography: Enhancing behavioral consistency through self-focused attention. *Journal of Personality and Social Psychology*, 36: 264–284.

Glass, D. C. & Singer, J. E. (1972). *Urban Stress: Experiments on Noise and Social Stressors*. New York: Academic Press.

Gödel, K. (1931). Über formal unentscheidbare Sätze der *Principia Mathematica* und verwandter Systeme. *Monatshefte für Mathematik und Physik,* 38: 173–198. (On formally undecidable propositions of *Principia Mathematica* and related systems.)

Grandin, T. & Johnson, C. (2005). *Animals in Translation.* New York: Scribner.

Greenberg, J. R. & Mitchell, S. A. (1983). *Object Relations in Psychoanalytic Theory.* Cambridge, MA: Harvard University Press.

Greist-Bousquet, S. & Schiffman, N. (1992). The effect of task interruption and closure on perceived duration. *Bulletin of the Psychonomic Society,* 30(1): 9–11.

Grob, C. S. (2002). *Hallucinogens: A Reader.* New York: Tarcher/Putnam.

Grover, S., Mattoo, S. K. & Gupta, N. (2005). Theories on mechanisms of action of electroconvulsive therapy. *German Journal of Psychiatry,* 8: 70–84.

Gualtieri, C. T. & Johnson, L. G. (2006). Reliability and validity of a computerized neurocognitive test battery, CNS Vital Signs. *Archives of Clinical Neuropsychology,* 21(7): 623–643.

Hakala, M., Karlsson, H., Kurki, et al. (2004). Volumes of the caudate nuclei in women with somatization disorder and healthy women. *Psychiatry Research: Neuroimaging,* 131: 71–78.

Hakala, M., Karlsson, H., Ruotsalainen, U., et al. (2002). Severe somatization in women is associated with altered cerebral glucose metabolism. *Psychological Medicine,* 32: 1379–1385.

Hasselmo (1999). Neuromodulation: Acetylcholine and memory consolidation. *Trends in Cognitive Science,* 3(9): 351–359.

Hawton, K., Salkovskis, P. M., Kirk, J. & Clark, P. M. (1989). *Cognitive Behaviour Therapy for Psychiatric Problems—A Practical Guide.* Oxford: Oxford University Press.

Heider, F. (1958). *The Psychology of Interpersonal Relations.* New York: Wiley.

Heise, D. (1975). *Causal Analysis.* New York: Wiley-Interscience.

Hines, D., Czerwinski, M., Sawyer, P. K. & Dwyer, M. (1986). Automatic semantic priming: Effects of category exemplar level and word association level. *Journal of Experimental Psychology: Human Perception and Performance,* 12: 370–379.

Hobson, J. A. (1999). The new neuropsychology of sleep: Implications for psychoanalysis. *Neuropsychoanalysis,* 1(2): 157–183.

Hobson, J. A. (2002). *Dreaming: An Introduction to the Science of Sleep.* New York: Oxford University Press.

Hoshikawa, M., Uchida, S., Sugo, T., Kumai, Y., Hanai, Y. & Kawahara, T. (2007). Changes in sleep quality of athletes under normobaric hypoxia equivalent to 2,000-m altitude: A polysomnographic study. *Journal of Applied Physiology,* 103: 2005–2011.

Hull, C. L. (1943). *Principles of Behaviour.* New York: Appleton.

Hull, J. G. (1981). A self-awareness model of the causes and effects of alcohol consumption. *Journal of Abnormal Psychology,* 90: 586–600.

Hull, J. G., Young, R. D. & Jouriles, E. (1986). Applications of the self-awareness model of alcohol consumption: Predicting patterns of use and abuse. *Journal of Personal and Social Psychology,* 51: 790–796.

Iacoboni, M., Woods, R. P., Brass, H., Bekkering, H., Mazziotta, J. C. & Rizzolatti, G. (1999). Cortical mechanisms of human imitation. *Science,* 286(5449): 2526–2528.

Ingram, R. E. (1990). Self-focused attention in clinical disorders: Review and a conceptual model. *Psychological Bulletin,* 107: 156–176.

Jennings, D. (2009). Pain beyond words, and an impulse just to endure. *The New York Times,* section D:5. September 21.

Jones, E. E. & Gerard, H. B. (1967). *Foundations of Social Psychology.* New York: Wiley.

Jones, E. E. & Nisbett, R. E. (1971). *The Actor and the Observer: Divergent Perceptions of the Causes of Behavior.* Morristown, NJ: General Learning Press.

Juliana, Y., Kolev, V., Verleger, R., Botaghava, Z., Born, J. & Wagner, U. (2006). Shifting from implicit to explicit knowledge: Different roles of early- and late-night sleep. *Learning and Memory,* 15: 508–515.

Jung, C. G. (1904). Studies in word association. In: *The Collected Works of C. G. Jung, Vol. 2.* Princeton: Bollingen.

Jung, C. G. (1934). Archetypes of the collective unconscious. In: *The Collected Works of Jung, C. G.* (Vol. 9). Princeton: Bollingen, 1954.

Jung, C. G. (1940). Psychology and religion. In: *The Collected Works of Jung, C. G.* (Vol. 11). Princeton: Bollingen.

Jung, C. G. (1946). The psychology of the transference. In: *The Collected Works of Jung, C. G.* (Vol. 16). Princeton: Bollingen.

Kalant, H. (2001). The pharmacology and toxicology of "ecstasy" (MDMA) and other related drugs. *Canadian Medical Association Journal,* 7: 167.

Kalivas, P., Churchill, L. & Klitenick, M. (1993). The circuitry mediating the translation of motivational stimuli into adaptive motor responses. In. Kalivas, P. & Barnes, C. (Eds.), *Limbic Motor Circuits and Neuropsychiatry:* 391–420. New York: CRC Press.

Kandel, E. R. (2006). *In Search of Memory: The Emergence of a New Science of Mind.* New York: Norton.

Kandel, E. R. & Schwartz, J. H. (1982). Molecular biology of an elementary form of learning: Modulation of transmitter release of cyclic AMP. *Science,* 218: 433–443.

Kant, I. (1781). *Critique of Pure Reason* (translated version, 1848). London: William Pickering.

Kelley, H. H. (1967). Attribution theory in social psychology. In: Levine, D. (Ed.), *Nebraska Symposium on Motivation:* 192–238. Lincoln: University of Nebraska Press.

Kemeny, J. G. & Oppenheim, P. (1956). On reduction. *Philosophical Studies:* 6–19.

Kemper, T. L. & Bauman, M. (1998). Neuropathology of infantile autism. *Journal of Neuropathology & Experimental Neurology,* 57(7): 645–652.

Kerlinger, F. N. & Pedhazur, E. J. (1973). *Multiple Regression in Behavioral Research.* New York: Holt, Rinehart and Winston.

Kernberg, O. F. (1988). Aggression and love in the relationship of the couple. In: Gaylin, W. & Person, E. (Eds.), *Passionate Attachments: Thinking about Love:* 63–83. New York: Free Press.

Kierkegaard, S. (1953). *The Sickness unto Death.* Princeton: Princeton University Press.

Kihlstrom, J. F., Barnhardt, T. M. & Tataryn, D. J. (1992). The psychological unconscious: Found, lost, and regained. *The American Psychologist,* 47(6): 788–791.

Kirk, S. A. & Kutchins, H. (1994). The myth of the reliability of DSM. *Journal of Mind and Behavior,* 15: 71–86.

Klein, M. (1932). *The Psychoanalysis of Children.* London: Hogarth.

Klein, M. (1946). Notes on some schizoid mechanisms. In: *The Writings of Melanie Klein,* Vol. 3, London: Hogarth Press.

Klein, M. (1975). Mourning and its relation to manic-depressive states. In: *The Writings of Melanie Klein,* Vol. 1, London: Hogarth Press.

Köhler, W. (1917). *The Mentality of Apes.* New York: W.W. Norton.

Kohut, H. (1977). *The Restoration of the Self.* Madison, CT: International Universities Press.

Kramer, P. D. (1993). *Listening to Prozac: A Psychiatrist Explores Anti-depressant Drugs and the Remaking of the Self.* New York: Penguin.

LaBerge, S. (1990). Lucid Dreaming: Psychophysiological studies of consciousness during REM. In: Bootzen, R. R., Kihlstrom, J. F. & Schacter, D. L. (Eds.), *Sleep and Cognition:* 109–126. Washington, D. C.: American Psychological Association.

Lamb, R. H., Weinberger, L. E. & DeCuir, J. W. (2002). The police and mental health. *Psychiatric Services,* 53: 1266–1271.

Lansing, K., Amen, D. G., Hanks, C. & Rudy, K. (2005). High-resolution brain SPECT imaging and eye movement desensitization and reprocessing in police officers with PTSD. *Neuropsychiatry, Clinical Neuroscience,* 17(4): 526–532.

Lanzetta, J. T. & Orr, S. P. (1986). Excitatory strength of expressive faces: Effects of happy and fear expressions and context on the extinction of a conditioned fear response. *Journal of Personality and Social Psychology*, 50(1): 190–194.

Lazarus, R. (1966). *Psychological Stress and the Coping Process*. New York: McGraw-Hill.

Leary, T., Litwin, G. & Metzner, R. (1963). Reactions to psilocybin administered in a supportive environment. *Journal of Nervous and Mental Disease*, 137: 561–573.

Le Bon, G. (1896). *The Crowd: A Study of the Popular Mind*. London: T. Fisher Unwin.

LeDoux, J. (1996). *The Emotional Brain: The Mysterious Underpinnings of Emotional Life*. New York: Touchstone.

Lerner, M. J., Miller, D. T. & Holmes, J. G. (1976). Deserving and emergence of forms of justice. In: Berkowitz, L. & Walster, E. (Eds.), *Advances in Experimental Social Psychology*: 1030–1051. New York: Academic Press.

Levin, F. M. (2003). *Psyche and Brain: The Biology of Talking Cures*. Madison, CT: International Universities Press.

Levin, P., Lazrove, S. & Van der Kolk, B. A. (1999). What psychological testing and neuroimaging tell us about the treatment of posttraumatic stress disorder by eye movement desensitization. *Journal of Anxiety Disorders*, 13: 159–172.

Levkovitz, Y., Harel, E. V., Roth, Y., Braw, Y., Most, D., Katz, L. N., Sheer, A., Gersner, R. & Zangen, A. (2009). Deep transcranial magnetic stimulation over the prefrontal cortex: Evaluation of antidepressant and cognitive effects in depressive patients. *Brain Stimulation*, 2: 188–200.

Lewin, K. (1931). Environmental forces in child behavior and development. In: Murchison, C. (Ed.), *A Handbook of Child Psychology*: 382–384. Worcester, MA: Clark University Press.

Lewin, K. (1935). *A Dynamic Theory of Personality*. New York: McGraw-Hill.

Lewin, K. (1936). *Principles of Topological Psychology*. New York: McGraw-Hill.

Lieberman, M. S. & Eisenberger, N. I. (2004). Conflict and habit: A social cognitive neuroscience approach to the self. In: Tesser, A., Wood, J. & Stapel, D. A. (Eds.), *Building, Defending and Regulating the Self*: 77–102. New York: Psychology Press.

Lilley, S. A., Andrade, J., Turpin, G., Sabin-Farrell, R. & Holmes, E. A. (2009). Visuospatial working memory interference with recollections of trauma. *British Journal of Clinical Psychology*, 48: 309–321.

Louie, K. & Wilson, M. A. (2001). Temporally structured replay of hippocampal ensemble memories during sleep. *Neuron*, 29: 145–156.

Maquet, P. (2001). The role of sleep in learning and memory. *Science*, 294: 1048–1052.

Marcel, A. (1980). Conscious and preconscious recognition of polysemous words: Locating the selective effects of prior visual contexts. In: Nickerson, R. S. (Ed.), *Attention and Performance*, 8: 435–457. Hillsdale, NJ: Lawrence Erlbaum Associates.

Marmot, M. (2004). *The Status Syndrome: How Social Standing Affects Our Health and Longevity*. New York: Owl Books.

Maslow, A. H. (1954). *Motivation and Personality*. New York: Basic Books.

Masterson, J. F. (1978). The borderline adult: Transference acting-out and working through. In: Masterson, J. F. (Ed.), *New Perspectives on Psychotherapy of the Borderline Adult*: 121–147. New York: Brunner/Mazel.

Masterson, J. F. (1988). *The Search for the Real Self*. New York: The Free Press.

McClelland, D. C. (1978). *Power: The Inner Experience*. New York: Irvington.

McClelland, D. C. & Atkinson, J. W. (1948). The projective expression of needs: I. The effects of different intensities of the hunger drive on perceptions. *Journal of Psychology*, 25: 205–222.

McClelland, D. C., Atkinson, J. W., Clark, R. A. & Lowell, E. L. (1953). *The Achievement Motive*. New York: Appleton-Century-Crofts.

McHugo, G. J. & Smith, C. A. (1996). The power of faces: A review of John T. Lanzetta's research on facial expression and emotion. *Motivation and Emotion*, 20: 85–120.

Meck, J. V., Martin, D. S., D'Anno, D. S. & Waters, W. W. (2003). Responses to intravenous tyramine is a marker of cardiac, not vascular adrenergic function. *Journal of Cardiovascular Pharmacology*, 41(1): 126–131.

Meyer, D. & Schvaneveldt, R. (1971). Facilitation in recognizing pairs of words: Evidence of dependence between retrieval operations. *Journal of Experimental Psychology*, 90: 227–234.

Miller, D. T. & Ross, M. (1975). Self-serving bias in the attribution of causality: Fact or fiction? *Psychological Bulletin*, 82: 213–225.

Miller, J. G. (1984). Culture and the development of everyday social explanation. *Journal of Personality and Social Psychology*, 46: 961–978.

Miller, N. E. (1944). Experimental studies of conflict. In: Hunt, J. (Ed.), *Personality and the Behavior Disorders*: 431–465. New York: Ronald Press.

Miller, N. E. & Dollard, J. (1941). *Social Learning and Imitation*. New Haven: Yale University Press.

Milton, J. (2000). Psychoanalysis and the moral high ground. *The International Journal of Psychoanalysis*, 81: 1011–1115.

Mishkin, M. (1982). A memory system in the monkey. *Philosophical Transactions of the Royal Society of London, Biology*, 298: 85–95.

Mishkin, M., Suzuki, W. A., Gadian, D. G. & Vargha Khadem, F. (1997). Hierarchical organization of cognitive memory. *Philosophical Transactions of the Royal Society of London, Biology*, 352: 1461–1467.

Mollon, P. (2005). *EMDR and the Energy Therapies: Psychoanalytic Perspectives*. London: Karnac.

Murray, G. (2007). Diurnal mood variation in depression: A signal of disturbed circadian function? *Journal of Affect Disorders*, 102: 47–53.

Najmi, S. & Wegner, D. M. (2008). The gravity of unwanted thought: Asymmetric priming effects in thought suppression. *Consciousness and Cognition*, 17: 114–124.

Naranjo, C., Shulgin, A. T. & Sargent, T. (1967). Evaluation of 3,4-methylenedioxyamphetamine (MDA) as an adjunct to psychotherapy. *Medical Pharmacology, Experimental*, 17: 359–364.

Neisser, U. (1976). *Cognition and Reality*. San Francisco: Freeman.

Osgood, C. E., Succi, G. J. & Tannenbaum, P. H. (1957). *The Measurement of Meaning*. The Urbana: University of Illinois Press.

Pascual-Leone, A., Bartres-Fax, D. & Keenan, J. P. (1999). Transcranial magnetic stimulation: Studying the brain-behaviour relationship by induction of "virtual lesions". *Philos. T. Roy. Soc. B.*, 354: 1229–1238.

Paterniti, S., Alperovich, A., Ducimetiere, P., Dealberto, M. J., Lepine, J. P. & Bisserbe, J. C. (1999). Anxiety but not depression is associated with elevated blood pressure in a community of French elderly. *Psychosomatic Medicine*, 61(1): 77–83.

PDM Task Force (2006). *Psychodynamic Diagnostic Manual*. Silver Spring, MD: Alliance of Psychoanalytic Organizations.

Piaget, J. (1928). *Judgement and Reasoning in the Child*. London: Routledge & Kegan Paul.

Piaget, J. (1954). *Construction of Reality in the Child*. New York: Basic Books.

Pillemer, D. B. & White, S. H. (1989). Childhood events recalled by children and adults. *Advances in Child Development and Behavior*, 21: 297–340.

Posner, M. I. & Petersen, S. E. (1990). The attention system of the human brain. *Annual Review of Neuroscience*, 13: 25–42.

Posner, M. I. & Snyder, C. R. R. (1975). Attention and cognitive control. In: Solso, R. L. (Ed.), *Information Processing and Cognition: The Loyola Symposion*. Hillsdale, NJ: Lawrence Erlbaum Associates Inc.

Pryor, J. B., Gibbons, F. X., Wicklund, R. A., Fazio, R. H. & Hood, R. (1977). Self-focused attention and self-report validity. *Journal of Personality*, 45: 513–527.

Pryor, J. B. & Kriss, M. (1977). The cognitive dynamics of salience in the attribution process. *Journal of Personality and Social Psychology*, 35: 49–55.

Reich, W. (1933). *Character Analysis*. New York: Farrar, Straus. & Giroux.

Reik, T. (1948). *Listening with the Third Ear: The Inner Experience of a Psychoanalyst*. New York: Grove Press.

Rind, F. C., Santer, D. & Wright, G. A. (2008). Arousal facilitates collision avoidance mediated by a looming sensitive visual neuron in a flying locust. *Journal of Neurophysiology*, 100: 670–680.

Rizzolatti, G. & Craighero, L. (2004). The mirror-neuron system. *Annual Review of Neuroscience*, 27: 169–192.

Rosenblatt, A., Greenberg, J., Solomon, S., Pyszczynski, T. & Lyon, D. (1989). Evidence for terror management theory: I. The effects of mortality salience on reactions to those who violate or uphold cultural values. *Journal of Personality and Social Psychology*, 57: 681–690.

Rosendal, M., Olesen, F. & Fink, P. (2005). Management of medical unexplained symptoms. *British Medical Journal*, 330: 4–5.

Roth, P. (1969). *Portnoy's Complaint*. New York: Random House.

Rowe, D. C. & Plomin, R. (1977). Temperament in early childhood. *Journal of Personality Assessment*, 41: 150–156.

Ryan, R. M. & Deci, E. L. (2000). Intrinsic and extrinsic Motivations: Classic definitions and new directions. *Contemporary Educational Psychology*, 25, 1:54–67.

Sacks, O. (1985). *The Man Who Mistook His Wife for a Hat*. London: Duckworth.

Sacks, O. (2007). *Musicophilia: Tales of Music and the Brain*. New York: Knopf.

Sarno, J. E. (1991). *Healing Back Pain: The Mind Body Connection*. New York: Warner Books.

Sartre, J. P. (1946). *No Exit*. New York: Vintage Books.

Schachter, S. & Singer, J. (1962). Cognitive, social, and physiological determinants of the emotional state. *Psychological Review*, 69: 379–399.

Scheier, M. F. & Carver, C. S. (1977). Self-focused attention and the experience of emotion: Attraction, repulsion, elations and depression. *Journal of Personality and Social Psychology*, 35: 625–636.

Schiff, W., Caviness, J. A. & Gibson, J. J. (1962). Persistent fear responses in rhesus monkeys to the optical stimulus of "looming". *Science*, 15(136): 982–983.

Schore, A. N. (2003). *Affect Dysregulation and Disorders of the Self*. New York: Norton.

Segal, H. (1967). Melanie Klien's technique. *Psychoanalytic Forum*, 2: 212–227.

Shaibani, A. & Sabbagh, M. N. (1998). Pseudoneurologic syndromes: recognition and diagnosis. *American Family Physician*, 15; 57(10): 2485–2494.

Shakespeare, W. (1984). Edwards, P. (Ed.), *Hamlet, Prince of Denmark*. Cambridge: Cambridge University Press.

Shapiro, C. M., Bortz, R., Mitchell, D., Bartel, P. & Jooste, P. (1981). Slow-wave sleep: A recovery period after exercise. *Science*, 11(4526): 1253–1254.

Shapiro, D. (2000). *Dynamics of Character: Self Regulation in Psychopathology*. New York: Basic Books.

Shapiro, F. (2001). *Eye Movement Desensitization and Reprocessing (EMDR)* (2nd Ed.). New York: Guilford Press.

Shaver, K. G. (1975). *An Introduction to Attribution Processes*. Cambridge, MA: Winthrop.

Shipley, T. E. & Veroff, J. (1952). A projective measure of need affiliation. *Journal of Experimental Psychology*, 43: 349–356.

Shorter, E. (1992). *From Paralysis to Fatigue: A History of Psychosomatic Illness in the Modern Era*. New York: Free Press.

Silva, P. J. & Duval, T. J. (2001). Objective self-awareness theory: Recent progress and enduring problems. *Personality and Social Psychology Review*, 5: 230–240.

Smith, C. A., McHugo, J. A. & Kappas, A. (2005). Epilogue: Overarching themes and enduring contributions of the Lanzetta research program. *Motivation and Emotion*, 20(3): 237–253. Netherlands: Springer.

Snyder, A. W. (2009). Explaining and inducing savant skills: Privileged access to lower level, less processed information. *Philosophical Transactions of the Royal Society of London, Biology*, 364(1522): 1399–1405.

Snyder, A. W., Bahramali, H., Hawker, T. & Mitchell, D. J. (2006). Savant-like numerosity skills revealed in normal people by magnetic pulses. *Perception*, 35: 837–845.

Snyder, A. W., Bossomaier, T. & Mitchell, D. J. (2004). Concept formation: "Object" attributes dynamically inhibited from conscious awareness. *Journal of Integrative Neuroscience*, 3: 31–46.

Snyder, A. W. & Mitchell, D. J. (1999). Is integer arithmetic fundamental to mental processing?: The mind's secret arithmetic. *Proceedings of the Royal Society of London, Biology*, 266: 587–593.

Snyder, A. W., Mulcahy, E., Taylor, J. L., Mitchell, D. J., Sachdev, P. & Gandevia, S. C. (2003). Savant-like skills exposed in normal people by suppressing the left fronto-temporal lobe. *Journal of Integrative Neuroscience*, 2: 149–158.

Snyder, M. L., Kleck, R. E., Strenta, A. & Mentzer, S. J. (1979). Avoidance of the handicapped: An attributional ambiguity analysis. *Journal of Personality and Social Psychology*, 37: 93–100.

Snyder, M. L., Stephan, W. G. & Rosenfeld, D. (1978). Attributional egotism. In: Harvey, J., Ickes, W. & Kidd, R. (Eds.), *New Directions in Attribution Research*: 91–117. Hillsdale, NJ: Erlbaum.

Snyder, M. L. & Wicklund, R. A. (1981). Attribute ambiguity. In: Harvey, J. H., Ickes, W. & Kidd, R. F. (Eds.), *New Directions in Attribution Research*: 197–221. Hillsdale, NJ: Erlbaum.

Solms, M. & Turnbull, O. (2002). *The Brain and the Inner World: An Introduction to the Neuroscience of Subjective Experience*. New York: Other Press.

Solomon, S., Greenberg, J. & Pyszczynski, T. (1991). Terror management theory. In: Zanna, M. P. (Ed.), *Advances in Experimental Social Psychology*: 93–159. New York: Academic Press.

Sörös, P., Marmurek, J., Tam, F., Baker, N., Staines, W. R. & Graham, S. J. (2007). Functional MRI of working memory and selective attention in vibrotactile frequency discrimination. *BMC Neuroscience* 2007, 8: 48.

Spence, K. W. (1956). *Behavior Theory and Conditioning*. New Haven: Yale University Press.

Stahl, S. M. (2008). *Essential Psychopharmacology: Neuroscientific Basis and Practical Applications* (3rd ed.). New York: Cambridge University Press.

Stark, M. (1994). *Working with resistance*. Lanham, MD: Jason Aronson.

Steffen, G., Bjorn, R., Ullrich, W. & Born, J, (2008). Visual-Procedural memory consolidation during sleep blocked by glutamenergic receptor antagonists. *The Journal of Neuroscience*, 28(21): 5513–5518.

Stephan, W. G., Bernstein, W. M., Davis, M. H. & Stephan, C. (1979). Attributions for achievement: Egotism vs. expectancy confirmation. *Social Psychology Quarterly*, 42: 5–17.

Stephan, W. G. & Gollwitzer, P. M. (1981). Affect as a mediator of attributional egotism. *Journal of Experimental Social Psychology*, 17(5): 443–458.

Stern, D. (1985). *The Interpersonal World of the Infant*. New York: Basic Books.

Stickgold, R. (2002). EMDR: A putative neurobiological mechanism of action. *Journal of Clinical Psychology*, 58: 61–75.

Stickgold, R. (2005). Sleep dependent memory consolidation. *Nature*, 437: 1272–1278.

Strachey, J. (1934). The nature of the therapeutic action of psychoanalysis. *International Journal of Psycho-Analysis*, 15: 117–126.

Sullivan, H. S. (1970). *The Psychiatric Interview*. New York: Norton.

Swerdlow, N. R. & Koob, G. F. (1987). Dopamine, schizophrenia, mania, and depression: Toward a unified hypothesis of cortico-striato-pallido-thalamic function. *Behavioral and Brain Sciences*, 10: 197–245.

Tauber, E. S. (1982). Preoccupation with immortality expressive of a negation of life. *Contemporary Psychoanalysis*, 18: 119–132.

Taylor, J. A. (1953). A personality scale of manifest anxiety. *The Journal of Abnormal and Social Psychology*, 48(2): 285–290.

Thompson, P. M., Vidal, C., Giedd, J. N., Gochman, P., Blumenthal, J., Nicolson, R., Toga, A. W. & Rapoport, J. L. (2001). Mapping adolescent brain change reveals dynamic wave of accelerated gray matter loss in very early-onset schizophrenia. *Proceedings of the National Academy of Science*, 98 (20): 650–655.

Thorndike, E. L. (1913). *The Psychology of Learning*. New York: Teachers College.

Tinbergen, N. (1951). *The Study of Instinct*. London and New York: Oxford University Press.

Tronick, E. Z., Als, H., Adamson, L., Wise, S. & Brazelton, T. B. (1978). The infants' response to entrapment between contradictory messages in face to face interaction. *Journal of the American Academy of Child Psychiatry*, 17: 1–13.

Tulving, E. (1972). Episodic and semantic memory. In: Tulving, E. & Donaldson, W. (Eds.), *Organization of Memory*: 381–403. New York Academic Press.

Tulving, E. (2002). Episodic memory: from mind to brain. *Annual Review of Psychology*, 53: 1–25.

Tulving, E. & Szpunar, K. K. (2009). Episodic memory. *Scholarpedia*, 4(8): 3332.

Van der Kolk, B. A. (2002). In Terror's Grip: Healing the ravages of trauma. *Cerebrum*, 4: 34–50. New York: The Dana Foundation.

Wagner, U., Gais, S., Haider, H., Verleger, R. & Born, J. (2004). Sleep inspires insight. *Nature*, 427: 352–355.

Wallach, J. V. (2009). Endogenous hallucinogens as ligands of the trace amine receptors: A possible role in sensory perception. *Medical Hypotheses*, 72(1): 91–94.

Wasson, R. G. (1980). *The Wondrous Mushroom*. New York: McGraw-Hill.

Weber, S., Habel, U., Amunts, K. & Schneider, F. (2008). Structural brain abnormalities in psychopaths-a review. *Behavioral Sciences & the Law*, 26(1): 7–28.

Wegner, D. M. & Erber, R. E. (1992). The hyper-accessibility of suppressed thoughts. *Journal of Personality and Social Psychology*, 63: 903–912.

Wegner, D. W. & Pennebaker, J. W. (1993). Introduction. *Handbook of Mental Control*. Englewood Cliffs, NJ: Prentice Hall.

Weil, A. T. (1980). *Marriage of Sun and Moon: Dispatches from the Frontiers of Consciousness*. New York: Houghton-Mifflin.

Wertheimer, M. (1923). Untersuchungen zur Lehre von der Gestalt (Laws of organization in perceptual forms). *Psycologische Forschung*, 4: 301–350.

Weston, D. (1999). The scientific status of unconscious processes: Is Freud really dead? *Journal of the American Psychoanalytic Association*, 47(4): 1061–1106.

Whittle, P. (1999). Experimental psychology and psychoanalysis: What we can learn from a century of misunderstanding. *Neuropsychoanalysis*, 1(2): 233–247.

Wicklund, R. A. & Brehm, J. W. (1976). *Perspectives on Cognitive Dissonance*. Hillsdale, NJ: Lawrence Erlbaum.

Wicklund, R. A. & Gollwitzer, P. M. (1982). *Symbolic Self-Completion*. Hillsdale, NJ: Erlbaum.

Wicklund, R. A. & Vida-Grim, R. (2004). Bellezza in interpersonal relations. In: Greenberg, J., Koole, S. L. & Pyszczynski, T. (Eds.), *Handbook of Experimental Existential Psychology*: 369–382. New York: Guilford.

Wilson, E. O. (1999). *Consilience: The Unity of Knowledge*. New York: Vintage Books.

Winnicott, D. W. (1953). Transitional objects and transitional phenomena: A study of the first not-me possession. *International Journal of Psycho-Analysis*, 34: 89–97.

Winnicott, D. W. (1960a). The theory of the parent–infant relationship. *International Journal of Psycho-Analysis*, 41(6): 585–595.

Winnicott, D. W. (1960b). Ego distortion in terms of true and false self. In: *The Maturational Processes and the Facilitating Environment*: 140–152. Madison, CT: International Universities Press, 1965.

Winnicott, D. W. (1970). The mother–infant experience of mutuality. In: Anthony, E. & Benedek, T. (Eds.), *Parenthood: Its psychology and psychopathology*: 245–256. Boston: Little Brown.

Winnicott, D. W. (1971). *Playing and Reality*. London: Routledge.

Winson, J. (1986). *Brain and Psyche: The Biology of the Unconscious*. New York: Doubleday.

Winson, J. (1992). The function of REM sleep and meaning of dreams. In: Barron, J. Eagle, M. & Wolitzky, D. (Eds.), *Interface of Psychoanalysis and Psychology*. Washington, DC: American Psychological Association.

Witkin, H. A. & Goodenough, D. R. (1981). *Cognitive Styles: Essence and Origins*. Madison, CT: International Universities Press.

Wolf, E. S. (1995). Brief notes on using the couch. *Psychoanalytic Inquiry*, 15: 314–323.

Wolfson, P. E. (1985). Testimony of Philip E. Wolfson, M.D. In the Matter of MDMA Scheduling. Docket No. 84–48. United States Department of Justice, Drug Enforcement Administration.

Wundt, W. (1904). *Principles of Physiological Psychology*. London: Swan Sonnenschein.

Zahm, D. S. & Brog, J. S. (1992). Commentary: On the significance of the core-shell boundary in the rat nucleus accumbens. *Neuroscience*, 50: 751–767.

Zeigarnik, B. (1927). Über das behalten von erledigten und unerledigten handlungen (On finished and unfinished tasks). *Psycologische Forschung*, 9: 1–86.

Zhang, J. (2004). Memory process and the function of sleep. *Journal of Theoretics*, 6(6).

Zillmann, D. (1983). Transfer of excitation in emotional behavior. In Cacioppo, J. T. & Petty, R. E. (Eds.), *Social psychophysiology: A Sourcebook*: 215–240. New York: Guilford Press.

Zillmann, D. (2006). Dramaturgy for emotions from fictional narration. In Bryant, J. & Vorderer, P. (Eds.), *Psychology of Entertainment*: 215–238. Mahwah, NJ: Erlbaum.

Zuckerman, M. & Kuhlman, D. M. (2000). Personality and risk-taking: Common biosocial factors. *Journal of Personality*, 68: 999–1025.

INDEX

RB homes. San Roque S09

Marbella Dreamhomes.
   3 bed Townhouse / fixed.

The Spanish Estate Agent Estepona
   3 bed village house

Yourviva
   3 bed townhouse S3 1

Island Properties San Roque
   S75 680   / 650 000 6 Gwos

Crystal Shore properties
San Roque Townhouse.
   (X homes.

* Affinity Property Group Affinity!
Used San Roque villa detached
   666 Gwos.   '15 30

Think Grau Sete 1 Sunits
1/ villa Las Rosas - La Chullera 30
2/ villa Sotogrande S15. Rafael de la